Also by Philip L. Fradkin

CALIFORNIA, THE GOLDEN COAST (1974)

A RIVER NO MORE (1981)

FALLOUT (1989)

SAGEBRUSH
COUNTRY

Philip L. Fradkin

SAGEBRUSH COUNTRY

Land and the American West

Photographs by the Author

ALFRED A. KNOPF

NEW YORK

1 9 8 9

THIS IS A BORZOI BOOK
PUBLISHED BY ALFRED A. KNOPF, INC.

Library of Congress Cataloging-in-Publication Data
Fradkin, Philip L.
Sagebrush country.
Bibliography: p.
Includes index.
1. Uinta National Forest Region (Utah)—History.
2. Land use, Rural—Utah—Uinta National Forest Region.
3. Fradkin, Philip L.—Journeys—Utah—Uinta National
Forest Region.   I. Title.
F832.U39F73   1989   979.2'14   88-45492
ISBN 0-394-52935-9

Manufactured in the United States of America

FIRST EDITION

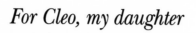
For Cleo, my daughter

Nothing is ever buried, the earth rolls in its tracks, it never goes anywhere, it never changes, only hope changes like morning and night, only the expectations rise and set.

—E. L. Doctorow, *Welcome to Hard Times*

If one searches for a scenario setting in which to examine, define, and analyze the twentieth-century West, the development of the West's natural resources—land, minerals, water—provides the theater (often of the absurd).

—Gene M. Gressley,
The American West: New Perspectives, New Dimensions

CONTENTS

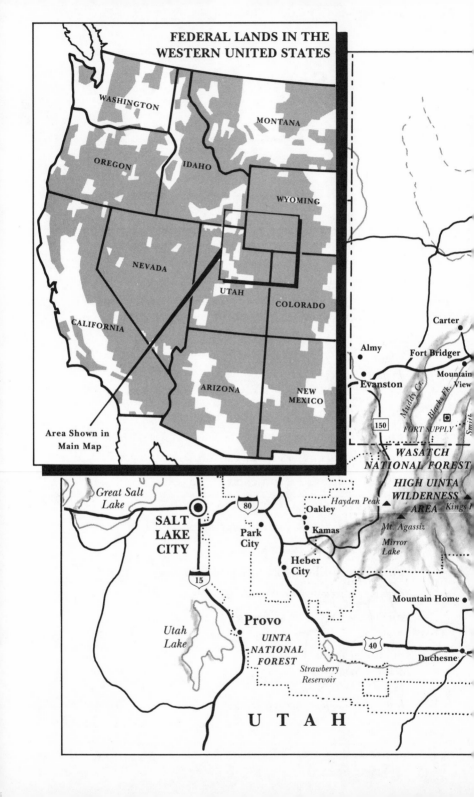

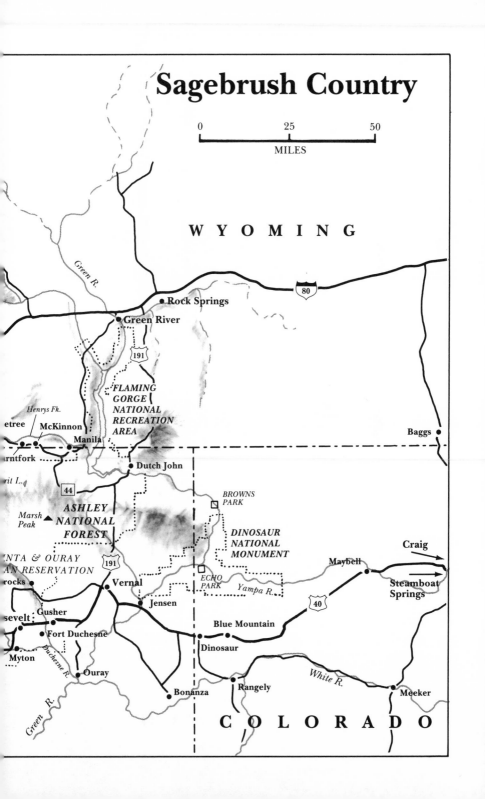

Sagebrush Country

0   25   50

MILES

WYOMING

Green R.

80

● Rock Springs

● Green River

191

Henrys Fk.

FLAMING GORGE NATIONAL RECREATION AREA

etree ● McKinnon

● Manila

Baggs ●

rntfork

● Dutch John

rit I...

44

Marsh Peak ▲

ASHLEY NATIONAL FOREST

BROWNS PARK

DINOSAUR NATIONAL MONUMENT

Craig

Maybell ●

NTA & OURAY AN RESERVATION

191

● Vernal

ECHO PARK

Yampa R...

40

Steamboat Springs

rocks ●

sevelt ● Gusher ●

● Fort Duchesne

● Jensen

● Blue Mountain

Duchesne R.

● Rangely

White R.

● Meeker

Myton ●

● Ouray

● Dinosaur

Green R.

● Bonanza

COLORADO

PREFACE

The arid region bounded by the Sierra Nevada and Cascade ranges on the west and the front ranges of the Rocky Mountains on the east has been called the West, the American West, the Interior West, the Mountain West, the Intermountain West, the Empty Quarter, and a number of other rather prosaic names.

I think of this region as Sagebrush Country. The sagebrush is the single most widespread plant in the West, growing and predominating in most places between the eastern Rockies and the Sierra and from Canada to Mexico. The hardy *artemisia* endures in a number of forms from the desert floor to the ten-thousand-foot level of mountain slopes. Its gray-green color and pungent, aromatic smell suffuse the landscape. The sagebrush lacks the pretensions of height and color, preferring to dominate by pure ordinariness.

The plant has an erratic history within its native region. The Indians used sagebrush extensively for various purposes related to physical survival. They wore it as clothing and inhaled it for medicinal purposes. With the coming of the whites, the plant fell into disuse and proliferated. Cattle, sheep, and horses mowed down the tasty grasses, thus allowing the sagebrush to expand. The objective in recent years has been to rid the range of the worthless plant, so large swaths of sagebrush were ripped from the ground by heavy chains dragged between two earth movers or poisoned with herbicides. Grasses more palatable to livestock were planted in its stead. Ripping out the native sagebrush and planting exotic grasses was like tearing out history and replacing it with fantasy. Myth has often been mistaken for reality in the West.

Besides being maimed, *artemisia* has been ignored. There are no special homages to the all-pervasive sagebrush, as there are to such rare sights as tall groves of *sequoia,* deep chasms, and repeating geysers—the freak shows of the West. Yet it is virtually impossible to approach these unusual sights without passing through voluminous amounts of sagebrush. How about a Sagebrush National Park? There are no votes, appropriations, or tourist dollars in that proposal.

Most recently sagebrush was resurrected for symbolic purposes. When westerners chose to differ with their dominant landlord, the federal government, they called it the Sagebrush Rebellion, which accurately located the dispute but did not define it precisely. "Rebellion" implies an armed conflict, and not the media event of the late 1970s. The brief dispute was over land, no small matter in the West, since land, provided that it is properly watered, is the source of wealth and power in Sagebrush Country.

This book is primarily about how land has been used and destiny determined in the West. It focuses on public lands, which constitute the vast bulk of holdings in the eleven western states. The public domain is a vast commons of some 730 million acres—about one-third of the nation's land area. What makes control of it a particularly western issue is the fact that over 90 percent of the federal lands outside of Alaska are in the eleven western states. For the three states touched by the Uinta Mountains, 64 percent of Utah is in the public domain, 49 percent of Wyoming, and 35 percent of Colorado.

These figures can be deceiving. State lands and other governmental holdings further decrease the private land base in these states. Distribution of public lands within the western states is also a factor. Virtually all of western Colorado is in the public domain, while most of the land east of the Rocky Mountains is in private hands. Life on the western slope of the Continental Divide is a far different proposition from what it is on the eastern side.

With Indian and military land holdings not strictly being classed as public lands, because of their special uses and lack of accessibility to the general public, the vast bulk of the remainder of the public domain is managed, in order of the size of holdings, by the Bureau of Land Management, the Forest Service, the National Park Service, and the Fish and Wildlife Service. The Forest Service is an agency of the Department of Agriculture, while the others are lodged within the Department of Interior. Those departments, Congress, the Supreme Court, and the President are in Washington, D.C. However, power over what happens on the public domain is geographically divided. What takes place on these lands is formally determined in the nation's capital and informally in the meeting rooms and on the ground in the West.

I have confined my inquiry mainly to what has happened in and around the Uinta Mountains: a historically rich, geographically cohesive, little-known region that takes in a large section of northeastern Utah and smaller parts of southwestern Wyoming and northwestern Colorado—the heartland of the American West. I believe that the particular place, if chosen well, portrays the general condition. That was the approach I took in a previous book on water and the West, *A River No More: The Colorado River and the West*. Because the use of water was the primary focus of that book, the issue is accordingly slighted in this second volume, which focuses on land. Together, the two works constitute a natural-resource history of the West. The use, abuse, and preservation of natural resources is, I believe, the most discernible trail across the mountains and through the deserts of the West.

What first attracted me to the Uinta Mountains was their ordinariness and their isolated unity. As I spent more time wandering around the Uintas, their uniqueness gradually became evident.

The Uintas are relatively uncontaminated by such ephemeral, outside influences as an overwhelming tourist trade or transient recreation seekers, such as skiers, who have so greatly altered other places. Resorts like Jackson Hole, Wyoming; Park City, Utah; and Aspen, Colorado, are floating islands that have been cut off from their past.

There is a clear continuum between past and present in and around the Uintas. That link needs to be clearly delineated because too many people, both within and outside the region, see the West only as a child of the present. The human occupants, be they Indians or of European origin, have overlaid this region with their comings and goings over the centuries. Every major and most minor currents of recorded western history have passed by these silent sentinels that straddle the center of the American West.

There were additional advantages to the choice of the Uintas. The mountains and the surrounding region that is dependent upon the heights contain lands controlled by every one of the federal land-management agencies, except the Department of Defense. All the natural-resource issues found elsewhere in the West are clustered in and around the Uintas. Water, wilderness, grazing, minerals, recreation, and wildlife concerns are all found here.

The Uinta Mountains not only unify, but they also divide; and as a barrier they have a number of unusual forms. The mountains mark the dividing line between the hot Colorado Plateau country to the south and the cold Wyoming plains to the north. Not only does the topography differ on the north and south slopes, but also the fauna and the flora. The crest is a cultural divide, there having been different Indian tribes on each side of the range who were followed by disparate, transient whites on the north and the homogeneous, rooted Mormons to the south. No one else has shared in the wealth of the West to the extent of these two separate Caucasian subcultures—neither Indians, Hispanics, nor the few blacks and Asians who form almost disenfranchised minorities within the region.

One hundred years ago, that most prolific of western historians, Hubert H. Bancroft, inadvertently stated this two-slope theme when he discussed Utah and Wyoming in separate books. Bancroft wrote: "In the history of Utah we come upon a new series of social phenomena whose multiformity and unconventionality awaken the liveliest interest. We find ourselves at once outside the beaten track of conquest for gold and glory; of wholesale robberies and human slaughter for the love of Christ; of encomiendas, repartimientos, serfdoms, or other species of civilized imposition; of missionary invasion resulting in certain death to the aborigines" but instead were concerned with "broad acres and well-filled storehouses for the men of practical piety." Not in Utah, said Bancroft, was there "a hurried scramble for wealth, or a corporation for the management of a game preserve." Across the border there was a different story. Bancroft wrote of Uinta County in the southwestern corner of Wyoming: "Historically, it is the most interesting portion of the [Wyoming] territory, having been occupied by adventurers ever since 1823." Adventurers and men of practical piety were separated by a mountain range.

The theme of cyclic extraction of natural resources to satisfy outside markets, and how those extractive forces have affected the natives, dominates the history of the two slopes and the remainder of the West. Throughout the last two hundred years the essence of the region, its rich lifeblood, has been repeatedly sucked and torn out of the ground and transported elsewhere to benefit others: whether it be in the form of beaver skins for gentlemen's hats, coal for railroads, oil for automobiles, natural gas for industries and homes, timber for housing, uranium for atomic bombs, cattle for food, dinosaur bones for museums, issues for conservationists, or color photographs to be shown at home after a summer vacation. The returns have been minimal—just enough to keep the natives quiescent.

Although I am an outsider, I have attempted to relate this history from the perspective, and using the voices, of the people who have lived within the region. Their words, which are too often drowned out by alien tongues, need to be heard by others, and themselves, in order to realize that there is a common past and the need for a unified vision of the future.

I once journeyed from the headwaters of the Colorado River system to its premature end in search of the essence of the West. I thought I felt its life force in the water that was drained off to give the land vitality—the river being depleted in the process before it reached the sea. This time, after searching the appropriate archives and talking to the relevant people, I floated down portions of the Yampa and Green rivers within the Uintah Basin and hiked along the crest of the Uinta* Mountains in order to locate myself within a

*The two spellings for the central geographical entity in this book and its progeny are in accordance with common usage.

landscape. From all these journeys I returned with a feeling of renewal, although I passed through bare lands made more barren by the activities of man.

The comfort of history is that it demonstrates that human intrusions are only temporary. All will pass, as did the dinosaurs who once roamed in profusion across these very same lands that were later invaded by people. Only the mountains and deserts and rivers will remain.

SAGEBRUSH
COUNTRY

Chapter 1

A RECENT
YEAR

Nineteen eighty-five was not the best of years for the administrators who oversaw Dinosaur National Monument at the eastern end of the Uinta Mountains. Then again, it was not the worst of years. What can be said with certainty is that the year began on the wrong foot, and the remainder of it was spent hopping about trying to catch up; which pretty well summarizes how public lands in the West are administered.

Joe Kennedy, the monument's superintendent, thought up the idea about changing the monument's name to the more prestigious designation of a national park. The legal difference is that a monument is established by an executive order of the President while a park has to clear all the hurdles of the legislative process. But Kennedy—a large, lumbering southerner who was fairly new to the area—was not knowledgeable about western ways. Emotional subtleties that were rooted in history, not legal technicalities, were the real issues in the controversy.

Kennedy ran into a buzz saw of opposition that chewed him up and came just short of spitting him out in the process. The man was dazed by his encounter with the realities of the West, and eventually he left for his native South.

The superintendent operated out of the administrative headquarters of the monument some two miles outside the small town of Dinosaur, Colorado, and a world apart in terms of orderliness from the disorder of the typical western hamlet. As the headquarters is physically removed from the town, so are the employees of the federal land-management agency distanced from the surrounding population. Park Service employees are transferred frequently and live and work in bureaucratic ghettos separated from their constituencies. They are remote, uniformed entities whose primary loyalty is to their careers and their agency. The stone walls of the monument headquarters are a bulwark against the unpredictable qualities of life as it is lived outside, not an invitation to enter.

The year began this way.

The superintendent had been looking at publications printed on slick paper whose carefully composed photographs seemed to pop out of the page and beckon the reader into a four-color scene that could never be duplicated in real life. Those fantasy pictures in books and magazines, be they written in English, French, Japanese, or German, depicted the "crown jewels" of the National Park system: such places as Yosemite, Yellowstone, Grand Teton, Glacier, Rocky Mountain, and Grand Canyon national parks. If the publication was particularly thorough, as was one published by Sunset Books, there might be a mention in smaller type of Aztec Ruins National Monument, Capulin Mountain National Monument, Capitol Reef National Monument (whose status was changed after publication to Capitol Reef National Park), and Dinosaur National Monument.

The accompanying descriptions told the story of relative status. Grand Teton was described thus: "Favorite park of many who know them all; once the gathering place of fur traders and trappers, in a setting of majestic beauty; its spires attract mountaineers from everywhere." Dinosaur, on the other hand, was located on a "semi-arid plateau in Colorado-Utah with deep gorges, rapid waters, and rich skeletal deposits of prehistoric reptiles." There was this warning concerning the national monument: "Back roads sometimes hazardous." In distant cities choices for summer vacations were made from such publications.

Kennedy had those publications stacked in his carpeted office, and he looked at them and showed them to visitors, along with a Utah State University graduate student's thesis on the drawing power of the different land classifications. A national park ranked higher than a monument, and national forest lands were considered third best. Federal lands rated higher than state lands. What Kennedy clearly saw was that national-park status meant bigger type size in such publications, more visitors, larger budgets, and more personnel. Park status could be a bureaucrat's dream come true, and Kennedy admitted that he had initiated the proposal, at least partially, for such reasons.

So the superintendent and his staff in the first month of that year put together a three-page summary entitled "The National Significance of Dinosaur National Monument." The document cited the richness of the dinosaur bone deposits, the drama of the Green and Yampa river canyons, the uniqueness of the Uinta Mountains (incorrectly termed "the only east-west mountain range in North America"), the sanctuary for such threatened species as the peregrine falcon, and the human history extending from the ancient Frémont Indian culture to the Escalante expedition to the river journeys of William Ashley and John Wesley Powell.

For some reason the Park Service's concept of the monument's history stopped in 1869, the year Powell and his men first descended the Green and Colorado rivers. This proved to be a decisive mistake for Kennedy. Had he carefully examined the historical record after it had been prematurely terminated, he would have found that similar attempts to change the monument's name failed in the early 1950s, when conservationists and dam builders fought over the destiny of the monument, and by implication the remainder of the national park system, in the first classic confrontation of the modern conservation movement.

Nothing that was publicly visible celebrated this western bloodletting in the monument. The locals, who had been around longer, were aware of that bitter controversy; and their emotional actions that year could be traced back to the prior disappointment of having the proposal for a cherished dam, which they thought meant prosperity, defeated by the actions of outsiders, whether

Park Service personnel or conservationists. Both were equally distrusted, feared, and disliked. So, in a sense, Kennedy was thwarted by history before he even began his quest.

Grumbling began to be heard to the west in Vernal, Utah, following the initial proposal to change the status of the monument. So the following month another document from the administrative headquarters found its way into the surrounding communities. This paper attempted to answer the concerns of the natives. No, such a name change would not dash hopes for greater energy developments in the area. A stricter air-quality standard for the surrounding desert, which might scuttle plans for future energy projects, was not automatic. Nor was the name change related to the issue of eliminating grazing in the national monument, or other restrictive management plans that might be put into place. Congress and the states of Colorado and Utah would have to rule on these matters. The document did not state that, if more people could be moved to visit a place because of a name change, the same shift in nomenclature might cause politicians to view it differently. This subtlety did not escape the locals.

The paper ended with a soothing thought: "For those of us who work at Dinosaur, the name change means greater national and international recognition. For the local communities a name change means that residents can take greater pride in their national park and enjoy the added income of more park visitors spending their money locally." Tourists represented a $1.3 billion industry to Utah; and the federal government was something of a mother lode itself, since its expenditures accounted for slightly more than 50 percent of all public monies spent on outdoor recreation in the state. For rural counties, such as Uintah County in the northeast corner of Utah, which were in the grip of a recession because of fading energy-related projects, the benefits of tourism were being rediscovered.

It was a good ploy; but the locals, when confronted with the alternatives, still put their faith in industrial development, though it was declining. Their choice was not logical, but it was consistent with the illusive search for quick mineral wealth that pervades the history of the West.

* * *

The best way to experience Dinosaur is to float down the Yampa and Green rivers. The most dramatic landscapes in the monument are the canyons of the two rivers, which form sinuous transportation corridors through the high, rolling plateau country and mountains of the 211,141-acre national monument. These uplands are duplicated elsewhere in the West with great regularity and greater grandeur. It is the canyons, and dinosaur quarry, that are different.

Located at the eastern end of the Uintas, the monument is drier than the remainder of the range because it lies in the rain shadow of the higher mountains. But the elevated desert has a certain austere drama. The nakedness of the landforms reveals the tremendous forces that wrenched this land in eons past. The land, with the twisted rivers forming the baseline for such observations, was torn this way and that by powerful forces and tilted on its side to reveal not only the bones of the past but almost a complete geological record of its existence. Both revelations drew the finest scientific minds of the nineteenth century to this remote region.

Science has given way to recreation. Currently eleven thousand persons float down the two rivers each year. When they begin their trip and when it ends, the equipment they take with them, where they eat and sleep, how they dispose of their wastes, and other essential matters are determined by a set of regulations known as a river-management plan. In 1972 there were 17,000 boaters on the river. After that year the waters within the national monument began to be rationed because of congestion and deterioration of the surrounding countryside by thousands of sets of tracks and the detritus people left behind. Studies were undertaken, public hearings conducted, and in 1979 the plan was adopted. A lottery was held each year to determine who among the private applicants could take a river trip. There were eleven commercial operators whose allotments were determined by historical use, and Don Hatch of Vernal had the largest slice of that pie.

The two seasonal rangers I would be traveling with for the next few days had a number of duties to perform. They would be maintaining the twenty-one campgrounds, performing rescues if needed, checking permits, giving interpretive talks, making wildlife observations, and answering questions, such as why do we have to conform to all of these regulations in the wilderness? (Answer: So it may continue to appear to be a wilderness. The major deception of the West is that each visitor believes he or she is the first, when along these two rivers habitation has extended back some 9,000 years, at the very least.)

I met Bill Ott and Jim McChristal at the maintenance yard behind the monument's headquarters. It has always amazed me how much mechanized equipment is needed to keep a so-called natural area in its natural state. The monument is not in its natural state, nor has it been for some time. So machines are necessary to patch roads, repair pickups, make trail signs, collect trash, and fix motors attached to boats that patrol a supposedly motorless river.

Both men were seasonal rangers, Bill being the senior of the two. He had a background in microbiology and river running. Jim came to rivers via a career as a technical writer for an aerospace firm. Both were in their late thirties and were part of the back-to-the-land movement that had invaded the West in the previous decade. While some of those footloose people had left the territory to seek more secure employment, others, like Bill and Jim, had found a temporary niche there.

On the hour-long drive to Deerlodge Park at the eastern end of the monument the two men talked with Elaine Adams, another seasonal ranger and the driver who would return with the vehicle. They used a combination of Park Service and river argot. The discussion ranged from Park Service jobs, pay, and housing, to river boats, oars, and rapids. "Cat" translated to Cataract Canyon and "Deso" referred to Desolation Canyon in their discussion of hazardous drops elsewhere that would not be encountered on this trip.

The best way to see Dinosaur National Monument is to float the sixty-two miles from Deerlodge to Split Mountain campground. The rapids are not fearsome, as are those in the Grand Canyon, and the steady movement of the current from east to west through the twisting, ribbed canyons provides a movable walkway through the landscape.

The weather was unsettled. A series of spring storms were traversing the high desert. The temperature the night before had been below zero, and today it was clear but chill. The spring flood stage of the Yampa was just beginning to subside, leaving driftwood amongst the cottonwoods in the flats above the slippery riverbank at Deerlodge Park, where we launched the rafts. The Yampa still has a seasonal ebb and flow, it being the last major tributary of the Colorado River system that has no major upstream impoundments or diversions. However, there have been more than twenty major proposals to change the river's free-flowing status. The West refuses to remain still.

After checking the permit of another party that was also readying to depart, we shoved off in the two rubber boats at 11:50 a.m. On the river there was a radio check with headquarters, and the base operator asked for my address and telephone number. Next of kin, I supposed. We passed some cows grazing peacefully on the north bank of Deerlodge Park shortly before we entered the confines of the canyon.

Grazing was on a lot of people's minds. In this portion of the monument and in a few other scattered locations it was supposed to conclude that year—a deadline that resulted in traumatic upheavals elsewhere in the West. The practice would not stop entirely within the monument, a blanket termination being only a remote possibility down the line a number of years.

The grazing of cattle and sheep is far and away the dominant activity on land in the Sagebrush West. Although Dinosaur National Monument is in the national park system, that does not exempt it from countless hooves and mouths altering and reducing the plant life and increasing erosion over the years while at the same time providing a livelihood for a few ranchers and small amounts of beef and lamb for distant markets. A Park Service report stated: "Grazing by domestic livestock is the primary perturbation persisting in most upland and some riparian communities." The condition of the range within the monument was judged to be fair to poor. Sagebrush had proliferated over the years, as there was no eradication program within the monument for the native plant, which moved in when more palatable species were decimated by livestock.

Grazing is permitted in some units of the national park system and prohibited in others. When Dinosaur was enlarged in 1938, grazing was allowed to continue on the new monument lands. A 1960 act provided for the phase-out of grazing in such a manner that those ranchers and their descendants who had used these lands in past years could remain; but newcomers or those who had temporarily leased their land in the intervening years would be forced out. Grazing was scheduled to continue on 60,000 acres and cease on 52,000 acres in 1986.

But nothing was ever definite, given the political situation and the lack of fencing. Cows could easily wander onto adjacent unallotted lands, since fencing in the monument was minimal. Such trespassing could either be accidental or planned—the illegal trespassing of cattle had occurred frequently during the last few years in Deerlodge Park.

On February 1, 1985, Superintendent Kennedy sent out a computer-generated form letter to the permittees of eleven of the twenty-two allotments, stating that their grazing privileges would be terminated at the end of the current grazing year, thirteen months distant.

The letter had been anticipated. The year before a Colorado rancher, Fred Blevins of Maybell, had appealed the termination of his grazing privilege through Congressman Ken Kramer of Colorado Springs. The flank attack on a western land policy via a congressman was not an unknown maneuver in the West. But the Reagan Administration held firm. G. Ray Arnett, an assistant secretary of the Interior Department, replied, "Although we appreciate Mr. Blevins' commitment to good management of the grazing lands, we believe the 25-year period provided for phasing out such activity was more than adequate for Mr. Blevins and any others affected by this change to prepare for the termination of their leases." Blevins had leased his base lands during the intervening years, and the law required continuous legal control in order to maintain grazing privileges.

Leo Snow, another permittee, inquired about the status of the allotment that he thought he had acquired in 1980. The previous owner was a Park Service employee, now dead, who had disguised his ownership of the base property, and thus the right to lease grazing lands within the monument—such an arrangement being against Park Service regulations—by registering the property in his wife's name. Land finaglings are a western tradition, and federal employees are not exempt from such illegalities. Snow threatened to go to his congressman to seek special legislation to exempt him from termination.

Other ranchers contacted their congressmen in either Colorado or Utah, state and national cattle associations, local chambers of commerce, farm bureaus, and newspapers that were likely to be sympathetic to their cause. This was also a year when grazing fees on public lands were periodically reviewed by the Administration and Congress. With energy projects also dwindling and the name change for the monument in the works, the atmosphere was charged at the eastern end of the Uinta Mountains and throughout the West in 1985.

Kennedy held the initiative on the name-change proposal until the movers and shakers of Vernal rose up in March to deftly shoot the proposal down. The chorus against the change consisted of the Vernal Area Chamber of Commerce, the Uintah County Farm Bureau, the Utah Farm Bureau, the Uintah Cattlemen's Association, the Uintah County commissioners, the Uintah Basin Natural Resources Association, and the Vernal *Express,* whose editor, Jack Wallis, wrote:

> If an iron-clad stipulation could be made that no change in the future industrial and agricultural use in the lands surrounding Dinosaur National Monument would occur as a result of the name change to a national park, much of the doubt would be erased.
>
> But because of the lack of faith and trust in federal policy, it is felt that the future development of northeastern Utah and north-western Colorado is better protected under monument regulations than it would be if changed to a park status.
>
> Why can't we have the national park status with its increased tourist attraction and also have the assurance that the surrounding industrial and agricultural resources can also be used to their fullest possible potential?

To the east in Craig, Colorado, seat of Moffat County, the major concern was less the limiting effect on industries that a stronger air-quality standard might impose, Colorado having already imposed a stricter standard than Utah, but rather how park status might limit upstream water developments on the Yampa River. The proposal contained a separate *bête noire* for each region; and, needless to say, local congressmen were not running to endorse it.

It all came to a head in late March when what was billed as "a fact-finding" meeting was held in Vernal at the Sheraton Inn. The sponsors were the chamber of commerce, farm bureau, and cattlemen's association, all of whom seemed less interested in facts than in the opportunity to air their opinions.

The gleaming new hostelry was a symbol of the dreams of industrial prosperity gone sour. Built a few years earlier in energy boom times to attract high-flying outsiders and serve as the business and social center for the town, the inn—actually a glorified motel—was less than half full. The bartenders polished glasses for nonexistent drinkers, and the waitresses stood about talking in clusters while waiting for nonexistent customers.

Outside the Grizzly Room, that particular species of bear having long ago departed from the region, the wind-burned ranchers whose tans stopped at their hat lines looked uncomfortable in the alien setting. The representatives of energy companies, whose firms had already or were about to pull out of town, huddled together in overdressed knots. The tall uniformed park superintendent, who wished he could have made himself invisible at that moment, wended his way between the two groups and entered the bear's den.

Kennedy knew he was about to be publicly drawn and quartered in a polite manner. That was the nature of these folks. In the past, when public land managers such as Harry Ratliff had more freedom, there would have been a contest. But not in this place nor at this time.

Kennedy played the good ole boy role. In his neat Park Service uniform with the campaign hat sitting on the table between him and the audience, as if it were a buffer, the superintendent attempted to disassociate the issues of air quality, grazing, and other fears from the name-change proposal.

"These things, which I call chickens, keep popping out of the woodwork," said Kennedy.

It didn't work.

An environmental specialist from the Chevron Oil Company took on Kennedy's interpretation of why a stricter air-quality standard would not be automatic.

He was followed by Joe Hacking, a local rancher, who spoke for the agricultural community. Referring to Kennedy's "chickens," Hacking cited grazing, sagebrush eradication, predator control, and insect-spraying programs outside the monument as other activities that would be jeopardized by the name change.

Other than the energy-company people, there were no city folks at this meeting, no representatives of those environmental organizations that were so active thirty years ago when dams were being proposed for Dinosaur, or ten years back when 80 percent of the monument was being proposed for wilderness status. Hacking had given an impassioned oration at the wilderness hearing. He asked then:

And how are you going to feed your families? I might feed them for you, but I might get a bellyful of it and say, "To hell with you." You don't understand the problems involved in getting the beef, the wheat or the bread onto your table. It's time that you have an environmental statement on that. Right now we're having a fuel shortage. You're probably driving 55 miles per hour just like I am. The price of your gasoline went up, too. You've got us in rural America backed into a corner and we've had a bellyful of it and we're starting to fight. You've got us outnumbered. We're a minority, but by hell you better hang onto your hats because we're going to be there.

The representative of the oil company and the rancher were followed by others on their side. Their voices merged into a common litany. The desire to determine their own fate and their distrust of the federal government were themes that were constantly reiterated.

Scott Chew, the fourth generation of a pioneer ranch family, was applauded when he stated, "When a woman goes from being a Miss to a Missus, she just doesn't give up her name."

Joe Haslow, an oldtimer who lived near the monument, said, "When those government men tell you something, have them sign it."

Don Hatch, whose father initiated commercial river-running operations on the Green and Yampa rivers, was the only person to support the name change unequivocally. He told his friends and neighbors, "I feel like a mouse in a cat pit."

Hatch could afford to oppose the strong current of community opinion, since he had social status and economic security. His family had been the first settlers in the region, and his successful river-running business depended on outsiders for income. Some thirty years earlier there had been threats of economic reprisals by locals when he publicly opposed the dams and aided the hated conservationists.

Others who were less well placed than Hatch, but of similar persuasion, said privately that they had not spoken up in favor of the name change at the hearing because they feared social ostracism and economic reprisals. It was an isolated area. One needed friends in order to survive.

Joe Kennedy had few friends in that crowd. He kept his head down and doodled on a pad while the testimony continued. At its conclusion he complimented the audience and added, "Boy, I'm coming out all right. I am getting out of here with my tail intact."

Kennedy's lack of grit, when word of his performance got back to monument headquarters, did not endear him to his colleagues. His stature had declined because of his poor timing, lack of an effective strategy, and retreat.

There were busy beavers on the river that year.

A short distance downstream from the departure point a United States Geological Survey team, consisting of three men in a flat-bottom boat, were taking a measurement of the streamflow. The USGS did survey work for both the Park Service and the Bureau of Reclamation, which have widely divergent views on dams. The bureau's job is to provide water; the service's duty is to protect natural features. Both do most of their work in the West, and when they lock horns the more powerful bureau is liable to override the more reticent service.

To a shouted question as we floated by, one of the surveyors replied that they were working, this time, "for you guys," meaning the Park Service, I assumed.

I was in Bill Ott's boat, mainly because he had floated the river many times and this was a familiarization trip for Jim McChristal, who had just come to work at Dinosaur. Bill was knowledgeable, and I listened carefully. The superintendent had cautioned Bill to offer facts, not his opinions, to the visitor; but the outspoken ranger had developed his own ideas on how the monument was run, or misrun, during the last three years of seasonal work. Short and wiry with a scrub of beard and a long-billed hat that was definitely not government issue, Bill looked and acted more like a freedom-loving river rat than a careful bureaucrat.

A few minutes later, as we were about to enter the canyon of the Yampa with the Vale of Tears on our right and Disappointment Draw to the left, Bill pointed out the site of the great-horned-owl massacres, which were one of Steve Petersburg's schemes.

At times, Steve Petersburg seemed as if he had his own agenda; and indeed, since becoming the wildlife ranger in 1973 and the resource-management specialist four years later, he had carved out a fair amount of bureaucratic turf within the monument's hierarchy. For the remainder of 1985, Petersburg tended to fill the vacuum that Kennedy's loss of face had created. It was the stocky, mustached naturalist, with an undergraduate major in forest management and a master's degree in wildlife biology, who took the lead on the ticklish Mormon cricket and peregrine falcon issues that threatened to rend the fragile skein of management that supposedly enveloped the monument.

Petersburg was definitely not of the "let it be" or purist school of conservation. He had been taught and believed in the management of natural resources. Management meant that man had fiddled with the natural environment so extensively over the years that it was no longer natural. What followed was that the only way to rectify past mistakes made in a haphazard manner was to employ rational solutions. The problem was that very little was known with certainty about nature, and more often than not personal and institutional biases crept into what was supposed to be a scientific solution.

For instance, in years past peregrine falcons were abundant within the monument. With the widespread spraying of DDT, egg-shells thinned and fewer peregrines survived birth to live and make their majestic flights from precarious eyries perched high along the rock walls of the two river canyons. In the early 1970s the Peregrine Fund, a conservation organization affiliated with the Cornell University Laboratory of Ornithology, began to raise falcons in captivity and release them in the wild, first in the East and then in the West.

With a mixture of nonprofit, state, and federal funds becoming available, Petersburg geared up in 1977 for the first peregrine relief measures in the monument. Three years later there were problems. The artificially hatched young falcons, who were being placed in artificial nests, fed, and protected by discreet observers who served as proxy parents—a process called hacking—were being slaughtered by predators, namely great horned owls.

Owls were numerous, the thinking went, and peregrines were scarce; in fact, they had been officially declared an endangered species. At first, an attempt was made to scare off owls and other predators like golden eagles with small explosive charges called cracker shells and M-80s, which were shot into the air. Then trapping was tried. Those measures failed, so Petersburg, faced with the possible loss of a cherished program, called on the experts to support the last option, euphemistically referred to as "removal" and less frequently as "lethal removal," meaning that the owls were to be shot by Park Service personnel. One species was to be killed to save another, which recalled the famous quote about destroying the Vietnamese village in order to save it.

The Peregrine Fund rode to the rescue. At Petersburg's suggestion, William Burnham, manager of the fund's Rocky Mountain program, wrote a letter to Superintendent Kennedy in January, 1983. The letter hinted that funding for falcon activities might go elsewhere, should the monument personnel not act decisively against the owls. Burnham pointed out, "The impact of man has greatly changed our world and no matter how hard we try not even the Park's ecosystems will ever be as they once were. Unfortunately, management and manipulation of all life forms may be a necessity." This was a classic statement of the management position.

From Gerald R. Craig, a researcher for the Colorado Division of Wildlife, who was also heavily involved in the peregrine program, came another letter of support, also solicited by Petersburg. It, too, contained the word "unfortunately." Craig wrote, "So, unfortunately it comes down to the value judgment of lives of peregrines versus lives of great horned owls. One is currently endangered and the other is a very common raptor."

The decision-making process involved only a seven-page environmental assessment, so outside opinions were not solicited as they would have been had a full-blown environmental impact statement been drawn up, nor did conservationists from the "let it be" school address the issue. The potential for conflict between the managers and the purists dated back at least as far as the clash between John Muir and Gifford Pinchot in the early years of this century.

One lone voice for the owls survives in the record. His was an outsider's opinion. Upon hearing of the proposed killings, a visitor to the monument from New York lodged a formal complaint with the staff: "The thought of shooting the great horned owl in order to save the peregrine falcon is revolting. It is natural evolution and should not be interfered with."

In his proposal, which Kennedy subsequently approved, Petersburg anticipated the criticisms of the New York visitor and the thoughts Bill Ott voiced on the river. The resource manager wrote: "Members of the monument staff or the general public, who either do not fully understand the biological reasons for taking owls or who are unalterably opposed to taking any species within the monument, may feel offended." Blasting owls with shotguns would be seen as being contrary to the basic tenet of the Park Service to protect wildlife, said Petersburg. But if they were not killed, an endangered species would be further threatened, a program negated, and credibility and cooperation with other agencies lessened.

Using a mechanical device that simulated a squealing rabbit to lure the owls within range, spotlights to fix them in gun sights, and shotguns to "remove" them, twenty-seven great horned owls were killed between 1982 and 1984. Along with the nonlethal pyrotechnics employed to scare off the predators, the entrance to the Yampa Canyon must have resembled a war zone at times. The massacres were one of the monument's better-kept secrets, as no one willingly talked about them nor did any mention of them occur in the more public of the park's documents.

At the abandoned eyrie, there being no hacking activities in Dinosaur that year, we entered the Uinta Mountains on the same east-west trajectory along which the mountains are laid out. The steeply rising cliffs served as a dramatic portal, and the water quickened. The dollops that came aboard felt like knife slashes, the water being quite cold. At Anderson Hole we halted to plant a heavy post that would serve as a hitching rack for boats.

After a quick lunch and short bake in the sun in order to stoke up on warmth, we were off. I sat as high as I could on the baggage so as to escape the cold water while Bill talked. Like one other boatman I knew, he had traversed the entire Grand Canyon on foot. Bill was building a replica of a historic river-running boat and hoped to launch it this season for a test run. Five acres and a log cabin in Oregon were his home base. From there he ventured forth. He was thinking about a trip to the Andes to watch the free, soaring flights of the Andean condor. The owl incident depressed him.

The rapids were not particularly threatening, but the spills of water into the raft were just enough to freeze my feet, which were encased in wet-suit booties. The cold took its toll. We were tired, so we put in at the Harding Hole campground at 5:30 after making twenty-six miles on the river that day.

We camped next to a boisterous group of men from Grand Junction, Colorado, who were sitting in collapsible lawn chairs and drinking beer. Bill checked and determined that, according to their permit, they were in the wrong campground. No sense to insist on their moving, since the river was not overly crowded. The paperwork back at headquarters did not always match the reality in the field.

Using relative standards, Harding Hole can be regarded as a wilderness. A black bear was recently spotted on the other side of the river. Bald eagles nest there in the winter. Arrow-like Canada geese fly by a few feet off the water. Golden eagles and great horned owls pursue young falcons, which in turn devour Mormon crickets. This was the year of the cricket.

A year, of course, does not exist unto itself in the West, or anywhere else, for that matter, but is connected to past years; and Mormon crickets, a type of wingless grasshopper, were endemic to the region and had figured in its mythic history. Miraculously, and in answer to fervent prayers, seagulls appeared to devour the crickets when the Mormons' first crop was about to be harvested in 1848. This year the pesticide Sevin was regarded as the savior.

To witness a heavy infestation of crickets is a grisly, unnerving experience. At the Escalante rest stop alongside Highway 40, and not far from the monument boundary, dense clots of reddish-brown forms scuttled across the sparse desert terrain. The crickets made a rustling noise, like swishing crinoline, when they moved across the dry terrain; and the ground appeared to heave as waves of the hard-shelled crickets, obeying some secret command or urge, rushed toward the Green River.

The voracious insects paused only long enough to devour their colleagues who had been crushed by the tires of passing automobiles. Should a car pass along the same track, the feasting newcomers were, in turn, flattened upon the asphalt. The whole glutinous mass of squashed cannibals formed a slippery hazard for subsequent vehicles.

The land snapped, crackled, and popped in the shadow of Blue Mountain as the hordes of single-minded wingless grasshoppers headed west, inexorably following their leaders toward gargantuan feasts in ripe fields or mindless destruction on roads or in rivers. The bands of crickets could cover two to four miles in twenty-four hours over a front as wide as twelve miles. They mowed down whole fields of grain and hay that appeared in their path. A river, such as the Green, was no great obstacle. They simply crossed such watercourses over the backs of their drowned comrades.

A sober-minded western range scientist wrote a heavily footnoted article in a technical journal which stated, "They appear to glide along, and when they are in close formation during migrations, the earth itself appears to be moving." The article continued, "When population densities are high, all vegetation, including sagebrush and other shrubs, is eaten or defoliated." For a rancher who depended for his livelihood on the well-being of the irrigated alfalfa and grain fields on his private lands and the forage on nearby public lands, these were fearsome times.

The Shoshone and Ute Indians, who ranged over these lands, valued the crickets as a source of protein-rich food. The insects were scorned and their destruction avidly sought by the white men who followed.

The last heavy cricket infestation came during the Depression years. Residents of small western towns armed themselves with brooms, sacks, and noisemakers and forced the moving crickets temporarily to detour from their routes. Metal barriers funneled the insects into pits, where they were doused with fuel and burned. Mashed crickets were so thick in places that "DANGER: SLIPPERY ROAD" signs were placed alongside western highways, and transcontinental trains were halted because they were unable to make headway along the cricket-slick rails.

There was a story, perhaps apocryphal since it fits so easily into the dude genre, about the chauffeur who stopped the large car he was driving. The lone passenger, described as a matronly lady, rolled down her window and asked the Works Progress Administration laborers what they were doing. One exasperated worker replied that they were gathering desert shrimp on Highway 40 for shipment back East.

Then, inexplicably, the crickets disappeared. There seemed to be something biblical about the quick arrival and sudden departure of such infestations.

The crickets began multiplying again in 1980 and were spotted on Blue Mountain, portions of which were within the national monument. By then pesticides had replaced burning as the favored means of eradication. Local ranchers pressured the Park Service to spray the insects so their grazing lands within and outside the monument could be saved. The ranchers suspected the national monument of being the home base for the rapidly multiplying crickets that scourged the surrounding countryside.

The Park Service refused to spray monument lands. Steve Petersburg and other park personnel were concerned about possible harm to the peregrine falcons from the spraying. A study was authorized in hopes of finding a biologically acceptable solution that would not affect the wildlife in the monument.

Cricket populations varied in the mid ranges during the early eighties. There was some spraying near the monument boundary in 1982. Much was made of the disappearance of two adult and four young peregrines from an eyrie on Steamboat Rock at the confluence of the Green and Yampa rivers that year. The truth was that no one knew why the peregrines were no longer about, if they were dead or alive, and, should it be the latter case, if they were in good health or bad health, wherever they might be. Officially their disappearance was blamed on an "undetermined cause," but unofficially Petersburg put it out that the birds had been done in by spraying.

When the cricket population rose dramatically in mid-decade, no one person or any agency was prepared for the onslaught.

Perhaps too late, and with an insecticide to which the wingless grasshoppers may have developed some resistance, the spray planes began taking off in the early-morning hours of the late spring to broadcast their deadly loads over tens of thousands of acres of sagebrush-covered lands in northwestern Colorado, northeastern Utah, and elsewhere in the West. The question was, what effects would the insecticide have on wildlife?

The evidence against Sevin, manufactured by the Union Carbide Agricultural Products Company, was mixed, although a believable argument was made for deleterious secondary effects on peregrines. The federal Fish and Wildlife Service had recommended a ten-mile buffer zone around occupied eyries, stating that the main problem was with the falcons' sources of food tending to vanish when an area was sprayed. Young peregrines preyed directly upon live crickets; and studies indicated that between 70 and 80 percent of small bird species, which adult falcons preyed upon, left an area to search for food elsewhere for up to one year after spraying. Theoretically, what remained was a biologically desolate zone where nary a bird call was heard nor insect chirped.

In its sales literature, Union Carbide claimed a 90 to 96 percent kill ratio of insects and said Sevin had a "low wildlife toxicity." The chemical had been in use for more than twenty-five years. There was widespread agreement that this carbaryl-based insecticide was an improvement over DDT and other more toxic chemicals, with their longer-lasting effects.

The Park Service and the Fish and Wildlife Service, which tend to band together in their wildlife policies, are under the jurisdiction of the Department of Interior. Their allies on this issue were the state wildlife agencies and conservationists. On the other side were the Animal and Plant Health Inspection Service (APHIS), which lies within the embrace of the Department of Agriculture and was in charge of the spraying program; state agricultural agencies; the manufacturer of Sevin; ranchers; and the Bureau of Land Management (BLM), also an arm of the Department of Interior. The split in interests and within entities of government is not unusual, as they have different responsibilities and constituencies to answer to.

Sevin was dumped within the recommended buffer zone by APHIS that year. When Petersburg and Otha Barham, the area director for APHIS, were in the same room there was bristling and caution. But the overt politeness of fellow bureaucrats prevailed.

One day in late June Barham walked into Petersburg's office at the monument accompanied by an insect specialist from the Colorado Department of Agriculture and a salesman from Union Carbide.

Petersburg was quietly fuming. It looked as if the Peregrine Fund, because of the heavy spraying around the monument, was going to take its falcons elsewhere that year. He was also plotting. Petersburg had surreptitiously gotten in touch with conservationists in Denver, who were now preparing to file suit to block further spraying.

Such a contact was a delicate matter that Joe Kennedy had rejected in the name-change controversy. The interference of outside conservationists could rile the hometown folks, Kennedy thought. There was a further risk. If it ever became known that a bureaucrat had sent out a covert alert, a career could very well stagnate or be terminated at the request of a congressman—a not infrequent happening in the West.

After the preliminaries, the two men got down to the heart of the matter.

"I got a letter from my staff," said Barham, "that says I can spray up to one mile of a peregrine eyrie." He added that, as a compromise, APHIS would in practice honor a five-mile limit requested by the Colorado Division of Wildlife.

With the Fish and Wildlife Service's ten-mile recommendation in mind, Petersburg sought clarification. He asked, "So you will spray within ten miles?"

"Yeah. I think the Colorado wildlife division and the Fish and Wildlife Service are in cahoots on that one," answered Barham, which told Petersburg nothing that he did not already know. Barham suspected the wildlife service of the common bargaining technique of asking for more and then falling back on what they could reasonably expect to get.

"The same thing goes on every year," said Barham, referring to the contention and bargaining process.

Petersburg bore in. "We are upset with what you have done this year. You said repeatedly that when you sprayed near the park you would tell us. We never heard."

"Well, we didn't know that you wanted to know about each job."

"The superintendent and I are distressed. We lost an entire eyrie in 1982 after you sprayed here."

"I heard about that," said Barham. Indeed he had, since the loss was being reported in the local press that year with the implication that the spraying was to blame.

So far, Barham said, they had treated forty thousand acres, a record under his supervision. Colorado's Moffat County was particularly bad off, he said. "The mayor of Dinosaur has just requested that we treat ten thousand acres."

"No, you're kidding," said a surprised Petersburg.

There was a discussion among all the participants as to the effectiveness of carbaryl-treated bait. The man from Union Carbide and the state insect specialist agreed that bait was safer, more effective, and more costly. "It just boils down to bucks," said the agricultural specialist.

A few days later a meeting on the cricket infestation was held at the district offices of the BLM in Vernal. The two federal agencies, which operated under the same department in Washington and shared common jurisdictional boundaries in the West, were a study in contrasts. Whereas at monument headquarters the concern had focused on the peregrine falcons, at the BLM office the harm to ranchers was the prime consideration. Petersburg had been invited but did not attend. Barham was represented by a stand-in, Ed Browning, who explained the procedures APHIS was using. He indicated that success was not complete. They had started too late and the crickets were reinfesting areas that had already been treated, said Browning.

However, he continued to push the program. "I still think we can do you a whole lot of good," said Browning. The agency was willing, but it needed more funds. "It's expensive, but just give me a name [client] and I'll cut a bloody swath out there," Browning promised the bureaucrats and ranchers at the meeting.

Scott Chew was a believer. Twelve acres of barley had been stripped overnight from the irrigated fields of the Chew ranch adjacent to the monument. Things were better on the open range, both inside and outside the monument. Along the creek beds where plant life was greener there had been some depredation, Chew reported. He, too, had seen crickets return to some treated areas but urged the willing man from APHIS to "just continue what you are doing."

But that was not to be. Two national conservation groups, the National Parks and Conservation Association and the Sierra Club, filed suit a few weeks later, and the spraying ground to a halt. "We are not trying to kill the spray program. We're just trying to make sure spraying is done with discrimination so peregrines and other endangered species aren't jeopardized," said Terri Martin, Rocky Mountain representative for the National Parks and Conservation Association. Others felt the environmentalists would like to put a permanent halt to the program. In the fall the Department of Agriculture declared the program, on which $35 million had been spent that year to spray thirteen million acres throughout the West, a success. There were fears that the cricket infestation would be even greater the following year, and APHIS went back to Congress to seek more funding.

Shortly after our departure the next morning from Harding Hole the rafts swung through a quick series of turns that climaxed in the Grand Overhang, a giant slab of rock that towered over the river. A month earlier, using the helicopter of a Denver television station, nine persons had milled about on top of the rock while three peregrine eggs were taken from a nest by Jerry Craig of the Colorado Division of Wildlife and replaced with dummy eggs. The false eggs would be retrieved and young birds placed in the nest after they had been artificially hatched. This operation was part of the monument's wild-eyrie augmentation program, and differed from hacking operations, which had been suspended that year because of the spraying. Adult birds and not people, it was hoped, would care for the young in these nests.

A television crew had been invited to Dinosaur to generate publicity that, it was hoped, would counter a threatened cut in program funding of the Colorado Division of Wildlife. While rappelling down, a cameraman tipped over backward in his sling and smashed a lens against the rock. It was a tight moment for the cameraman and all who were watching. He continued his descent to the nest and filmed the event. The adult male and female flew about, wailing loudly. The last report for that day's activities was that the female had perched on the dummy eggs.

The overall report for that year's falcon activities noted: "Removal of the eggs was somewhat delayed from the optimum time to facilitate use of a television station's helicopter and to allow the station to photograph the manipulation for a special documentary program." Bird manipulation and media exploitation were part of wildlife management.

So was the internal-combustion engine. In order to save money and time, Steve Petersburg recommended that the monument purchase an Avon rubber raft and a twenty-five-horsepower outboard engine. "It is quite inefficient to float the full length of the river in a 'normal' raft to observe these sites," wrote Petersburg in a memo to Kennedy. The superintendent approved the purchase, and then thought better of it since all other boating activities on the Green and Yampa rivers were restricted to motorless craft. The newly purchased raft and motor were then designated for patrol purposes.

Part of our job while floating the river on rafts was to look for peregrines. We saw none, but later that summer I hiked out to the Grand Overhang site with Patty Schrader, a natural-resources student at the University of Michigan and a seasonal ranger, to see how the four baby falcons that been placed in the nest were doing. We sat inside a tan tent that we hoped camouflaged our presence and watched the eyrie through binoculars. At first we saw nothing, and Schrader thought all the chicks had been victims either of predators or fatal falls from the heights. Then one chick emerged into view. That was all we saw that day except for a distraught adult bird that circled above our heads.

I wondered if that noisy machinery and those milling people a few weeks earlier and our presence on this day wouldn't make any falcon leery of showing itself. We left feeling dejected, but later sightings confirmed that all four young birds had fledged.

Just beyond the Grand Overhang there were constant reminders of the ever-present cattle culture. We passed four bloated cow carcasses, this being one reason why we carried our drinking water with us.

Reminders of past cultures intermingled with the present one. Remnants of the Fremont Indian culture and the leavings of Shoshoni and Ute Indians were scattered along this stretch of the river. Mantle Cave, a short hike from the river, was a prime site for Indian artifacts. At a nearby ranch, a private inholding within the monument, modern artifacts were strewn about the yard. A covey of snowmobiles were beached in the sagebrush and scattered about were irrigation pipes and rusting fuel drums, and other ranch trash. Archaeologists had sifted through the Indians' junk piles in the cave. Today's junk would be tomorrow's find.

The only rapids of any consequence, Warm Springs, were passed without incident; and we ended that day at Echo Park, whose green lushness encased within rock walls recalled estate lands in wet northern climates rather than the parched canyonlands of the West. As we stood on the bank after unloading the rafts, a single kayaker flashed by with an offhand comment and a wave of his hand between hasty paddle strokes. He was insouciance personified. There was nothing the two rangers could do about the illegal river runner. Their boats were too slow and their radios ineffective from that isolated enclosure.

Such illegalities were a problem that year. The position of a certain segment of river runners was not much different from that of other users who were testing the limits of restrictions on public lands. What the boaters wanted was a larger piece of the river, and their target was the Park Service regulations that halved the permits between private parties and commercial outfitters. The river runners contended that the lottery they were subjected to was not equivalent to the outright granting of a permit to a commercial concessionaire. "Can you imagine calling an airline to reserve space during the busy holiday season and being told to apply to a lottery? Like airline seats, river permits should be available by advance registration," they maintained.

To test the law in an American tradition that goes back at least as far as the Boston Tea Party and forward to the recent Sagebrush Rebellion, ten river runners publicized their pending attempt to run the river without permits and then quietly slipped downriver in a raft and several kayaks one night of the Fourth of July weekend. Park Service rangers observed their departure and then used megaphones to direct the river runners to come ashore. The boaters proceeded downriver and came up against a Park Service flotilla of two motordriven craft. The rafts were boarded and towed ashore. Two of the kayakers evaded the net and made their way to Echo Park.

Those who were apprehended upstream and the two who landed at Echo Park were taken before a federal magistrate. Some were released, some fined, and the two who had a free but apprehensive night and day on the river later went to trial and were fined and jailed for a few days. The federal judge noted that the Park Service had a difficult choice to make between preserving the natural resources and providing the very public access that might result in frayed lands and rivers.

For managers of western lands survival often means finding the middle line and then dividing the pie, or permits, in half or thirds or quarters—a concept called multiple use. For a land administrator like Kennedy, whose tenure at Dinosaur spanned the Carter and Reagan administrations and adoption of the river, natural resources, and general management plans for the monument, adaptation was the key to survival.

Of the two presidential administrations, each having opposing philosophies of land management, Kennedy said, "For a while we were very heavy into protecting the resources, as far as I could see. More recently the direction that has been coming down is to mind what you have; don't expand." That meant upgrading existing facilities but not taking on new responsibilities, especially those that lay outside the monument's boundaries. A good administrator during the Reagan years did not comment upon or attempt to affect the course of events outside immediate jurisdictional boundaries.

To enforce river-running regulations within the monument was all right, but the Reagan Administration dictum meant not protesting proposals for upstream dams and nearby energy developments. Of course, dams would affect the flow of water and river running through the park; and energy developments had a bearing on air quality and visibility within the monument. The Carter Administration had encouraged such interference. The Reagan Administration did not.

Land managers in the West had been through these policy swings before. It was their job to endure. They were professionals. They had been trained.

That Kennedy and others like him in the West can function effectively, if not consistently, under such policy upheavals is a tribute to the education system that has bred western land managers. Earlier that year I had visited Utah State University, which turns out the largest number of graduates who take on such jobs, and the Albright

Training Center in Grand Canyon National Park, where ranger skills and Park Service *esprit* are instilled.

At Utah State a separate Department of Range and Forestry was formed from the Department of Agriculture in 1928, making the Logan college the first to grant such a specialized degree in the West. Since that time 3,500 bachelors, 800 masters, and 200 doctoral degrees have been awarded in natural-resource subjects. Undergraduate enrollment, with three-fourths of the students coming from out of state, soared during the environmental fervor of the seventies and then plummeted during the eighties, when interest in such issues lessened and federal jobs were cut back because of shrinking agency budgets. At present the majority of students are from Utah.

The College of Natural Resources, as it is now called, is housed in a striking new building above the lush Cache Valley and below the heights of the Wasatch National Forest at the northwestern end of the Uinta Mountains. It is the smallest of eight colleges at the land-grant university. The endowment was for an institution that would offer courses in agricultural and mechanical arts. The college's graduate programs have been supported by $4 million in federal grants, some of which come from the Departments of Interior and Agriculture. As a state school it is also supported by tax monies allocated by the legislature; thus there is a built-in conflict should federal and state interests ever clash, as they did during the Sagebrush Rebellion.

The college and its faculty were almost totally paralyzed when state mining and livestock interests took on federal land-management agencies during the late seventies. One noticeable exception was Bernard Shanks, an associate professor, who labeled the movement that was attempting to assert state control over the federal lands "the new McCarthyism." Shanks claimed he lost his job at the university when powerful Utahans, such as Calvin Black, complained to the university's president. The college's version of this incident was that Shanks had been denied tenure purely for academic reasons before he had made the remarks that were widely disseminated.

Not only at Utah State, but elsewhere among the western academic community that dealt with natural-resource issues, there was a noticeable silence on the politically explosive issue. Shanks said, "To my knowledge not one academic leader in the natural resources profession from the western states has spoken out against the Sagebrush Rebellion. But several academic personnel have spoken out in favor of the movement." Counterbalancing Shanks's attack on the movement was the active role that Doyle F. Matthews, dean of the College of Agriculture at Utah State, took in backing the movement. However, most of what little debate there was on the subject was internal. The academics hid behind their cloak of objectivity.

The natural-resources-policy class that Shanks taught was the single, concentrated attempt within the curriculum of the college to widen the perspective of students beyond rather narrowly focused subjects, such as vegetation management and livestock nutrition. Neither Shanks nor his successor, Rosemary Nichols, had much luck teaching the course, which touched on such sensitive policy alternatives as conservation. Shanks was not granted tenure nor was Nichols, the first woman on a tenure track at the college. As she was about to leave the school, Nichols said that broad policy issues, and the different viewpoints that were brought to bear upon them, were neglected at "the captive college," which was dominated by western land users. She thought the college was back in the dark ages. For instance, there were no energy-related courses offered for future managers of federal lands that had recently been overwhelmed by such projects.

To the south, in a piñon-juniper forest just short of the south rim of the Grand Canyon, the Park Service mystique and such practical matters as how to apprehend a burglar and put together a budget are being taught at the Albright Training Center, named after a former director of the Park Service and sometimes referred to as "the academy." Typical trainees at the seven-week Rangers Skill course are graduates of such institutions as Utah State. They are in their mid-twenties and already have had two years of permanent service at such divergent places as Dinosaur, Hawaii Volcanoes, Gates of the Arctic in Alaska, or Independence Hall in Philadelphia. Their supervisors also occasionally visit the training center for updates in their specialties.

The Park Service is a benign paramilitary outfit. Its personnel dress in uniforms and some wear guns, but they are primarily dedicated to preserving either a natural or a historical site. To forge a brotherhood, or increasingly a sisterhood, they come together briefly early in their careers at the training center, where "participants develop a better feeling for their role in the NPS," according to a training manual, and then depart to their far-flung postings as part of a network that is called a "fraternity."

Such an institution is sometimes difficult to control for those who are nominally its superiors. An enraged assistant Secretary of the Interior once denounced a Park Service report as having "the quasi-religious sound of a manual for the Hitler Youth Movement." John Carver went on to state in an impassioned speech at Yosemite National Park, which subsequently became part of Park Service folklore: "When all else fails, the Park Service seems always able to fall back upon mysticism. . . . The National Park Service is a bureau of the Department of the Interior which is a department of the United States government's executive branch—it isn't a religion, and it should not be thought of as such." Carver, an appointee, soon left government; but the Civil Service employees he was addressing remained for many years.

A sympathetic history of the Park Service written by a former employee, William C. Everhart, and endorsed by the Park Service director serving at the time the book was published commented: "Since Carver's outburst was rated on a par with so many of his peevish pronouncements, the mystique was in no danger." Furthermore, wrote Everhart, a former Park Service historian, "In case any reader may have missed the clues, the Park Service comes closer to being a tribal clan than a government agency."

When I visited the training center, Ray Murray, chief of technical services, was teaching a course for supervisors that featured the faces of such go-getters as Lee Iacocca and Peter Ueberroth being flashed on the screen, interlaced with quotes from social critic Vance Packard. These men had the right stuff, it was intimated. They could communicate as could that ace communicator Ronald Reagan.

Thirty middle-level bureaucrats were arranged in a semicircle around Murray in a room whose walls were hung with color photographs of wondrous natural scenes. They were encouraged to be bold in an agency better known for its timidity. These were the lessons of the day:

Keep the Park Service image out there so that budgets will not suffer. Your first allegiance is to your staff, then to the service as a whole. Play office politics. Keep your outside networks intact. Think of the whole organization, not just your own turf. Job security, in a time of declining budgets, is the main concern at this time.

It was a message delivered with fervor and the easily digested visual aids favored by the military. The realities that were occurring on the ground in such places as Dinosaur National Monument were a distant reflection of what was being taught in these classrooms. David O. Karraker, who was in charge of the training center, said, "It is kind of a bittersweet thing. We do not want to destroy their idealism in what the National Park System is all about, but they will have to deal with reality."

The politics of the abortive name-change effort was one such reality.

The name-change controversy came up on the river.

Dave Whitman, who had just joined the monument staff as Chief of Interpretive and Visitor Services, met us at Echo Park, having been trucked in from above. Whitman wanted to get the feel of the river that has carried so much history along with it on its headlong rush through the Uinta Mountains.

Sleeping, eating, and cavorting about in the nearby campground was a noisy group of suburban Denver high school students. We planned to meet the students and their teachers at the Jones Hole campground that night for an interpretive talk around a campfire. The get-together would be a significant "visitor contact" for the rangers, and they could log it as such.

The noontime departure was in a broad swing around Steamboat Rock, radiant in the bright sun, and then another gentle arc brought us into a zone of darker, more constricted rock, where Bill Ott told me to watch carefully for a two-inch pipe and some writing on the rock wall to the left. We saw no pipe or writing, and Bill guessed that the high water had obscured those fitful reminders of the great dam fight of the fifties. But on the opposite bank there was a rock cairn, which I took to be a remnant of that conflict. The mystique of the Park Service had not been well served by its secretive maneuverings during the administrative and legislative battles. Other forces had been in the forefront.

The weather was threatening and the run from Colorado into Utah and on to the Jones Hole campground was uneventful. We beached the two boats, made camp, and ate all the leftovers, which, when lumped together, vaguely resembled Chinese food. The two seasonal rangers stationed at Jones Hole and a visiting ranger from Rocky Mountain National Park joined us. Shortly before nightfall we marched over to the students' camp in what must have been an imposing procession.

There were about twenty students and five instructors, comprising half of the senior field-studies program of the Jefferson County public schools, an outgrowth of the more loosely organized alternative-school concept of the seventies. The emphasis was on direct experience with the real world, which meant being involved in an urban project, working on a farm in eastern Colorado, hiking through the desert wilderness of south Texas, and running the rapids of the Yampa and Green rivers—all the time applying the more traditional academic subjects of English, Social Studies, Science, and Physical Education to what was being encountered around them.

The students, now reaching the end of the course and the safe years of high school, were exuberant about what they had learned. There had been lessons in independence, teamwork, limitations, denial, danger, solitude, fitness, and compromise. The hope was that from this smorgasbord of learning they emerged with independent minds. There would be a test tonight.

The students sat in a circle, some reclined on foam pads, and a few gave each other back rubs. It was that kind of crowd. There were crickets nearby, a great horned owl in the distance, and the constant, reassuring murmur of the river, of whose boating history Bill Ott spoke in learned detail.

Then Dave Whitman, who had been to all the appropriate

training schools, took over. His formal training was apparent. He captured the immediate attention of the students by stating in a decisive tone, "How about stretching?" The suggestion did three things at once. It established his presence, his consideration, and the fact that he was in charge now.

After the students sat down, Dave asked: "When you picture a dinosaur, what do you think about?"

Nothing like a little audience participation to start things off, I thought. There was silence, and finally a few tentative answers like big, cold-blooded, ancient.

Well, said Dave, dinosaurs were the reason for this park. He then launched into a short discussion of the ancient beasts and ended by asking, "What do you think of our park?"

The answers ranged from "great" to "beautiful."

"It is a national monument now, but we think it has most of the qualifications for a national park. Would you like to see it a national park?"

The pitch was out in the open. The question that Dave had asked had all the badly disguised subtlety of priests asking visitors in a cathedral if they believe in God.

There was a chorus of yeses that I found disappointing, given all the work that had gone into developing independent minds within the past year. But, in their defense, the students were in the grip of a revival-meeting mentality. Whitman said he would let their leaders know to whom to write, and thus another national-park constituency was born.

I then spoke to say that the Park Service ranger had not outlined all the current considerations that were involved in such a decision —the monument's history and the history of the surrounding mountains and deserts that made up this distinctive entity called Sagebrush Country. Perhaps the students should immerse themselves for a while in that web, I suggested, before rendering an opinion.

From the silent faces that surrounded me in the firelight I did not sense a great deal of assent to my remarks. It was easier to feel than to think, and plenty of feeling was going on in the West that year.

*   *   *

Not surprisingly, the strongest emotions in the West came from the extreme ends of the land-use spectrum, the large middle ground being rather docile. Two men I visited that summer represented the two poles in the western natural-resource controversy—use and preservation. What they said within their respective spheres of influence had some effect on what happened on the land. Their counterparts were elsewhere within the region and on both coasts.

Dick Carter had devoted his life to the creation of officially declared wilderness lands. In his mid-thirties, tall and intense, and sporting a well-trimmed beard that did not offend mainstream western sensibilities, Carter had gained a reputation as a minor miracle worker. In a state, Utah, and amongst a theocracy, the Mormons, that was oriented toward use, Carter had been the main driving force in getting state leaders, the congressional delegation, and major land users to unite that year behind a bill that set aside the High Uintas as a wilderness area. From that victory he immediately went on to lobby for the preservation of certain Bureau of Land Management lands as wilderness areas and came head to head with such people as Calvin Black.

Carter was of the Mormons, but not one himself. He was related to the church hierarchy, but had not been baptized in the church. He dealt with wilderness issues with the same messianic zeal and hard work that his Mormon relatives used in missionary work, or that Cal Black employed to oppose such measures.

At the age of twelve Carter went on a ramble through the mountains on Forest Service lands that surrounded Salt Lake City and in the process discovered wilderness. With an assist from the romantic image of the Forest Service ranger, a myth he was able to evaluate more realistically in later years, Carter's career as a professional wilderness advocate was launched. He attended the College of Natural Resources at Utah State, that breeding ground for federal land managers, and subsequently worked as a wilderness ranger for the Forest Service in Idaho and at the western end of the Uinta Mountains. He began to roam those mountains with his restless energy and inquiring mind, and what he saw was a vast preserve that needed the sanctification of Congress and the President.

Carter took a staff job with the Wilderness Society in Washington,

D.C., a place he hated, and then returned to Salt Lake City in 1976 to open up the society's regional office. Three years later the eastern conservation organization decided to close the office, so Carter and a small group of like-minded people formed the Utah Wilderness Association and began their drive to establish the High Uinta Wilderness Area in a state where such areas were conspicuous by their absence. Over the next few years the association grew to six hundred members with an annual budget of over $30,000. This supported two staff members and a low-rent office with duplicating equipment to grind out the newsletters, alerts, and announcements that gave the impression of a larger organization with vaster resources.

Utahans, albeit a minority of them, felt more comfortable belonging to a home-grown group rather than to such organizations as the Sierra Club and National Audubon Society, which are headquartered on both coasts. Although all these conservation groups appeared to work together, their leadership had separate agendas and considerable egos that needed to be satisfied periodically by institutional victories and flailed villains, such as former Interior Secretary James G. Watt. The Utahans, however, were more intent on shaping their own destiny within their own particular framework.

To a person like Cal Black, the environmentalists, whoever they might be, were the enemy, united and intent on destroying his way of life. And he and those who were like-minded fought back. Sometimes the fighting got a little dirty. The more radical conservationists committed industrial sabotage, while Black and his supporters sometimes retaliated by bulldozing roads into proposed wilderness areas so they would lose that potential.

Carter could remember being nudged to the edge of a cliff by two large antagonists while on a Bureau of Land Management field trip to inspect wilderness areas in southern Utah. A witness to the incident stated, "They were making statements that 'We can't have even one more wilderness in this state,' and Dick replied, 'Well, fortunately there are other people on this planet who feel a need for wilderness, and this may be one of those areas.' The man responded to him, 'Well, in about a minute there is going to be one less [such person] on this planet.' "

Black, appointed by the Reagan Administration to the National

Public Lands Advisory Council, had done some pushing of his own. It was the council's job to recommend to the Secretary of the Interior policies and programs for the nation's public lands, which included lands administered by the Park Service and the Bureau of Land Management. Black had other distinctions. He was the model for Bishop Love in Edward Abbey's *The Monkey Wrench Gang.* The bishop and his gang pursued a bunch of sabotaging eco-freaks around the canyon country. Black, a county commissioner in southern Utah, was also one of the more vocal supporters of the Sagebrush Rebellion.

During that rebellion Black's threats mirrored Abbey's fiction. As Bureau of Land Management personnel were explaining the agency's wilderness policies at an open house in southern Utah, County Commissioner Black strode into the room and began berating the BLM personnel. He shouted, "We've had enough of you guys telling us what to do. I'm not a violent man, but I'm getting to the point where I'll blow up bridges, ruins, and your vehicles. We're going to start a revolution. We're going to get back our lands. We're going to sabotage your vehicles. You had better go out in twos and threes because we're going to take care of you BLMers."

An employee of the federal agency said, "Mr. Black, I hope you are not threatening me."

"I'm not threatening you. I'm promising you," Black replied.

"They tried to run the BLM people out of Nevada, and we *are* going to do it here," promised Black.

A few years later at the Elk Ridge Café in Blanding, Utah, Black was the very picture of western reasonableness. Of medium height and chunky, he had parted his hair to disguise his partial baldness in front, a touch, along with bifocals, that made him seem quite human. His fabled anger only arose when discussing outsiders, whether from the Salt Lake area, California, or the East. "They make me furious," he said. "They snatch our destiny from our hands and make it their own." To Black, the conservation organizations were anathema. He referred to the Sierra Club as the Sahara Club and the Friends of the Earth were the Fiends of the Earth.

In a burst of passion, Black continued: "I've always felt that it was unfair for the people of the United States to own most of the thirteen western states, or colonies; but we don't own any part of their states. Land is the only source of wealth in the West. Land is the means to make a living. It is the source of energy, food, fiber, and minerals. Land is wealth. Land is power. I believe the definition of colonialism is when someone elsewhere exercises control and authority and dominion over someone else and exports the natural resources. The royalties and wealth from these lands go elsewhere, and little is returned."

Black's thoughts were not unlike the writings of Bernard DeVoto some thirty-five years earlier. DeVoto, who advanced the colonial theme in an evocative manner, was a conservationist and a Utahan-cum-easterner. However, DeVoto and Black parted company on who should be the dominant landlord. DeVoto thought the federal government was the proper repository for the bulk of western lands while Black advocated their partial and gradual privatization. By such means those lands would be put on the tax rolls and become more productive, and the wide swings between economic highs and lows that have historically plagued the West would be evened out. Black had personally experienced those wide fluctuations. He had bought a truck and hauled uranium and witnessed the wide swings in the price of that deadly mineral while raising six children off his earnings in good years and bad.

There would be a limit on how much land an individual or corporation could own, a concept that was not far from the Jeffersonian ideal of independent yeomen tilling their small plots throughout the West. Such a concept was true democracy, Black believed, while government control was at the very least socialism if not outright communism.

On his departure from the café, Black was asked by friends if he was on his way to The Lake that weekend. Yes, he allowed.

There was a basic western contradiction at work here. Black was going motorboating on Lake Powell, a government-created reservoir. The water from that federally funded development and other similar projects throughout the West—be they dams, canals, roads, railroads, airports, predator-control programs, or grazing-enhancement programs—allowed Black and those like him to survive in that harsh desert environment. Help us, but don't control us, Black and others like him seemed to be saying. From such a dichotomy comes anger when the scale appears to tip toward control.

The next morning we departed from Jones Hole campground and drifted through Whirlpool Canyon and then Island Park, a marked departure from the land of twisted rock. More than one hundred years previously John Wesley Powell had passed from the canyon into the park and subsequently wrote: "The river meanders through the park, interrupted by many wooded islands; so I name it Island Park, and call the canyon above Whirlpool Canyon." That simple description is a good example of unencumbered writing and interpretation.

A swing to the east, and back again, and we were in Rainbow Park, where state fish personnel were taking a census of the river in their motor-driven craft. We put in at the boat ramp and ate lunch while a Colorado couple readied their raft for the eight-mile run to the boundary of the monument where we were to take out.

We set off and successfully navigated Moonshine, S.O.B., and Schoolboy rapids and then emerged wet and cold at the end of our trip at Split Mountain campground.

Of course, Dinosaur National Monument does not exist as an island unto itself.

Various people enter the monument for many purposes and then quickly depart. They take various things away with them; photographs, notes, dinosaur bones, memories, livestock, the knowledge of where minerals do or do not lie buried beneath the surface, and other continuing facets of the western dream that occur in different forms for different people. The process has been one of gradual depletion, since little is left in return.

The tiny national monument is surrounded by the vast sea of Bureau of Land Management territory that constitutes the majority of federal lands in the West. The problems are of greater dimensions on those lands of less outright aesthetic value, which possess far greater reserves of expendable natural resources than the parks.

Their administrators are in greater sympathy with the needs of the surrounding residents, since those people are more prevalent on these lands than the tourists who favor the national parks.

The BLM office in Vernal is a good example of this compatibility. It looks just like another hastily erected building, housing a transient energy company. One can wander through it with virtual impunity, while a closed door that is watched over by a receptionist separates the visitor section from the administrative section of the monument headquarters. The people who work for the BLM are not in uniform, but rather in the informal garb of western wear—snap-button shirts, bolo ties, boots, and Levi's. The effort to look the same seems almost as forced as the effort to be different. The emphasis is on unison with the agency's immediate surroundings. The BLM district's December newsletter is apt to send holiday greetings "from our family to your family."

One result of this exercise in compatibility is that massive energy-development plans put together by the BLM district hardly attract notice, while a simple name change raised a hue and cry at Dinosaur. Even among BLM districts, Vernal is a special case. Whereas environmentalists and others have protested BLM resource-management plans throughout the West, the Vernal District ushered the Book Cliffs final plan and environmental statement through the process without a protest, the first such document to emerge in its virgin state. In another instance, nine synfuel projects proposed by seven companies for the Uintah Basin were lumped together in a single environmental-impact statement that sailed through the adoption process with virtually no hitches.

The irony—and the saving grace—is that nothing resulted from this last extraordinary exercise in paperwork and planning time because the oil-shale and tar-sand projects began to disappear for economic reasons even before the final plans were adopted. As the energy crisis of the seventies abated and oil prices dropped, such developments became less feasible. But for a while energy was king. The population of the Uintah Basin, it was thought, was going to increase to 150,000 people, two and one-half times its present population. The air quality and other qualities of life would lessen, but there would be more jobs and more money with which to raise families.

The bubble did not so much burst as slowly lose air over a couple of years: a planned $40 million oil-shale facility that was partially built was quietly abandoned, and the paved highway that led to it began to revert back to desert. For $1 million the BLM agreed to act as caretaker for the White River Oil Shale Corporation facilities, just in case someone decided to reopen them. The government and the people in this region never entirely gave up hope for a bonanza.

For a little more than ten years, before he was transferred again, BLM District Manager Lloyd H. Ferguson looked over the ascendancy of energy and the descendancy of ranching concerns, only to see the process reverse itself once again near the end of his tenure. Ferguson, who had studied range management at Utah State, was a westerner and a Mormon who understood his compatriots. And there was harmony between them. Outsiders tended to focus on more accessible and dramatic areas, such as what went on in and around the Grand Tetons, and thus Ferguson was left virtually alone to deal with his more immediate constituents. The silver-haired land manager easily weathered the change in presidential administrations, noting only a difference in rhetoric, not substance. He was more attuned to the voices around him, which tended to remain a constant.

While the Park Service personnel at the national monument seemed to worry smaller issues to death, such as falcons versus owls, it seemed that Ferguson and his staff, which tripled during his tenure, never could entirely control everything that was going on in their gigantic district. Besides grazing and synfuel issues, there were oil and natural gas, wild horses, archaeological finds, phosphate and other mining ventures, wildlife, railroads, roads, electrical generating plants, wilderness, recreation, pipelines, electrical transmission lines, and a host of other lesser issues to resolve. The BLM efforts, as elsewhere in the West, resembled the attempt to stem a flood by putting one's finger in an earth-filled dam. The impending disaster was only relieved when the water level dropped, or the cycle of boom and bust came full circle again in the West.

It was while the circle was being closed that the Vernal District Advisory Council met in the conference room of the district office one summer evening. The council was the closest thing to a governing board for a region vaster than any neighboring city or county, yet no member of the public (except me) and no member of the press was present at the public meeting.

The rancher Dean Chew was once again elected chairman. His father, Douglas, was an original permittee of the Grazing Service, the forerunner of the BLM, and the family had lived in the area for eighty-five years, a period of time that goes back into ancient history for the West. One of Dean's sons, Scott, had represented the family interests at the Vernal meeting. The Chews took an active role in helping to determine their fate, which this year hinged on the possible creation of a nearby wilderness area, the name change, and the infestation of Mormon crickets.

District Manager Ferguson and Dean Evans, area manager for the Book Cliffs region, went over the major provisions of the resource-management plan.

The chairman asked a question.

A tract of land adjacent to Dinosaur National Monument and near the Chew ranch had been reinstated as a candidate for wilderness designation, and Chew, who grazed livestock on it, wondered if he would get another shot at deleting it. Ferguson said he would.

The district manager, citing the fact that grazing permittees (read Chew) had not been consulted, had originally deleted Daniels Canyon from further study as a potential wilderness area; but it had been reinstated at a higher BLM level.

Ferguson was in a delicate position, not unusual for a federal land manager. The immediate problem for Ferguson was the criticism being directed at him from above for not having more such areas designated for wilderness study. The district manager cautioned that he did not have complete control over the selection process. Carter's group, the Utah Wilderness Association, had accused Ferguson of issuing oil and gas leases on potential wilderness lands, thereby ruining them for that consideration. Carter was lobbying at the state BLM level for the creation of more wilderness study areas, and Calvin Black was pushing to delete them.

Concerning grazing, Ferguson said, "There is a lot of potential out there, and there should be more use." He was selling a program of range improvements, and almost all of those at the meeting were takers. Wild horses would be gotten rid of, as would piñon and juniper trees. The horses competed with livestock for the grass, and the trees occupied space that was needed to grow feed. An adoption program for the horses, along with herbicides dumped from airplanes and chains dragged between tractors to rid the range of the native trees, were solutions that were discussed at the meeting.

A fair amount of herbicides and pesticides had been used in the district that year. The herbicide 2,4-D was sprayed on piñon and juniper trees to aid commercial woodcutters. The justification for such an action, contained in the one-page environmental assessment, was: "Dead wood brings a higher price than green, and there is a scarcity of areas that contain a concentration of dead wood." Additionally, there was a scarcity of firewood and room for grazing would be created by the removal of the trees. The district, as differentiated from the monument, aggressively sprayed Mormon crickets with the pesticide Sevin, which was also used to rid ponderosa pine trees of a beetle infestation. "BLM EMPLOYEES ARE 'HOPPER HATERS,'" trumpeted a headline in the district's newsletter.

Then Ferguson proceeded to energy matters. There was a little ongoing exploratory work being done on tar sands; but most of the oil-shale companies were just marking time. None at the meeting wanted to come right out and say that, even as they talked about the resource-management plans and the environmental-impact statements in which their wish lists for more energy projects were imbedded, the likelihood of those developments' ever materializing was remote now. There was a vast difference between wish and reality that was not being openly addressed, let alone reconciled, in the West that year.

It was left for Clay Johnson, who represented the Uintah Basin fly fishermen, to sound a note of reality. The local environmentalist said, "The assumption here is that those companies will stay in business fifty to one hundred years and be around to clean up their mess. Some will not stay in business for one more week, and we know that. You are just a little too blasé about what is going to happen."

Referring to wilderness and wildlife issues, Johnson said, "Maybe you will be a little bit more open-minded on this, though it is difficult because of where and how we grew up."

The others, who represented ranchers, energy companies, local and state governments, hunters, and the local public, sat back in their chairs and looked noticeably bored while Johnson talked. What the fly fisherman had to say was absorbed by the placid responses of his fellow council members.

The representative of the neighboring Ute Indians, who was a member of the advisory council, was not present. The tribe, which had a history of absences from such meetings, considered itself an independent entity; yet it was equally as dependent upon federal largesse as the other representatives of special interests, if not more so.

Not long after the meeting I started on my journey of discovery. I hoped to fit together what I had seen and heard that year with what had gone on before in this quintessential part of the West.

Chapter 2

INDIANS

It was a Monday in August, a sparkling day, too early for the smog to have settled over Salt Lake City or for the afternoon thunderheads to have built up over the Uinta Mountains, some thirty-five miles to the east. The city, unable to squeeze into the canyon where Interstate 80 pierced the Wasatch Range, was quickly left behind. Where the curtain of the Wasatch-Cache National Forest is rung down decisively at the point of departure into the mountains, the sagebrush immediately intrudes. The long grade ascends toward Parleys Summit, from where the Uintas appear to be a low mass of virtually undifferentiated ridges, a minor backdrop in the vast space of the western landscape through and over which transcontinental travelers hurry. This is the great American void: the place where the Eastern European poet, Czeslaw Milosz, said his imagination "encounters a zero—the empty, wrinkled surface of the planet crossed by jets in a matter of hours."

Those wrinkles, the peaks and ridges of the Uintas, extend an average of 7,000 feet above the surrounding bare countryside, with the highest point, Kings Peak, 13,528 feet above sea level. There are twenty-five other mountains above 13,000 feet in the range, and most of the high country—rocky plateaus, narrower ridges, spurs, and glacially-carved valleys strewn with grass and wildflowers and pockmarked with lakes—hovers above the 12,000-foot mark. Timberline is at 11,000 feet. The Uintas are no mean mountain range.

The 150-mile length of the Uintas is slightly bowed and resembles a fish which swims as a caterpillar crawls. The arched back is toward the cold northern plains and the softer underbelly gets the full advantage of a southern exposure. The average width of the Uintas is thirty-five miles, with a maximum forty-five near the western end. The head of this rather odd amphibian abuts the north-south-trending Wasatch Range, much as a fish confronts the glass wall of an aquarium. Toward the east, the tail tapers off to an almost indeterminate end in the mesa and plateau country of northwestern Colorado.

In an effort to make the mountain range seem unique, much has been made of the fact that the Uintas lie in an east-west direction. The mountains are referred to as the only such horizontal range in the country or, hedging a bit, the "most prominent" or the "major" such range. One source lists twenty-nine other east-west-trending ranges in the United States, and suggests that the Uintas might simply be the longest range in that rather obscure category. The fact is that these mountains are rather ordinary, and there really is no way around that unadorned truth.

The Uintas are, in a sense, invisible. Little traffic crosses the mountains since the major transportation corridors parallel them. People zoom by on both sides and overhead. The mountains loom as a barrier only if an infrequent journey, mainly by local inhabitants, is made across or into them.

Geographical vertigo is another by-product of their unusual axis. Most western mountains have an established pattern of vegetation that can be counted upon: lush growth on the west-facing slopes where most of the moisture is dropped by the prevailing westerlies and scant vegetation in the rain shadow lying on the eastern sides. The abrupt dividing line on these north-south ranges is the crest. In the Uintas, this wet-dry pattern takes place more gradually along the length of the mountains. To traverse the crest of a typical western mountain range for an extended period of time normally means going from a warmer to a colder climate, or vice versa, and experiencing all the concomitant changes in the flora and fauna.

These changes occur within a much more compressed space in the Uintas, whose slopes face north and south and reflect those climatological orientations.

There are other distinguishing characteristics of these mountains. Dramatically walled amphitheaters, sparkling lakes, and gentle meadows were produced by extensive glaciation, which spread over fifteen hundred square miles hereabouts during the Great Ice Age. Mountain amphitheaters of shallow depth but great extent were carved in both directions from the crest, and within these bowls more than five hundred lakes were scooped from bedrock or formed when moraines blocked the melt water. Surrounding these lakes or standing by themselves, both above the treeline and within the lodgepole pine, spruce, and fir forests, are large expanses of grassy meadows. Taken as a whole, there is a rounded gentleness to these mountains.

The Uintas are not a great wildlife preserve; too many people and too many domestic animals have criss-crossed them over the years. There are moose and elk. As in other mountain areas of the West, beaver are making a comeback to the detriment of the clear, flowing streams that they dam and to the advantage of the meadows that will be created in their stead. Mule deer are a common sight, but bighorn sheep have become rare. Black bears are about, as are mountain lions and coyotes. Grizzly bears vanished years ago. The smaller animals are fairly prevalent: porcupines, muskrats, skunks, bobcats, badgers, rabbits, squirrels, and, at the higher elevations, pikas and marmots. Along the Green and Yampa rivers are Canada geese and blue herons. Turkey vultures, an occasional golden or bald eagle, and peregrine falcons circle on the updrafts. There is other wildlife but, again, nothing out of the ordinary for the West.

The Uintas are not regarded in an abstract, Thoreau-like manner. These mountains are heavily used by the people who come up from nearby cities, towns, crossroads hamlets, isolated oil fields, and ranches. These are mountains to work and play in, not to write nature essays about. It is a rare Salt Lake youth who did not experience his wilderness baptism as a Boy Scout in the Uintas. At an older age they return with their fishing rods and horses, the former being the dominant recreational activity and the latter the

preferred mode of transportation. Also emerging in the summer
months are large herds of sheep and smaller groupings of cattle,
which eat and defecate in the high mountain meadows. In the
winter the mountains close down, except for pincer attacks by
snowmobiles from the roads at either end. They need that time to
recuperate.

Past Bald Mountain and beyond the entrance to the Mirror Lake
campground, congested with large recreational vehicles and earnest fishermen, is the turnoff to the parking area for the Highline
Trail. We were at the 10,347-foot level of Hayden Pass, and my
friend who had driven from Salt Lake left me off shortly after noon.
I did not drive my own car here and leave it because the previous
year it was broken into and various treasured goods were stolen at
the trailhead to an Oregon wilderness area. Besides, I will be
leaving these mountains far to the east, where I have arranged for
another friend to pick me up.

At the departure point, a mountain transportation terminal really,
there was a swirl of activity. Horses and riders, backpackers, Boy
Scouts, and curious tourists were either arriving or departing in
vehicles. I wanted to leave the melee of the trailhead behind as
quickly as possible, so I quickly changed into my boots, shouldered
the heavy backpack, and departed into what seemed like a very
stable landscape.

Within the context of geological time, the Uinta Mountains are
only a very recent phenomenon. More than two billion years ago, a
length of deep time that can only begin to be appreciated if it is
written out as 2,000,000,000 plus a few millions more, the now-
upraised Uinta region was a slowly subsiding basin, part of a great
trough through which the water sloshed from the Arctic Ocean to the
Gulf of Mexico. The sediments left by the moving water weighed the
basin down, more toward the western end than the east, an ancient
indentation that influenced the axis of subsequent mountain ranges.

The earth rose ever so slowly over a number of years, and the
bottom of the basin was uplifted, folded, metamorphosed, and
faulted. The result was the Red Creek Mountains, higher and more

extensive than their eventual successors and also possessing the same unusual orientation. Those ancient mountains, the eventual victims of erosion, have long since disappeared; but their stubs, like worn teeth, can still be seen north of Browns Park.

What was mountainous became hilly and remained so until the sea again intruded during Paleozoic time, some 570 to 225 million years ago. The oldest forms of life in the Uintas were deposited during this era in the form of brachiopods and trilobites, the primitive ancestors of the contemporary horseshoe crab. The organic-rich sea life filtered down to form deposits of phosphates that would later be avidly sought and mined by humans.

Slowly the sea drained toward the west in Mesozoic time, some 225 to 65 million years ago, and the land rose again to form a vast desert. The waters advanced, retreated, again flooded the area as far east as central Colorado and then ebbed away. A thick alluvial plain, known as the Morrison Formation, spilled out onto this ancient sea bed. Within it were trapped the remains of dinosaurs found later in Dinosaur National Monument and the deposits of uranium mined in the postwar years for use in atomic weapons.

Volcanic ash settled over these deposits like a shroud, and once again the sea returned, this time laying down the Frontier Formation, in which the coal deposits in Wyoming were found. In late Cretacean time, high mountains rose to the west; and the Uinta region was under a shallow sea, which retreated in the face of the mountain-building forces that gave birth to the present-day Rocky Mountain system.

Finally, what became known as the Uinta Mountains began to coalesce some seventy million years ago along the indentation of that ancient east-west-trending basin. As the mountains rose and faulting occurred along both flanks, basins formed to the north and south and filled to become lakes, whose sediments, named the Green River Formation, would later yield trona (a source for sodium compounds) on the north and the promise of oil shale to the south. The lakes quickly disappeared and left in their place the Green River and Uintah basins.

During recent geological time all but the higher peaks and ridges in the western half of the mountains were covered by glaciers, which spread like fingers as far as thirty miles down and out into the barren basins. The glaciers on the south slope caught more snow, expanded, and thus gouged larger amphitheaters and longer descending valleys than the glaciers on the north side of the divide, which accounted for the more precipitous northern flank of the mountains.

To the east the twisted canyons of the Yampa and Green rivers pose a riddle. Like the chicken and the egg, the question here is which came first, the rivers or the mountains? Or, as Wallace R. Hansen phrased it in a United States Geological Survey publication: "How could rivers establish and maintain their courses across a great mountain range in utter disregard for the structural complexities within the range?" There has been much professional debate on this subject. Hansen favored the stream-capture theory, which supposed that at one time the Uintas formed the Continental Divide. Then the eastern portion of the Uintas collapsed; and the Green River, whose flow to the east was stagnated by the new Continental Divide rising in that direction, breached the lowered crest of the Uintas at Ladore Canyon and joined a stream flowing to the south. In this manner the Colorado River system took shape and the landscape reached its present-day proportions.

The path led down through the forest to a new sign, which told me I was entering the High Uintas Wilderness Area of the Wasatch National Forest. Up to this year, and for some years previously, the mountains' higher elevations were within what was called the High Uintas Primitive Area. The name change took an act of Congress, which Dick Carter and others had promoted. All the traditional forces in western land matters focused on the rocks, forests, lakes, and wildlife of the Uintas for one session of Congress and then handed down their decree in the form of a name change that Superintendent Kennedy of Dinosaur would have been envious of.

Another sign instructed me to leave any motorized vehicles behind, carry out all refuse, tether or pasture stock no closer than 200 feet from the shoreline of lakes and trails, camp no nearer than 150 feet from certain lakes, and light no open fires along the

Highline Trail, my principal route. In the course of the following days and nights I obeyed some of those rules some of the time but not all of the rules all of the time, which probably put me in the category of the majority who want the wilderness to remain untrammeled but do not believe that one's singular activities will be detrimental.

Actually, there are few restrictions in the Uintas compared to other similar places in the West. The Forest Service does not require wilderness permits, as it does elsewhere in areas of similar heavy use. Nor does it ration use, an action that would greatly anger locals, who regard the Uintas as their personal mountains and the Forest Service as an agency of convenience rather than a strict regulator. Other Forest Service and Parks Service wilderness areas are rationed in order to provide the quality of experience that their nomenclature would lead the visitor to expect. A relative free-for-all exists in the Uintas because it is difficult to tell friends and neighbors that there is no more room in the inn.

From this rumination on a sign two factors emerge that are pertinent elsewhere in the West. They are the essential timidity of the federal land-management agencies and the strong proprietary feelings of the locals.

Federal lands are public lands, meaning that, in theory, they belong to the nation as a whole and each taxpayer has an equal share in them. In practice, few taxpayers have any interest in these lands, let alone a virtually unknown place like the Uintas. So the custodial agency bends to whoever exerts the most pressure, and most of the time the input comes from the locals, either individuals, their trade associations, or elected representatives. The only countervailing forces are the few congressmen who have taken the time to master the byzantine intricacies of western land and water laws; the courts; a rare presidential administration; and, more frequently, the private conservation groups on both coasts who believe they are acting in the "public" interest. The situation is fraught with conflict.

The trail was crowded, as I expected it to be on the first day. The usual rule of thumb is that beyond one long day's hike lies relative serenity. People rarely want to make an extended physical effort to get far from their vehicles. Couples and groups predominated, not unusual for the family-oriented Mormon population from the Wasatch Front that uses this end of the mountains.

The trail was a quagmire wherever moisture and horses' hooves had combined to churn the softened earth into a pockmarked frenzy that resembled the wasteland surrounding stock ponds in the desert. To get through the gook meant being coated to the calves with mud, so extensive detours and hopping from islands of solid soil, wood, and rock to similar dry points were necessary. The numerous horses also left their wastes behind. At times the journey felt like a walk through wet kitty litter.

After a few mouthfuls of dried fruit for lunch, I began to pass one Boy Scout troop after another, their presence on the trail being heralded by empty beef jerky cans and a virtual snowfield of Tootsie Roll wrappers. Around a bend, I came upon a fat scout who had dropped his pack in pain and frustration. I felt immediate sympathy, having once been a fat camper who was forced to keep up with others on hikes in the New Hampshire mountains.

"How are you doing?"

"Horrible," the scout said, tears in his eyes.

He told me his troop had left him behind with some vague directions. I offered the boy reassurance and more precise directions to his destination, then moved on.

The scoutmaster was hiding behind some trees just down the trail, observing the boy. "This is a learning experience," he told me. I said that the boy had a different metabolism and just felt terrible.

"Well, just wait for a few days from now," said the scoutmaster.

I silently wished them all good luck and pushed on. A few minutes later I began to narrow the distance between myself and three scouts who were talking derisively about the fat boy's predicament. I saw a canteen lying in the trail and yelled ahead, asking if it was theirs.

"Yes," one replied, "but the scoutmaster can bring it. I'm not going back for that."

The Boy Scouts and I were only the most recent in a long succession of temporary inhabitants of this region. The total span of human life in this place—some ten thousand years—seems infinitesimal when compared to two billion years of geological time. Human activities diminish even further in importance when the historical record is considered. They have been distinguished in a general manner for up to one thousand or so years ago; but it has only been within the last two centuries that a clear historical record has existed for the wanderings of men and women in and around the Uinta Mountains.

The first people in this region who left some faint traces, the Desert Archaic culture, used the land as they wished within a very narrow but necessary spectrum. They were almost totally preoccupied with survival and were ceaselessly on the lookout for food, clothing, and shelter. If these roving bands failed in their vital quest, then the results could, indeed, be disastrous. The mutuality of the small group was the decisive factor in survival.

Those ancient bands were extended families who knew how to seek out the scant resources of the stream courses across the arid basins and the moderate heights. They retained no fixed bases—the seasonal cycle of plants and animals determined the paths of their wanderings. Because numbers were small and the region was vast, the assumption is that these people did not disturb the natural balance. One authority wrote of early man: "He exploited selected econiches without significantly altering the delicate balance achieved by other species." That was only an assumption, since no proof was available.

Depletion, however, would have been possible on a relative scale. A ravenous band could arrive in a valley of abundance and denude a saline area of pickleweed and destroy the populations of black-tailed jackrabbits. Then they would move on when food became scarce, and time would eventually eradicate any trace of a transgression. Was this the first human example of boom and bust in the West? Human is specified here, but would it not have been possible for a dominant animal population, such as the dinosaurs, to have at least partially eaten themselves into extinction? In the present-day West the fierce competition for food between wildlife, feral horses, and domestic livestock has denuded large swaths of land.

Some fifteen hundred years ago, following the earliest-known

humans, a remarkable culture began to expand across the upper
Colorado Plateau from the southern slopes of the Uinta range to
the Colorado River. There is also evidence of its existence in
southern Wyoming, where there is a sparser early record. The
Fremont culture was similar to but distinct from the Anasazi culture,
which blossomed to the south. It bore little relationship to the Utes
who were to follow.

One cultural group, or individuals within a culture, pushing
others off the land they occupied—that is one way to view the
history of the West. The Utes were interlopers and displaced existing
peoples, who in turn had displaced others, just as the whites were
to displace the Utes.

The Fremont people usurped those early nomadic bands, with
whom they had few cultural similarities, when they began to migrate
from the south into the region around A.D. 400 or 500. Their
pattern of settlement was to build a handful of pit houses and
more elaborate granaries or storage facilities of adobe or stone.
They were a more settled, agricultural people than their prede-
cessors and remained in one place, at least on a seasonal basis,
to grow a number of crops. Crops were irrigated by water diverted onto the fields from nearby streams. The Fremonts' plain
gray pottery was of good quality, as were their baskets, which
in the Uintah Basin were coated with gilsonite, an asphalt-like
substance that served as waterproofing. It was more recently mined
for use in the paint and nuclear industries. Another characteristic
of the Fremont was their animal-skin moccasins, which distinguished
them from other surrounding peoples, who wove their sandals
from plant fibers. Like the Pima Indians to the south, the Fremont
played games with polished stone balls.

The culture reached its artistic zenith in the Barrier Canyon
murals, wherein recognizable animals from the local habitat swirled
around huge ghostlike human images. An expedition mounted in
1928–30 by the Peabody Museum of Harvard University reported:
"It was in pictographs that the artistic ability of the Fremont people
appears to have found its highest expression, and in quantity, quality,
and variety the pictographs of the Fremont area are unrivaled in
North America." The anthropomorphic figures were painted in red,

although sometimes details were rendered in white or bluish gray. There were no facial features, except two blank circles representing the eyes; and the faces as well as the trapezoidal bodies were covered with lines and dots. The author of the report, James H. Gunnerson, found the pictographs "stiff, unrealistic, awe-inspiring and in no sense mundane." Gunnerson saw some Hopi influence in the Fremont murals and thought they were the work of a religious specialist, not unlike Michelangelo when he created the ceiling of the Sistine Chapel.

The Fremont culture may have been represented by a peak population of some ten thousand persons spread over a twenty-thousand-square-mile area, which encompassed most of Utah. There were distinct units, one of which was the Uinta Fremont. People from this branch penetrated the canyons on the south slope of the mountains and ascended at least to the amphitheaters, if not to the crest, in the summer months. The High Uintas, easily accessible from the long canyons on the south slope, were hunted for bighorn sheep. At lower elevations pine nuts were gathered. The most extensive settlements were in the foothills at elevations from five to six thousand feet, the same well-watered, temperate zone later favored by the Utes and whites. One ancient site, Caldwell Village, is presently bisected by a fence, roads, and an irrigation ditch that draws its water from Deep Creek, just as the Fremont people did one thousand years ago.

At this site, occupied by several extended families for more than a century, twenty-two pit houses have been uncovered. Timbers supported the roofs of the houses, which rose from a shallow pit varying from twelve to twenty-seven feet in diameter. Some of the houses had second floors. On the bottom level, underneath the compacted dirt floors, were storage and burial pits. In this village the skeletons of two dogs, one with its head bashed in, were found along with the skeletons of nine humans, including a year-old infant. The guess is that the village site was first occupied in 1050 and abandoned around 1200, the approximate time that the entire culture began to slip into oblivion. The Anasazi to the south also vanished during the same period. The disappearance of these relatively sophisticated cultures underlines the fragility of existence in this region.

What caused their disappearance eight hundred years ago? Gunnerson wrote: "Drought was probably the major or initial cause for the disintegration of the Fremont culture." As conditions worsened, there may have been competition for the resources of the land. Such competition bred antagonisms and warfare, and archaeologists have noted that the granaries that were built later were located in more defensive positions. Drought and the depletion of natural resources may have also caused the disappearance of the Anasazi.

The Fremont people did not live in any garden of Eden to begin with, and it would have taken only a moderate reduction in rainfall to make the region uninhabitable and send a settled people off into a nomadic existence. "After about two centuries of growth, the Fremont culture was probably approaching a balance with its environment and technology," noted Gunnerson. But they dispersed, to be replaced around 1300 by the Shoshoni-speaking Utes, who probably emigrated from southern California and Nevada and spread across the territory once occupied by a superior culture. When they first arrived on the scene, the Utes represented a throwback to the foraging desert bands of earlier times.

So far the white man's version of the creation of this small part of the earth and the arrival of the Ute Indians on the scene has been told by various geologists and anthropologists. The Indians' story, as related in their tribal history book, goes thus:

Senawahv, the Ute creator, made the land for the use of the Indians, and upon it he placed buffalo, deer, roots, berries, and other plants and animals. In the beginning, there were no people on the earth. Senawahv began to cut sticks, and he placed them in a large bag. This went on for a long time until the bag was full. One day when Senawahv was away Coyote, who was known for his curiosity, opened the bag to see what Senawahv was doing. Many people came out speaking different languages. When Senawahv returned, only a few people were left. He was angry with Coyote because he had planned to distribute the people equally upon the land. The result of the unequal distribution was war between the different peoples. Each tried to gain land from his neighbor. Of the people remaining in the bag, Senawahv said, "This small tribe of people shall be Ute, but they will be very brave and able to defeat the rest."

Generally, the early Indians within this region had little concept of territoriality. What was regarded as "ours," in a limited sense, was the ability to use certain natural resources that grew upon the land, that roamed over it, or that swam in the waters, such as seeds, game, and fish. For the Utes there is no evidence that they asserted even this limited claim of use because different groups within the common culture trespassed upon each other's preserves, as did outsiders. The Utes hunted on the north slope, where the Shoshoni were dominant, and the Shoshoni rode south to do the same. Raids and wars were conducted on neighboring tribes for honors and later to capture horses, rather than to acquire land. "It was only in the wars with the whites that resources were the major issue," wrote Julian H. Steward, an authority on the Utes and Shoshoni.

Nor was there any concept of tribe before the whites began their confused labeling and the Indians responded to their incursions by joining together in larger groups. The small, wandering bands were named according to the localities they inhabited or the foods they preferred. The word "Yuta" was first used by the Spanish in the seventeenth century at a time when the Utes referred to themselves, in an overall sense, by a form of the word meaning "The People," a common practice among Indians, who knew little about what extended beyond the limits of their range. From "Yuta" came Ute, Utah, Uinta Mountains, Uintah and Ouray Indian Reservation, Uinta National Forest, and Uintah County in the Uintah Basin, all within Utah.

In contrast to such highly organized eastern tribes as the Iroquois, there was no sense of a common culture and certainly no political unity among the various groupings of Utes. They shared a language but were some of the most primitive people in the world at the time when the colonies were detaching themselves from England. At most there were small groups based on an extended family structure, and sometimes a few families combined to form a small village or a nomadic band. Leadership was in flux, since it was not hereditary but based on ability, with no powers of enforcement. The leader suggested when it was time to move camp, where to look for food, or how to conduct a raid. The concept of a single, unifying chief was imposed by whites, who wanted a contact with whom they could deal.

The Uintah Utes, a distinctive geographical branch of this common linguistic grouping, were not farmers and depended on wild seeds, fish, and game for their sustenance. Their settlements, when they did halt their frequent peregrinations across the basin, tended to be where the Fremont people had established their more stable communities—the same well-watered, temperate locations that the whites would covet upon their arrival on the scene. There were just so many habitable places along the southern slope of the Uinta Mountains.

Without agriculture, which stabilized a community and provided for a limited future if crops were stored, the Utes were dependent upon what was immediately available within a relatively short distance. Like the people of other Great Basin cultures, the Utes became practiced in making a few items serve a variety of needs.

Take, for instance, the common sagebrush plant. Women wore skirts woven from the tough inner fiber of sagebrush bark, and both men and women clothed themselves in a poncho-type shirt made out of the same fabric. To complete the outfit, the legs were wrapped in sagebrush bark to protect them from the cold, and on the feet were sagebrush sandals or inserts of sagebrush material within an outer wrapping of muskrat or beaver skin. At night the people slept on woven sagebrush sleeping mats; and if it was chilly, they drew sagebrush blankets over them. A newly born baby was wrapped in a soft sagebrush blanket.

Sagebrush was also used for medicinal purposes. Inside the sweat lodge the men would stuff their nostrils with sagebrush bark or it would be placed on the hot stones upon which water was poured to produce a sauna-type effect. The plant gave off a pungent, invigorating smell that tended to make one feel cleansed.

To the north, sagebrush was also an important factor in the quality of life. For the Shoshoni, of the same Uto-Aztecan stock as the Utes, sagebrush was used to reduce fevers, and it was a prime ingredient in fire making on the north slope of the Uintas. The dry, light bark was used as tinder in the following manner: a three- to nine-inch piece of sagebrush was bound to a willow stick, then twirled in the round hole of a larger piece of wood until smoke emerged and the heat ignited the tinder. Torches were made from bound pieces of sagebrush. If a rabbit ran into a hollow log, the animal was suffocated by such a torch, the result being a tangy treat.

This all-purpose plant, regarded as a nuisance today if it is thought of at all, was worn as an adornment by Shoshoni women. The Shoshoni called the plant "po ho," and in turn were referred to by other tribes as the sagebrushers, or buffalo-eating people.

These Indians were not necessarily the best keepers of the land. Their advantage lay in smaller numbers and greater resources. The sagebrush was rooted out around populated places, and there are stories of the large-scale slaughter of animals. Anne M. Smith, an anthropologist, gave this account of an antelope hunt in the Uintah Basin:

> In late fall when antelope were fat, a stout corral was built below a low cliff, possibly ten feet high, and the edge of the cliff was disguised with green brush. Long converging wings were constructed of piles of brush at intervals, with people standing along the lines of the V, between the brush piles. (Women never participated in an antelope hunt.) When an antelope herd was located, hunters would drive it to the area enclosed by the wings and over the cliff. Sometimes as many as 200 antelope were driven over the cliff into the corral, where they were killed by arrows, spears or clubs.

Fires were set on the dry flats to smoke out rabbits and other small game, and undoubtedly these fires occasionally got out of control, as they did elsewhere in the West. There were buffalo in the Uintah Basin in early historic times, and there is little doubt that the Utes, in conjunction with white trappers, contributed to their extinction in that region by 1830. The horses and guns that the Indians acquired from the whites hastened the process.

The horse, introduced to the continent by the Spanish, irrevocably changed the lives of western Indians by greatly aggravating the differences among groupings. The Colorado Utes obtained horses before the Utah Utes, and Omer C. Stewart, an anthropologist, wrote: "In some ways the coexistence, side by side, of the skin tents of the well-mounted Ute buffalo-hunters and the small huts of the walking Ute is a parallel to the coexistence of poor Ute hunters and gatherers and their more affluent [ancient] neighbors who planted maize and built their homes of stones and earth postulated for 700 years earlier." A mounted Indian looked down upon his poorer cousin who traveled on foot. Mounted whites referred to such pedestrian Indians by the derogatory term "diggers."

The spread of the horse north and west from the Spanish settlements along the Rio Grande was in the shape of a T tipped on its side, with the long shank facing west. The primary route went north along the western slope of the Rockies and on up into the northern plains. Thus, the Colorado Utes probably acquired horses around 1640. When the Wind River Shoshoni arrived in western Wyoming at the start of the eighteenth century, they quickly became mounted and spread the horse culture to the north. The dispersal of the horse was much slower to the west. When the trappers entered the Uintah Basin in the 1820s, they found an Indian population that was fairly well mounted; but when the Spanish crossed the basin some forty years earlier there had barely been any sign of horses.

Not surprisingly, the horse was first desired for its flesh among the Indians, who were of a practical turn of mind, and only later appreciated for its transportation values and potential in warfare. A mounted tribe was different from an unmounted one, just as a nation armed with nuclear weapons is different from one with conventional arms. The mounted Comanches chased the Uintah Utes out of the basin, and the latter did not return until they, too, had horses. For a time the mounted Shoshoni extended their domination from southern Colorado to Saskatchewan, then retreated to southwestern Wyoming in the face of newly acquired horses, superior guns, and diseases. There were no ultimate weapons, just temporary advantages.

The animal symbolized wealth and meant increased mobility, much as the automobile does today. The possession of horses enabled the Indians to range far in search of food, especially the buffalo; and the meat could be hauled back long distances to the villages. The result of all this new activity was to consolidate these people: such a prized possession needed to be guarded closely, and the activities horses made possible required a larger support base. Horses became so greatly desired that the Utes would trade their children to the Mexicans for the animals. After they obtained the horse, the Uintah Utes ranged widely in search of the disappearing buffalo and more horses. As the traffic in horses increased, so did the traffic in young slaves. The beast was fed, then the people ate; and overall consumption rose accordingly.

In his study of the Wind River Shoshoni, the band that roamed across the northern slope of the Uintas, the anthropologist D. B. Shimkin pointed out that a horse needed feed, and that basic necessity prohibited extended stays in one place, where the grass would be stripped from the ground. With an average of two horses per person, and an average population of some 1,500 persons, "nomadism became inescapable" for the Shoshoni. The more extensive migrations resulted in the loss of an intimate knowledge of one place. Such a horse economy was cyclic, and, according to Shimkin, resulted in "gorging and starvation, great assemblies and complete solitude, elaborate ermine tippets and the crudest of basketry," or, in more modern terms, boom and bust.

Each spring these wanderers of the cold Wyoming steppes gathered in the Wind River Valley near present-day Lander and began their annual trek south to the northern slope of the Uinta Mountains. Along the way they would look for seashells in the fossil beds near Fort Bridger, where they would linger when a trading post was established there in the 1840s, and then journeyed up Blacks Fork into the mountain canyons. There they gathered seeds, pine nuts, and berries, and hunted mule deer, beaver, marmots, and mountain sheep; the last were chased by Indian dogs along the heights of the range until they fell exhausted. During the warm months there was socializing with other Indians in this land of relative abundance.

Names give some indication of the utilitarian sense with which the Shoshoni regarded the mountains. Their name for Blacks Fork was Pine River. A favored place on upper Blacks Fork was referred to as "Beaver, its-rock-house." The Uinta Mountains, where Blacks

Fork rose in the snow along the crest, was called "Pine river, its-mountain range," and, perhaps indicating the dominance of others, "Utes, their-mountain range." With humor or the habit of naming things with reverse perceptions, Kings Peak, the highest point in Utah, was called "Small-peak." From Bear River to the Great Salt Lake the region was known as "Good-land" before the whites arrived to make it their land.

The Shoshoni would cross over from the Blacks Fork drainage to the drainage of the upper Bear River and then make a side trip to the lake for salt. On their return, when the first snows fell in late August or September, they headed for the Wind River Valley and the fall buffalo hunt. These wanderings were typical of a hunting-oriented society, with the bison being the most important food and trade source. Enough buffalo were killed to provide perhaps two thousand skins for trade in a given year. Others were slaughtered for food. Shimkin described the Indians' buffalo hunt as "an endless slaughter merely for skins and tongues." The Shoshoni also aided the whites in the virtual extermination of the beaver. The anthropologist, who closely studied the tribe in the years before World War II, concluded that conservation of resources was not practiced by the Indians.

Virtually all the Wind River Shoshoni made this cyclic journey during their lifetimes until the incursions of an alien culture shrank their land base to a small reservation. It was a Shoshoni from another band, Sacajawea, who led Meriwether Lewis and William Clark across the northern portion of this range in 1805, and thus inadvertently brought about the undoing of the Indians.

Before the Americans could claim what lay to the north and the south of the Uintas, the Spanish and later the Mexicans made intermittent use of this region. First their surrogate, the horse, arrived on the scene, then the people themselves: that strange race of conquering Europeans, who searched endlessly for tangible riches and quick profit in the name of God, King, and themselves and then disappeared to the south again with little to show for their sporadic efforts. The Hispanic era is usually dismissed as a brief aberration, but its legacy to the Sagebrush West has been of vast importance. The Spanish came bearing myths about the land of plenty—plenty, that is, of what they had in mind, not necessarily plenty of what existed there. This imposition of wish upon reality, a condition that was bound to result in great disappointment, was their greatest contribution to the West.

The Spanish always had a myth handy to guide their *entradas* over the hot deserts, where they fractured the stillness with the alien sounds of clanking armor and religious chants. In the far West it was the exotic Island of California, rich in gold and populated by black Amazons, who were ruled by a strong-willed queen named Calafia, while the rumors of the Seven Cities of Cibola, where the natives were adorned with precious jewels, lured Francisco Vásquez de Coronado north to New Mexico on a fruitless chase after riches. Less known, but firmly established within the pattern, was the legend of a "fabulously rich" region somewhere to the north of New Mexico, where many people lived around a lake, most probably Utah Lake near present-day Provo.

According to the legend, after the deluge these people were present at the Tower of Babel. Following that second catastrophe, they migrated to America and founded a kingdom on the shores of Lake Copala in the country of Teguayo. For the Spanish this was believable history, so, with the permission of authorities in Mexico City, expeditions were mounted and sent north in the 1550s and 1560s to search for this lost civilization, presided over by a great king who did not deign to look upon his subjects. The nearest they got to that mythical kingdom was the Gila River in Arizona. One leader of an expedition reported that he had to abandon the effort after his horses became mired in a swamp, an unlikely happenstance in that arid region.

The myth persisted, nevertheless, and took on some credibility when a Spanish priest in 1623 recorded a similar tale related by an Indian held prisoner at Jemez Pueblo in New Mexico. At that moment the word "Yuta" was given birth in a written language. Before the appearance of the Spanish on the scene and afterward, the Utes traded with the Pueblos in New Mexico; so it is likely the priest did hear about the primitive Indians grouped around Utah

Lake. But what he may have wanted to hear and what the prisoner, who most likely wanted to please, told him bore little resemblance to the place, a discovery not made until 1776, when Fray Silvestre Vélez de Escalante found the Utes grouped around the lake and reported they were "very poor as regards dress" and ate fish and a gruel made from seeds.

There were no riches here, and the small party of Spanish explorers quickly departed. But they could not help but leave another myth in their wake. Just out of sight of the lake to the west, the expedition's cartographer created a thick river flowing west from an amalgamation of the Great Salt Lake and Utah Lake, called Laguna de Los Timpanogos. Another river was shown flowing west from Sevier Lake, named Laguna de Miera by the cartographer, it being the continuation of the Green River, which, by a stroke of the stylus, was lifted out of the Colorado River Basin and plopped into the Great Basin. This river became known as the San Buenaventura, and became the fantasized waterway from the interior of the continent to San Francisco Bay. The cartographer, Bernardo Miera y Pacheco, did not confine his imagination to drawings, but with words described a large civilized tribe, living just to the west of Utah Lake, who tipped their weapons in gold.

Some priest-explorers in California picked up Miera's broad hint and declared that there was a navigable water connection between the interior and the Pacific Coast, which could be used as a passage to the Orient—not a Northwest Passage but a southwest one. Later mapmakers perpetuated this enormous error. In 1804 the explorer Alexander von Humboldt presented President Thomas Jefferson with a copy of his map, which was a duplicate of Miera's version. Lewis and Clark departed with such a river connection in mind, but disproved its existence to the north.

The mythical river persisted on paper, although any self-respecting trapper who had crossed this region, or heard others tell of such a journey, knew differently. But the mountain men had no official status. It was not until 1843, when the government explorer John C. Frémont saw on his map a blue line that pierced the various heights of the Basin and Range Province in Nevada and California's Sierra Nevada and went looking in vain for water and feed for his horses, that official notice was taken of the truth. There simply was no such river. Two years later the map drawn as a result of Frémont's expedition corrected the seventy-year-old error.

The Spanish legends of quick mineral riches available in the West have survived to this day in the Uinta Mountains, where treasure seekers spend weekends poking about. The Spanish, according to one written account, mined huge amounts of gold in the mountains but were massacred by the Utes on the way out with their riches, which were then buried or cast into lakes. Interestingly enough, there were supposedly seven "famous and very rich Spanish mines," which matched the number of fabled cities in the Southwest. A current book, popular in Utah and appropriately published by Dream Garden Press, rather baldly states that "an occasional cache of gold bullion attests to the truth of the Indian legends." If such caches have been found, or such nuggets taken out as are described in the book, then those facts have been lost to serious, documented history. The Uintas, like other mountains in the West where mineral pickings have been slim, attracted such myths.

Regretfully, all the firm historical evidence points to the rather dismal fact that the Spaniards and Mexicans had to scratch for a living in this spare land, where beaver skins, horses, and slaves were the prime economic incentives. The entire Hispanic era in the heartland of the West encompassed perhaps one hundred years, yet it is difficult to cite anything with precision because the Spanish presence, except for one official expedition, was shadowy. The western historian William H. Goetzmann wrote: "One of the great and virtually unknown stories of Western exploration was the story of Spanish penetration westward and northward into the San Juan, the Green, and finally over the Wasatch Range onto the Sevier River and the Great Basin." To the north of the Uintas, the record becomes something less than a bare shadow, but there are hints of Spanish penetration as far north as the state of Washington.

One reason for the lack of a historical record was the prohibition by the Spanish authorities on trade with the Indians and the illegal circumvention of this edict by enterprising traders, who did not choose to keep diaries or publish their memoirs. These traders slipped north in the 1760s, if not earlier, and lived for months with the Utes and Shoshoni before returning surreptitiously with beaver pelts, "it being to the advantage of the persons concerned to cover up all trace of their activities," noted Joseph J. Hill, an authority on the fur trade. The trade of Spanish horses and trinkets for the beaver skins and slaves that the Indians gathered is the first known example of resources being extracted from this area by outsiders.

The first written record of Spanish intrusion, or for that matter of anyone's journey across this land, was the journal of the Domínguez-Escalante party in 1776. Like the tourists who traverse Highway 40—a paved route that parallels the tracks of the Spanish, who, in turn, followed in the footsteps of Indians—the small party sought to cross the Uintah Basin as quickly as possible. The young Jesuit priests, about whom little is known other than their *entrada,* were officially charged with saving souls and finding a route from New Mexico to the Spanish settlements in California; they failed in both purposes. However, they were the first persons to leave a map and a written record of the heartland of Sagebrush Country.

Crossing from east to west along the foothills of the Uinta Mountains, Escalante, whose name is most prominently linked with the expedition because he was the principal keeper of the diary, noted that when they came to the Green River, the San Buenaventura of that day, there was "good land for farming with the help of irrigation," an observation that the Mormon settlers one hundred years later made for themselves. The West was constantly being rediscovered. Those first explorers left a record of their passage by carving their names and dates on trees and rocks on the banks of the Green River.

At a pass through Asphalt Ridge, pierced now by Highway 40 to the west of Vernal, Utah, the Spaniards found horse tracks and surmised that they had been spied upon by Indians, whom they suspected of coveting their mounts. There was smoke from Indian campfires at the base of the Uintas, and the group passed by ruins of the Fremont culture. Escalante noted that the Uintas were capped by snow in mid-September, and named them the Sierra Blanca de los Lagunas. Neither Escalante's name nor Miera's designation of them as the Sierra Nevada stuck.

The party hurried on, apprehensive at the signs of approaching winter. The wind from the west was piercing and cold. The water next to the fire froze at night. The predominance of sagebrush was noted time and again. Eight days after entering the basin, they left it for their disappointing encounter with the Indians surrounding Utah Lake. Silence descended again upon the region after that first recorded journey.

When Mexico gained its independence from Spain in 1821, little changed, since the new regime was preoccupied with surviving threats to its existence that were mounted from a more immediate distance. Besides, nothing of value had been found to the north, where sovereignty was a paper presence. The trade in horses and slaves continued. An old trapper recalled of the 1830s, "It was no uncommon thing in those days to see a party of Mexicans in that country buying Indians, and while we were trapping there I sent a lot of peltries to Taos by a party of those same slave traders." The Indians willingly participated in the practice until the Mormons attempted, not with complete success, to stem the drain of human resources. The Mexicans, who were themselves intruders, resented the influx of American trappers; but in the end, when they surrendered their ghost territory in 1848, they had been overwhelmed by the reality of far greater numbers.

Seven miles from the parking lot I called it quits for the first day at the base of Rocky Sea Pass. Sixty pounds was no minor load, and the pack straps were beginning to bite into my shoulders and hips. As usual I had over packed and was carrying more food and books than I needed. I did not want to starve the body or the mind, and so I paid the penalty.

I pitched my tent in a small meadow of leafy bract aster, whose lavender presence was bisected by the lengthening shadows of the trees. High, puffy clouds slowly crossed from west to east, the direction of the prevailing wind and my journey. I was suffused with the feelings of self-reliance and freedom, those ultimate western mirages.

Chapter 3

TRAPPERS

Like the West, the mountain men have come down to us in outsized proportions. They were not free spirits and independent souls. Like the Indians, the trappers mostly journeyed in bands. Both in travel and work, which involved hostile terrain and unfriendly Indians, a fair degree of cooperation was required. Most were family men, one study showing that 84 percent of the trappers were married. And most were not American, another study indicating that 60 percent were of French descent.

They were also company men, since most worked for or depended upon highly competitive fur-trading firms and suppliers that were headquartered outside the region. True, a so-called free trapper supposedly had his choice of whom he could sell to; but in practice that freedom was severely curtailed by who was available at the time and whether he was operating on credit, which tended to tie him to one supplier-buyer. The trappers were poorly paid, tended to squander their money, and went deeply into debt with the company store, whose goods were sometimes marked up 2,000 percent. It was a life of economic servitude and dependency, or, as one trapper put it, "a toilsome occupation," whose profits went to outsiders, rather than the "romantic adventure" involving "knights errant," as described by Hiram M. Chittenden almost ninety years ago in what was widely regarded as the definitive account of the era.

These men were credited with opening up the West, whatever that meant. The Indians had been there far longer and in much greater numbers than those of European descent who were involved in the brief interlude of the fur trade. It began in the mid-1820s with five or six hundred men concentrated in a few areas and ended twenty years later with perhaps half that number in the field.

The trappers passed on no maps and little published knowledge of use to those who followed, and the hunters who remained to serve as guides for emigrants, explorers, and the military were few in number. Many parties either got through or would have gotten through on their own, although it helped to have the way smoothed by experience. The impetus to cross the West was just too great to be halted from lack of firsthand knowledge of the terrain.

The derivation of the folklore and the myths surrounding the mountain men was commented on by the western historian Howard R. Lamar, who wrote: "Part of it can be explained by the Victorian romanticism of the nineteenth century. But a major part stems from the fact that we can still go into the woods today and experience the thrill of hunting, danger, and death. It is simply a variation of the eternal adventure story, American style." The movie *Jeremiah Johnson,* which was filmed in the Uintas and starred actor Robert Redford, perpetuated those myths in the 1970s, when the high country of the West was inundated by would-be mountain men with high-technology equipment strapped on their backs and freedom in their hearts. Mountain-man fairs that resurrect the mystique and the skills of the trappers are held throughout the West.

The principal contribution of the trappers was actually quite substantial, even though it has not been widely recognized. They were the first to exploit on a large scale a natural resource that was available in the West, desired elsewhere, and depleted in the process of satisfying that passing fancy. In a recent appraisal of the trapping era, David J. Wishart of the University of Nebraska wrote:

> In contrast with later stages of frontier settlement the fur trade barely scratched the surface of the West. The trappers and traders were too few in number, too limited in technology, and too focused in their objectives of exploitation for it to be otherwise.

The fur trade did, however, set the pace for subsequent Euro-American activity in the West. The attitude of rapacious, short-term exploitation which was imprinted during the fur trade persisted after 1840 as the focus shifted from furs to minerals, timber, land, and water.

For those who got their hands dirty in the field, the financial rewards for providing the raw material for gentlemen's hats were minimal or nonexistent. Most trappers eventually left the mountains to make a living elsewhere. For others, like John Jacob Astor, who remained at home, there were decent profits to be enjoyed in the early years of the trade. These entrepreneurs were the first to raid the West from the outside. It took a mixture of audacity, irresponsibility, and desperation—the essential characteristics of economic adventurers—to carry off their bold plans.

Both goods and profits flowed out of the region, which was abandoned when the goods were depleted and fashions were no longer dependent on that particular four-legged animal. From beaver to the recent energy crisis, the essential forms of the story do not differ. An accurate model for the future was the most valuable legacy of those two decades in the last century: a time that has become so distorted that it is unrecognizable in the Paul Bunyans who have come to be known as mountain men. Howard Lamar wrote: "In re-examining the main determinants of frontier history, I would like to argue that we have neglected a dual tradition of trade and mercantile capitalism by overstressing the mythic figures of explorers, pioneers, and settlers."

William Ashley, who made his fortune and then disappeared from the scene, was the prototype of the merchant-adventurer. Born and raised in Virginia, Ashley at the age of twenty moved to frontier Missouri, where he began to put his restless, entrepreneurial talents to work. He was a wheeler-dealer who desired wealth and social status. Marrying well three times helped him partially to achieve these goals. But his real love was politics, at which he was only moderately successful, his instincts being most keenly attuned to making money from the land. The secret was to remain ahead of the rest of the pack. He accomplished this by utilizing his driving energy, innovativeness, and discipline. It also helped that Ashley participated in the field activities of his company and that he had the good fortune, or astuteness, to sell out at the peak of success.

Ashley's fortunes rose and fell during his early years in Missouri. He made money transporting coffee by pack train to Missouri, then lost it shipping lead and cotton to New York. From mining saltpeter and producing potassium nitrate, Ashley moved into the associated business of manufacturing gunpowder during the War of 1812. Following the end of the war, and several explosions and deaths as the result of that operation, Ashley switched to real-estate speculation in St. Louis. When Missouri was admitted to the Union in 1821, Ashley was elected lieutenant governor. For a man of business, it was a good idea to have one foot in politics. Meanwhile, he had moved up through the ranks of the state militia until he was a brigadier general, a title he assumed for the rest of his life. The militia, like lawyering or the right college, allowed one to plug into the "old boy" network.

Always attempting to be one step ahead of the other economic adventurers, Ashley quit real estate and, neglecting his state post, which was mostly titular anyway, formed a partnership with his friend Andrew Henry to search further west for riches. They ran an advertisement in a St. Louis newspaper in 1822 seeking "enterprising" young men to journey up rivers and across deserts in order to trap beaver in the mountains for one to three years. This and subsequent advertisements attracted a mixed group, from which were to emerge the most colorful and competent trappers of the time. Among those who answered the call were Jedediah Smith and Jim Bridger.

In comparison to the likes of Smith, Bridger, and Kit Carson, Ashley's name pales in terms of popular recognition. Yet it was Ashley who set up and profited greatly from the system that allowed these men and other trappers to remain in or near the mountains, while others worried about the logistics of sending supplies out and transporting the furs back to the market. Ashley, for whom a national forest in the Uintas was named, reaped most of the monetary rewards; but he was not a remote parasite upon the West, as were others.

A man of slight build with a thin nose, Ashley was out in the field
directing his men, sharing in the dangers, and doing a goodly share
of the exploring in the early years of the trade. His expeditions
were conducted with precision and discipline. The trappers did not
haphazardly wander about alone or engage in drunken hee-hawing,
but rather marched and camped within the confines of a quasi-
military system imposed by Ashley. He got them through difficult
country with a minimum loss of life and a maximum amount of furs—
which, after all, was the nature of the business.

An attempt by Ashley to pierce the Interior West via a river route
was foiled by Indians in 1823. Deeply in debt once again and
becoming desperate, he decided to use horses and try an overland
route to the central Rockies. His partner, Henry, led one party, and
Smith, a young but promising New Yorker, commanded the other
group, which was to produce more important results. After wintering
with Crow Indians near present-day Dubois, Wyoming, Smith
rediscovered South Pass, through which emigrants were to pour
west in another twenty-five years, and dropped into the upper
Green River Basin, where he surprised the dozing Shoshoni Indians
and spied the Uinta Mountains in the distance.

A few Spanish, British, and American trappers had been through
the basin before, but Smith's penetration of the region and subsequent commercial success would greatly increase the traffic. He
divided the band of eleven men into two groups and trapped along
the north slope of the Uintas, most probably along Blacks Fork, one
of whose tributaries is named Smiths Fork. At the same time, and
unbeknownst to each other, Étienne Provost and a party of Mexican
trappers from Santa Fe were working the south slope.

On their return across the Green River, the second group of
Smith's men treated some Shoshoni Indians to a feast of roast
beaver, and the Indians reciprocated by stealing their horses. By a
stroke of luck, the trappers again came across this band and at
gunpoint forced the return of the horses, then went on their way
with no loss of life or face on either side.

The incident was illustrative. The trappers, who did not desire
land but, like the Indians, were mostly interested in what lived
upon it, were a brief, ephemeral intrusion into the Indian way of

life—except as a source of deadly diseases. They either lived with the Indians or fought them, whichever served their mercantile purposes, fit their natures or the particular set of circumstances at the time. When land became more the object of desire in coming years, the Indians were regarded with more universal aversion, a feeling that was returned.

The promise of an abundance of furs caused Ashley to hurry into the field with twenty-five men in the late fall of 1824. His government license allowed him to trade with the Shoshoni for furs within United States territory, a limitation the general paid no attention to as he extended his hunt south of the 42nd parallel into Mexican territory. Government control within the Louisiana Purchase was almost nonexistent, as was the Mexican presence outside it.

On this trip Ashley revolutionized the fur trade by relying on pack trains and a wagon, rather than boats, to carry supplies. He foolishly chose the winter months to make his journey, so it was not until the following April that Ashley and his men reached the Green River and sighted the snow-capped mountains to the south. The first large rush of Americans into the region was toward the Uintas, those silent witnesses to history.

Ashley wasted no time. He split his party into four bands and directed that three of them spend their time trapping, then rendezvous with his group in July at a point further down the Green, where he guessed that a river might enter from the west or, if there should be no such river, at a place just before where the Green met the mountains. After having dispatched the remainder of his party, the leader and six men embarked in a fragile bullboat, made from buffalo skins stretched over a willow frame, on a voyage into the unknown. The river was a mysterious region thought to contain a giant whirlpool that sucked everything down into the center of the earth. For all they knew, according to the maps of the time, they might end up on the shores of the Pacific Ocean.

As a measure of the man and his determination, it should be noted that Ashley could not swim.

The river trip began gently enough. Things were a bit crowded in the one vessel, so the party halted, shot some buffalo, and quickly constructed a smaller boat. Lots of beaver were spotted along the banks, and a few were trapped. The general fell from a cliff while chasing a buffalo and bruised his side, which gave him a lot of pain for a week. Two weeks after shoving off, the hoped-for river from the west flowed into the Green. Ashley made the agreed-upon marks to designate the site for the meeting at the mouth of Henrys Fork, which he called Randavouze Creek. The weather was cold, dark, gloomy, windy, stormy, and snowing—the words Ashley used most frequently in his diary.

On May 3, the leader gazed ahead and what he saw did not please him: "The Mountains around present a variety of scenery altogether exceedingly gloomy. They are mostly covered with a verry small growth of pine, some of them in many places appear to be Entire rock & which has undergone severe fire. The gap through which the river Enters appears hardly large Enough to contain the water." The unsuspecting party proceeded down the river. As they entered Flaming Gorge, where the serpentine river began to pierce the Uinta Mountains, it seemed that the world dropped out from under their wildly bobbing craft.

Looming red-rock walls, as if guarding the gates of Hell, towered over the minuscule men and their craft. There was no escape over the precipitous heights. The river, picking up speed, propelled them inexorably forward and down a deceptively smooth tongue of water into the turmoil of the boiling rapids. It was "not possible for boats of any description" to float through this maelstrom, Ashley said, so they portaged; and the general, or one of his party, took the time to inscribe "Ashley 1825" on a rock.

The turbulent waters continued through narrow canyons, forcing the party to portage many times. The Green was no smooth Missouri River, which just kept rolling along. Roiling was a better word through the Uinta Mountains. Nor were there many beaver along its banks. "Destitute of provisions" was a frequent comment. There was no turning back from a bad decision.

As the days passed, the going became worse. Encountering in Split Mountain Canyon a series of rapids—now named Moonshine, Schoolboy, and S.O.B.—the two boats approached a "verry great & dangerous fall" on May 14. They attempted to pull for shore, but the current swept them downstream. The general then pointed the way down the middle of the river, and the steersman responded, "but soon after entering the heavy billows our boat filled with water but did not sink." The bullboat struck a rock and its momentum forward was halted by a back eddy, enough so that "two of the most active men then leaped in the water took the cables and towed her to land just as from all appearances she was about making her exit and me with her for I cannot swim & my only hope was that the boat would not sink."

Two days later they sailed out from the confines of the canyons into the open spaces of the Uintah Basin and camped beside a small stream that came to be known as Ashleys Fork. Had the trappers camped on the east bank of the river instead of the west and looked in the right place, they might possibly have seen a cottonwood tree inscribed with "Year of 1776," and lower down the word "Lain" surrounded by two crosses. A half century earlier Escalante and his party had camped on the other side of the river for two days, then forded it slightly higher, turned south and crossed "another rivulet" (Ashleys Fork), where the priest made his observation about the possibility of irrigation. Ashley was ignorant of Escalante's earlier presence. Different nationalities serving different purposes had passed a common point in the West.

Two members of Provost's party from New Mexico stumbled across Ashley and his men and told them there was little game and there were hostile Indians further down the river. But Ashley persisted, hoping to find Provost and obtain horses from the Utes. They floated on down the river through barren hills and mesas that hid vast reserves of energy that would be avidly sought in the next century, but yielded no game in that year. To partially compensate for empty bellies, the weather was warmer than they had encountered on the Wyoming side of the mountains.

Finally they saw another human: a Ute, who, according to Ashley, greeted them "as if he had been accustomed to being with white men all his life, calling aloud, 'American.'" Yes, said Ashley, that's who we are; and the Indian put out his hand and the two men shook, just as if they were meeting in downtown St. Louis. Then the conversation lapsed into sign language. The general asked the

Indian to tell his compatriots that he wanted to buy some horses and to please visit him.

Two days later some Indians arrived at the riverside campground. Most likely they were a roving band of Colorado Utes, rather than their poorer cousins from the Uintah Basin. Ashley was surprised at their prosperous appearance, their ease of manner in front of whites, their good horses, and the English rifles they carried. No, said the Indians, they hadn't obtained the abalone shells they were adorned with from the Pacific Ocean; rather, they got them from Indians that lived around a large salt lake (who in turn had acquired them from Indians further west, and so on to the coast). The Indians would sell only two horses to Ashley, who now decided to leave the unrewarding river.

In early June Ashley headed northwest up what he called the "Euwinty River" (in reality the Duchesne) and eventually intersected the Indian trail along which Escalante had paralleled the southern slope of the Uintas. The Duchesne, swollen with late spring runoff, blocked Ashley and his men when they killed an elk that fell on the opposite bank. They were hungry and found no further game.

On June 7, much to his relief, Ashley met Provost and his party of twelve men, who knew their way around the countryside. Although Provost was born in Montreal, he had lived in Santa Fe for the last eight years and operated out of that territorial capital of Mexico with a number of trappers of French and Spanish descent in his entourage. Thus, within the space of a few days, Indians, French, Hispanics, and Anglos had come together in the Uintah Basin. The country was beginning to shrink.

At the fork of the Duchesne and Strawberry rivers the two parties followed the latter through the Strawberry Valley, to the point where Escalante had veered off toward Utah Lake. Then they descended Center Creek to the Heber Valley, which, Ashley noted, was fertile, thickly wooded, and filled with beaver and bears. Provost, Ashley, and their men turned the western end of the Uintas at Kamas then headed east at Coalville up Chalk Creek, where, in late June, ice a half inch thick formed overnight in their water buckets. The route they followed along the north slope of the Uintas to the rendezvous site was the same that incoming immigrants were to take in reverse some twenty years later and the railroad and state highways were to duplicate years after those first migrations. There were just a few ways to cross the broken countryside with relative ease, and from the Indians on, subsequent visitors tended to follow in each other's footsteps.

Ashley and his party, as far as is known, were the first outsiders to circumnavigate the Uinta Mountains; certainly not a voyage equal to Magellan's multi-ocean epic, but one of immense importance to the Interior West. Ashley profited from his venture, and the prospect of others also profiting initiated a fur rush.

By early July of 1825, 120 trappers were ensconced in two camps a short distance from each other on Henrys Fork near present-day McKinnon, Wyoming, for the first in a succession of annual trading and social sessions. It was Ashley, the entrepreneurial innovator, who set up the first trappers' rendezvous. Being the man that he was, the general did not dally at the rendezvous, which was a quiet, businesslike affair that first year. After two days of lively trading he left with beaver pelts worth $50,000 in St. Louis. On arriving home, Ashley described the country he had passed through. There were no woods, he said, but in their stead was "an herb, called by the hunters, wild sage: which grows from one to five feet high, and is found in great abundance, in most parts of the country."

The next year, at the rendezvous held at the western end of the Uintas, Ashley functioned as the middleman, trading supplies for beaver pelts. Then he sold his business to Smith and others and returned to St. Louis, where he built himself a fine home, speculated in real estate, and unsuccessfully ran for governor and the United States Senate. The general did manage to be elected to Congress for three terms. Overall, he estimated that he had grossed $200,000 buying furs from the trappers and selling them supplies.

His was one of the few stories of profit in the fur trade, which was at its peak when he retired from the field. William Goetzmann wrote of Ashley in his study of western exploration: "In the four short years he had been in the fur trade, Ashley had done more than any other man to revolutionize the trade and reopen the West to American enterprise." Ashley also established the enduring prece-

dent of the western entrepreneur calling for federal help. He wrote
a report in 1831 that advocated reduced tariffs on trade goods and
asked for a company of cavalry to protect trappers and traders.
Seven years later, at the age of sixty, Ashley died after achieving the
respectability he sought by exploiting a natural resource.

I was up at 6:30 a.m. on the second day and hastily dressed in
the coolness of the shadow cast by the boulder-strewn ridge immediately to the east. Cold was added to coolness when I splashed
water on my face from Pigeon Milk Spring, where the ice had
formed overnight. I stuffed my hands in the warm pockets of my
synthetic jacket to warm them. I added hot water heated over a gas
stove to instant oatmeal and more such water to a mixture of hot
chocolate and coffee, and breakfast was over quickly.

It was another fine day. I had reduced my food bag by one
dinner and one breakfast—a small divestiture, to be sure, but more
would go until there was a substantial reduction. One of the few
injustices about backpacking is that as the legs and back get stronger,
the load gets lighter. My legs felt strong, there being no general
soreness or blisters following the first day.

The short climb up Rocky Sea Pass was along a gently inclined
trail. Not long before I reached the pass at 11,200 feet, the trees
dropped away and the high country emerged in all its rolling,
cresting glory for the first time on this trip. The dominant feeling
was one of emergence into a simpler, cleaner world. I paused to
savor the scene.

The pass not only marks a spiritual demarcation but also a
bureaucratic boundary. At this point the Ashley National Forest
takes over jurisdiction of the wilderness area, while previously my
brief journey had lain within the Wasatch National Forest. I would
pass back and forth between these two different administrative
entities during the remaining nine days. Who had charge of what
meant nothing to me, but a great deal to the federal managers and
the commercial users of public lands.

A map showing the public domain and private lands in the
eleven western states resembles a scattered archipelago of private

holdings within a vast governmental sea. Starting with the trapping era in the nineteenth century, the national policy has been one of unrestricted use, as practiced by the mountain men, and later in the century the outright disposal of the public domain. Those lands shrank by about 1.1 billion acres over the years. A few people got rich and many more went broke or just managed to eke out a living as the lure of virtually free land drew people onto the western landscape.

Towns grew, railroads were built, and colleges and universities were established with the help of public land grants. A nation expanded, and that was what people desired, until they realized near the end of the century that natural resources were being depleted and that western lands were valuable for purposes other than as commodities to be traded and sold.

A policy of retention and control gradually replaced disposal, but it took many more people to manage land than to sell it, so a specialized federal bureaucracy grew and then, amoeba-like, divided and subdivided as additional responsibilities and specialties developed. There were mining, water, logging, grazing, wildlife, wilderness, and recreation to manage along with a host of other activities.

Conflicts and jealousies arose over the spoils, and justice was not always well served. Where I sat was once part of the old Uintah Indian reservation, whose boundaries were shrunk to create the Uinta National Forest, which, in turn, was partially dismembered and added to the more powerful and acquisitive Wasatch and Ashley national forests. Now the boundaries of the Uinta, the first forest reserve created in Utah, barely took in the mountains from which the national forest derived its name.

Before all that bureaucratic shuffling there were no boundaries. Rocky Sea Pass, over which Indians once padded, was a seasonal territory shared by the Utes and the Shoshoni. The trappers took only beaver and desired no permanent hold on the country. Then came the settlers, who sought extended occupancy and coveted Indian lands. The lines were then drawn and redrawn again and again until they became meaningless to all but a few.

* * *

Following the Ashley era, when only an invisible boundary separated Mexican from American territory, the Uintas retreated from prominence in the fur trade as the streams were depleted of beaver. Accordingly, the rendezvous site shifted further north. As the years went by and the profits lessened, the trappers became a leaner, more desperate lot. They turned to other activities that were peripheral to trapping, such as hunting meat for trading posts, guiding parties of immigrants and explorers, loafing, drinking, interpreting, horse thievery, or leaving the region altogether for retirement in the balmier climates of California, Oregon, and Missouri.

Near the end of the era there was a minor spurt of activity at the eastern end of the Uinta Mountains with the establishment of a trading post in Browns Park. The proper name for the post was Fort Davy Crockett, since it was constructed in the same year, 1836, or shortly after the Tennessee frontiersman and politician lost his life at the Alamo. But the trappers knew the place as Fort Misery.

Browns Park, then known as Browns Hole, was one of the few relative garden spots in the West. Over the centuries it had served as a refuge for men and animals seeking shelter, food, and warmth from the howling winters that ripped across the surrounding countryside.

The park is both a refuge and a natural fortress. Some thirty-five miles long and six miles wide, it is hemmed in and defined by the mountains and bisected by a placid section of the Green River. The Green plunges into the flat bottomlands of the park from the frothing rapids of Red Canyon, then departs via the precipitous drops in Lodore Canyon. In between there are serenity and safety. When Ashley floated by in 1825 he saw the remains of a winter encampment of thousands of Indians.

Two years after Ashley's passage a French-Canadian trapper by the name of Baptiste Brown may or may not have wandered into this haven and settled down. If he did—and the man's existence, let alone where he chose to live and how he lived, is in doubt—then he could very well have been the first settler of European descent in this region. Monsieur Brown may have stabbed a man, or broken both legs when his horse failed to jump an arroyo while being pursued by Blackfeet Indians. There is no word how he survived this predicament, or what injuries the horse sustained. He may also have been a horse thief. However, he is most often described as an old trapper who wanted to build a cabin, trap a little beaver, and hunt deer in peace for the rest of his years.

There were other claimants for the honor of having this remote place named after them. They include Bible-Back Brown, Bo'sun Brown, and Old Cut Rocks Brown. Some said the Brown of Browns Hole was killed by Indians, and others, members of a party searching for a legendary tribe of white Indians called the Munchies, said it was named for a trapper who was isolated there one winter by heavy snows. The history of Browns Park has always been slightly out of kilter.

What is known with some certainty is that some type of trading post, perhaps skin tents, existed in the park as far back as 1832. It was not until some four years later that the fort was built. "Fort" was a euphemism for the rude structure described in 1839 by a St. Louis doctor: "The fort itself is the worst thing of the kind that we have seen on our journey. It is a low one-story building, constructed of wood and clay, with three connecting wings, and no enclosure. Instead of cows, the fort had only some goats. In short, the whole establishment appeared somewhat poverty stricken, for which reason it is also known to the trappers as Fort Misery (Fort de Misère)."

Nor were the trappers at the fort much better off than their immediate surroundings. When there was no meat available from wild animals, Indian dogs at $15 apiece provided sustenance. One traveler to the fort judged such fare as "excellent, much better than our domestic beef and next to buffalo." It was Kit Carson's job to supply the meat as post hunter. Also on hand were two other trappers who would become legendary figures—Joe Meek, who was down on his luck and about to leave the Interior West for the coast, and Joe Walker, who specialized in trekking about the West with unusual ease. These three and the remainder of the restless souls at the fort were involved in an incident in the fall of 1839 that indicated to what depths the trappers had sunk.

A hunting party consisting of Carson, six other whites, and two squaws were drying buffalo meat on a fork of the Yampa River when it was attacked by Sioux Indians in the early-morning hours. One trapper was shot five times, but the others managed to make it behind the logs of the horse pen, from where they returned the fire, wounding and killing several Indians in the process. The Indian chief made the sign for peace, and the trappers motioned for him to come forward so that they could talk. The story, as told by Carson, continued: "When they [the Indians] were within shooting distance, they [one or a number of trappers] fell back behind some trees and gave the signal to his companions, who fired and killed the head chief and one or two others. The Indians kept up a firing for a short time and then retreated. When the chief was shot he jumped up and fell down, the others were very much excited, and raved and tore around. He was a distinguished chief."

A couple of months later the Sioux retaliated, running off 150 of the trappers' horses from the park. Apparently one distinguished chief was worth that many horses because the Sioux are no longer part of the story. Some of the trappers were angry, so they struck out blindly and stole fourteen horses from Fort Hall in Idaho and another thirty horses from the friendly Shoshoni to the north. The "good" trappers, who included Carson, Meek, and Walker, condemned their colleagues for this breach of frontier etiquette, which might bring retaliation upon them all. They set out to recover the stolen horses from a ruined fort on an island in the Green River to the south, where their comrades had retreated. By a series of stratagems and threats the horses were surrendered and all ended peacefully when the animals were returned to the Shoshoni. But it was not the trappers' finest hour.

After that episode, times were dull except when there was an occasional delivery of rum or Taos lightning. For a diversion, Meek and several other trappers walked one hundred miles down the Green River on ice one winter, and in the summer they went hunting in the High Uintas—"a beautiful and romantic country and then a hunter's paradise for small game," according to one trapper. Walker talked about floating down the Green and Colorado rivers to California, where he would cross the desert to the coast, a trip he never made but others were to partially accomplish thirty years later.

The fort was abandoned in 1840, the year of the last rendezvous, and four years later, when the explorer John Charles Frémont passed through, all that remained was ruins. Time erased even these partial marks so effectively that when the settlers arrived thirty years later they claimed that no such place had ever existed.

After soaking in the view, I dropped down the east side of the pass into the upper Rock Creek drainage. Here the softening effects of grass and lakes took over from the hardness of the rock-encrusted ridge. I walked past two unnamed lakes, where the wet ground had been turned into a quagmire by hoofs, and then followed the Highline Trail down a long grade through dense woods to Rock Creek, where, after a brief lunch, I began the long ascent to Dead Horse Pass.

To traverse the Uintas is like walking on ocean waters. There is an undulating rhythm of wave ceaselessly followed by trough; wave and trough, wave and trough. There is a lulling quality once the rhythm is discerned and the body and mind adjust to it. I knew generally what to expect over the next ridge without the aid of a topographical map once I had caught the rhythm.

I felt the end-of-day fatigue coming on as I climbed Dead Horse Pass. The pass marks the crest of the Uintas and is another dividing point between the two national forests. The topographical map shows that the national forest and the "old Indian treaty boundary" are one and the same here. There should have been a sign stating "Broken Promises," rather than the anonymous rock cairn at the pass.

Below the crest of the precipitous north slope, along which the switchbacks of the trail are but shallow indentations, is Dead Horse Lake. I surmised that the horse fell from the pass to the cold waters of the lake, and took care on the descent, lest it be renamed Dead Backpacker Lake.

The government-supported explorers, such as Frémont, were an addendum to the trapping era. They made official through published words and maps what the trappers already knew and had failed to pass on in a lasting format. The trappers' directions were oral or written in the bark of trees and engraved on rocks. The explorers, who were required to submit reports to justify government appropriations, left a paper trail and thus had a more lasting impact, although they passed in the tracks of others. These government employees used their expeditions and reports as a tool for their advancement, which was their way of extracting profit from the West.

No one used this medium more effectively than Frémont, an officer in the Corps of Topographical Engineers, who managed to popularize the concept of westward movement, furnish a practical field guide complete with accurate maps for western travel, and further his career—all at the same time. Frémont came to embody the expansionist concept of Manifest Destiny in a Byronic character, a combination guaranteed to attract attention. Handsome, intelligent, articulate, well-connected, shallow, and a Virginian, Frémont mined the Interior West for the fame that he thought would give him riches and high political office. He achieved neither, but along the way the captain carefully delineated the central route to the coast and in the process passed by the Uintas. Emigrants later headed west with his reports in hand.

Rescuing Kit Carson from obscurity by employing him as his guide, Frémont and his party of some forty men mounted South Pass in mid-August of 1843. The Great Pathfinder, as he was called, wrote: "The road led for several days over dry and level uninteresting plains; to which a low scrubby growth of *Artemisia* gave a uniform dull grayish color." Frémont was on the Oregon-California trail at the time, and the traffic had picked up to the point where it was a badly rutted path through a wilderness on either side.

At noon on August 16, the party halted at the ruins of Jim Bridger's first trading post on the Green River; and Frémont commented that little was known about the river, and that the Indians had many strange stories concerning it. No mention was made of Ashley's voyage part way down the Green River. Not really a pathfinder but a pathfollower and pathpublicizer, the explorer noted: "The heavy wagons have so completely pulverized the soil, that clouds of fine light dust are raised by the slightest wind, making the road sometimes very disagreeable." Time was speeding up for the West.

Sagebrush was again on the explorer's mind as he crossed the high Wyoming plain to the north of the Uintas. Two days later he noted, "Since crossing the great dividing ridge of the Rocky Mountains, plants have been very few in variety, the country being covered principally with *Artemisia.*" A trained observer with a semi-scientific mission, Frémont made botanical observations and collections throughout the journey.

Further along, past Blacks Fork, where Bridger's second fort lay abandoned that year, Frémont found the fossils that so enchanted the Shoshoni and took brief notice of beds of coal, to which he attached no value. The trail began to get crowded. They camped where immigrants' livestock "razed the grass as completely as if we were again in the middle of the buffalo" and passed one wagon train after another.

The Army explorer rode on to Oregon, then south along the rim of the Great Basin. After a dash into California, he continued along the western edge of the Great Basin in search of the imaginary Buenaventura River. After a futile search, Frémont concluded there was no such stream—the Columbia River being the closest thing to a waterway from the interior to the coast. Frémont's subsequent report and accompanying map finally put that fable to rest. On his map the Buenaventura shrank to a California coastal stream, and the Uintas emerged as an unlabeled rise with named rivers flowing from both slopes. With no river corridor, the land route across the West became of paramount importance.

Frémont, the romantic who played to an outside audience, fastened on the mountains as the dominant physical feature of the West, not the extensive deserts he had come to know so well while crossing the Great Basin and other barren lands. He wrote: "In height, these mountains greatly exceed those of the Atlantic side, constantly presenting peaks which enter the region of eternal snow; and some of them volcanic, and in a frequent state of activity. They are seen at great distances, and guide the traveller in his courses." However, he did note accurately that grazing rather than farming "would claim a high place" on these lands.

For the return trip, now along the south side of the Uintas, Joseph Walker had joined the party as chief guide, relegating

Carson to the role of an assistant. Frémont, who was credited with making the first botanical collections in the Uintah Basin, noted the widespread use of sagebrush by Indians and the self-contained nature of the basin that sheltered the Utes "from the intrusion of their enemies." Passing east against the westward trek of Escalante and Ashley, the party came to the trading post of Antoine Robidoux at the junction of the Uinta River and Whiterocks Creek, where a settlement of Fremont Indians once thrived. At the post, known variously as Fort Robidoux, Fort Wintey (a corruption of Euwinty), or Fort Uintah, they found "a motley garrison of Canadian and Spanish *engagés* and hunters, with the usual number of Indian women." They obtained some supplies and left in June of 1844. The men at the post were killed shortly afterward and their women carried away by Ute Indians.

Making good time across the badlands to the east, the party reached Ashleys Fork that night. Two days later, using a bullboat that they had purchased at the Robidoux establishment, they crossed the Green River and entered Browns Hole, where the remains of the old fort were passed. Although Walker and Carson were present, no mention was made of its short history in Frémont's narrative. Of course, the recounting of prior activities would have diminished Frémont's "pioneering" accomplishments. At the site of the duplicitous killing of the distinguished chief, the explorer briefly noted: "We passed during the day a place where Carson had been fired upon so close that one of his men had five bullets through his body." That was one view of the incident. And then Frémont, too, passed from the scene.

On the way down from Dead Horse Pass, I squeezed past three members of a Forest Service trail crew, being careful to claim the inside track on the narrow trail. As they passed one asked, "Is there a good view?" My brakes were shot so I did not pause for trail pleasantries and simply replied out of the corner of my mouth, "Not bad, not bad."

I figured we would meet again, as I saw their tents and horses clustered below near the lake where I planned to camp that night.

At the end of a long day on the trail indecisiveness tends to set in if I don't select a place to camp before 4:00 p.m. It was later, perhaps by one hour, so I spent twenty minutes fussing over the exact location for my tent. Finally, like a dog circling frantically before lying down, I found the right spot and pitched my tent, then lay down in the last of the warm sun to watch the turquoise lake and shadow-blackened mountains meld together.

I was jolted awake by an apologetic voice. It was one of the Forest Service people I had passed earlier, looking very official with a badge fastened to his chest. There were Regulations. Would I mind moving the tent back from the lake? "I know it's a bummer," he added apologetically.

Oh shit, I thought. "Yes, sure, no problem," I said. I knew I was in the wrong because of the sign I had read yesterday.

After dinner I wandered over to their campfire and was offered coffee. The talk was of what I was doing in the mountains, abstract versus representational art (one crew member was an art major), the noise seismic crews and oil-company helicopters make in wilderness areas (another had worked on such a crew), the sheep that are denuding the lower part of Blacks Fork valley, and the advantages of working summers for the Forest Service. Six dollars an hour and a lot of fresh air were the big pluses.

The crew was restless. There was a big fire burning to the north, and they had not been summoned on the radio. Fires meant overtime pay, good chow in the fire camp, and relief from the tedium of trail work.

I remembered when I was their age and was a very small part of the bureaucracy that was managing public lands. One summer I piled brush and the next I shingled roofs in the Randle District of the Gifford Pinchot National Forest in Washington. It was tedious work, and I hoped a fire would relieve me of it. Every hour on the hour our brush crew made a radio check, always with the hope that we would be spirited away to adventure. When we were finally called in the middle of a rainy night, I smelled my first rank bear while climbing a ridge in a storm to get to a single tree that had been set on fire by a bolt of lightning. When we arrived, there was a blackened stump. The rain had done our job. One of the crew members fell off a cliff, and we had to carry him out. So much for the adventure of fire fighting.

However, there were other compensations to such jobs. On days off I fished for salmon, played poker and pinball, cruised the main street of Yakima drinking beer and looking for girls, and climbed such mountains as Mount St. Helens, whose shape has been drastically altered in the intervening years. For a young man from the East, it was not bad work; and that exposure to the West, along with an earlier visit, was enough to bring me back after educational and military commitments had been completed. In the last twenty-five years I had continually sought the feeling of emergence in the mountains and deserts of the West, which was one reason why I was sitting around that campfire in the middle of the Uinta Mountains.

Besides working for the same agency, we had something else in common. The four of us were clad, sheltered, and fed by the marvels of a technological society. When I returned to my Gore-Tex tent, I took off my fiberpile jacket and climbed into my Gore-Tex-covered, down-filled sleeping bag. I was clad in long, polypropylene underwear. Dinner was freeze-dried beef Stroganoff, and breakfast would be similarly prepared oatmeal. I was warm, dry, and well fed and have been so in these and other mountains in the midst of winter. Although I have some cotton and wool garments, I am essentially clad in the products of the petrochemical industry. Those seismic crews were working for me.

As I dozed off I marveled at how the trappers had endured in these mountains without such amenities.

Chapter 4

EMIGRANTS

With the establishment of Fort Bridger, the trapping era ended and the emigrant period began. Like the Uinta Mountains, on whose northern slope the fort lay, the crude structures were an axial point in the history of the West. Bernard DeVoto wrote in reference to Fort Bridger that "the history of the West through the next fifteen years could be written along radii that center here."

If the fort was the locus, then Jim Bridger was the personification of such a history. From the start of the trapping era, through the comings and goings of the emigrants, and on to the dawn of the railroad era, Bridger participated in it all. He was another restless Virginian, who came west to St. Louis at the age of twelve with his family and then became one of those "enterprising" young men who joined Ashley. Bridger was perhaps the first white American to see the Great Salt Lake, was present at the first rendezvous in 1825, was one of the first to describe the wonders of Yellowstone. He also had some other noteworthy experiences of a different kind. He participated in the massacre of a band of Shoshoni, 488 of whom supposedly lost their scalps to the trappers on a particularly bloody day along the Green River. The actual number of slain Indians may not have been that high because the teller of the tale, another trapper, tended to exaggerate.

In time, Bridger came to be regarded as the prototypical mountain man, partly because of his exploits and character and partly because he had a good press. Writers sought out the trapper for colorful quotes, and he obliged them with tall tales and the proper stance. One admiring writer who was present at the 1837 rendezvous described Bridger in heroic terms that could have fit either a man or a beast. "The physical conformation of this man was in admirable keeping with his character. Tall—six feet at least—muscular, without an ounce of superfluous flesh to impede its forces or exhaust its elasticity, he might have served as a model for a sculptor or painter, by which to express the perfection of graceful strength and easy activity."

There was another less flattering viewpoint. To a missionary's wife who witnessed Bridger and his men dancing about with a scalp, "they looked like emissaries of the devil worshipping their own master." Some saw Bridger as a braggart. William A. Carter, the sutler who accompanied the Army, wrote, "At first his conversation was very interesting, but I soon became wearied by his excessive egotism." But then Carter was a different sort of person. An illiterate who spoke Spanish, French, and a number of Indian dialects, Bridger without question knew the territory well and was a survivor. His career in the field spanned forty-four critical years of western history before he retired with failing eyesight to a farm in Missouri.

In 1841, when the first sizable group of emigrants came through South Pass on their way toward California, Bridger was thirty-seven years old—a man in his prime with the second half of his life ahead of him but a calling that was no longer in demand. What was a trapper to do? There were a number of choices. He could continue in a declining trade, take to drink and loitering, quit the mountains, hire out as a guide, or adapt. He chose the latter two alternatives. Old Gabe, as he was called, was a transition figure. With the trappings and mannerisms of the past he served what was coming— the hordes who quickly passed by on their way to the lands of milk and honey.

Some type of temporary trading facility was erected by Bridger and then abandoned on the Green River; a party passing by in July of 1842 noted only one dog in residence. At the site of what came to be referred to as Fort Bridger on Blacks Fork, three dogs and the grave of an Indian woman were discovered a few days later by the same party. The following year the "fort" became more of a reality. Bridger, through a literate intermediary, wrote a St. Louis merchant that he had established a small fort with a blacksmith's shop and hoped to take the "ready cash" of the emigrants in exchange for "all kinds of supplies, horses, provisions, smithwork etc." He looked forward to "considerable business" with the passersby and noted the fort's "beautiful location on Blacks Fork of Green River, receiving fine, fresh water from the snow on the Uintah Range." In applying for credit, the ex-trapper became a local booster in the manner of later chambers of commerce.

Bridger had a partner in the new venture by the name of Louis Vasquez, who wound up minding the store more often than the peripatetic entrepreneur, who never completely surrendered to the sedentary life of the trader. The two had been together on and off since 1822, when they both answered Ashley's call. By the time they went into business, they were visual opposites. The educated Vasquez, of Mexican descent, was aristocratic in manner and dress—at least in that setting and in comparison to Bridger. Supposedly the portly Vasquez rode around the countryside in a coach and four, which sounds a bit too effete and impractical for that desolate region. A visitor to the fort noted, "Opening upon a court were the rooms occupied by the Bridger family. Mr. Bridger, with a taste differing from that of his partner (who has a white wife from the State) made his selection from among the ladies of the wilderness—a stolid, fleshy, roundheaded woman, not oppressed with lines of beauty." Neither man was a good credit risk, Vasquez being judged irresponsible because of his "drinking and frolicking," and Bridger not being regarded as a good manager of men.

But they happened to be in the right place at the right time. When the emigrants began flowing by, they found Fort Bridger was a place to rest, resupply, and gain firsthand information on what lay ahead.

Each year, as the rate increased, the fort was improved, so that in 1849, the year of the California gold rush, Captain Howard Stansbury, who was sent to explore and survey the Great Salt Lake, reported to the War Department: "It is built in the usual form of pickets, with the lodging apartments and offices opening into a hollow square, protected from attack from without by a strong gate of timber. On the north, and continuous with the walls, is a strong high picket-fence, enclosing a large yard, into which the animals belonging to the establishment are driven for protection from both wild beasts and Indians."

In its time the fort served much the same purpose as a combined gas station, convenience store, and café-motel on the nearby interstate. The dust, heat, cold, searing wind, dryness, and forlornness of all that sagebrush country were enough to drive the travelers a short distance out of their way to seek the temporary shelter of the cottonwood trees, cool water, and plentiful grass along Blacks Fork. At any one time there were Shoshoni and Ute Indians, white trappers, their squaw wives, half-breed children, and emigrants milling about the bottomland. Movement was constant: wagon trains in, wagon trains out.

Hard cash was exchanged for goods. One passerby remarked that the squaw wives of the trapper-traders "have a good supply of [buffalo] robes, dressed deer, elk and antelope skins, coats, pants, moccasins and other Indian fixins, which they trade low for flour, pork, powder, lead, blankets, butcher knives, spirits, hats, ready-made clothes, coffee, sugar, etc." Such a trade was the beginning of the colonial pattern of surrendering, at a low price, products made from natural resources for manufactured goods.

As with the men, opinion was divided on the services they offered. Bridger and Vasquez got good marks from the majority of tourists. An Indian agent on his way to a posting remarked, "They are gentlemen of integrity and intelligence." As the ill-fated Donner Party passed by in July of 1846, one of the members wrote that "Vasquez and Bridger are the only fair traders in these parts." The partners were promoting a variation of the usual route to California, called the Hastings Cutoff, which brought them more trade since it passed right by the door of their establishment. The dallying of the Donner Party along this route, and their poor judgment, cost half of the eighty-nine emigrants their lives in the snow and the cold of the Sierra Nevada.

A traveler on his way to the gold fields of California noticed the Uinta Mountains, "which loom up grandly above the beautiful, fertile valley surrounding the trading post." Most were simply thankful that there was a cool, fresh place to rest; and some treasured the bare touch of civilization that the fort provided, one noting that Mrs. Vasquez "entertained us in an agreeable and hospitable manner, notably by inviting us to 'sit on chairs.' "

However, not all were happy with the place. Some were distracted by the filth of the French-Canadian trappers, their squaws, and the many half-breed children running about. "I cannot imagine how the term 'Fort' came to be applied to these trading stations, for they have no one point of resemblance to such a structure, Fort Bridger being even more completely destitute than the others of any such feature," wrote one forty-niner. Others found the prices too high, but the opportunities for shopping in the region were quite limited until the Mormons arrived on the scene.

Financial panic in the East, free land in the West, Manifest Destiny, Oregon and California becoming United States territories, then gold being discovered in California—these were the oblique forces and tangible factors that drove and lured the people westward. So many trekked west in 1849 that the sorely pressed Indians wondered if it wouldn't be a good idea to go east to settle on what they supposed were newly vacated lands. Bleached skeletons of horses and cattle lined the trail through the alkali deserts of the Green River basin, with not a few unmarked human graves along the way. All the edible grass between Fort Laramie and Fort Bridger was stripped from the ground by the passing livestock.

The third day dawned clear and I ate, packed, and departed, my living room, dining room, bedroom, kitchen, and study once again firmly attached to my back.

I retrieved my pipe, which I had left the previous night by the fire, and talked briefly with one of the trail crew, who had just made a radio check. Still no summons, though there was hope. The outlook was for more hot, dry weather, which certainly fit my needs for the higher elevations but was conducive to the spread of wildfires.

I said goodbye, then took the trail that paralleled the West Fork of Blacks Fork for a short distance.

If I had followed the West Fork all the way down through the glacially-carved canyon, taken the rutted dirt road past the ruins of the Blacks Fork logging commissary and the new Meeks Cabin Reservoir, and then finally emerged onto the empty sagebrush flats through which the stream meandered, I would have eventually found myself in the irrigated pastureland surrounding Fort Bridger.

I had visited the fort earlier on Rendezvous Weekend, an annual paean to the mountain men. The participants had ranged from an Irish setter named Budweiser to Big Dave, Tater, and Pawnee, all, except the first-named, dressed in authentic fur-trade costumes. A Shoshoni woman was delivering a Jesus message over a portable electronic megaphone. Milling in and around the costumed participants were the folks up for the day from Salt Lake City and elsewhere.

This mountain men's fair was, in addition to being an exercise in living history, a commercial event. Guns, knives, beadwork, cattle skulls, peace pipes, Indian headdresses, furs, and books with such specialized titles as *Muzzle Loaders* and *The Book of Buckskining* were displayed on blankets and shelves. A headpiece made out of coyote fur from northern Colorado was priced at $125, and it cost $1,700 to buy a .54-caliber Bridger Hawkin rifle. Then there were the period eats: buffalo burgers served by the Lyman Lions Club and scones made from Western Family Enriched White Bread Dough by the hardworking members of the First Presbyterian Church of Mountain View. Eight thousand scones were produced by the diligent Christians that weekend.

At the center of the rendezvous, spread out in a peaceful setting amidst the neatly trimmed grass and cottonwood trees of the Wyoming state park, was the gun in all its myriad blackpowder forms. People were carrying, handling, stroking, talking, and thinking guns. Men, women, and children fired away in a perpetual haze of smoke during sight-in and practice time or participated in such contests as the blanket shoot, four-man team stake shoot, individual stake shoot (Santa Fe Hawkin rifle), cartridge rifle shoot, four-man buffaler shoot, squaw and buck buffaler shoot, flint rifle upside-down match, big toe shoot, junior and sub-junior rifle shoot, and, following Sunday church service at the old Mormon wall, the ladies' knife- and tomahawk-throwing contest.

This gathering was a dream come true for the National Rifle Association, of which many of the participants were members. An insert in a magazine handed out at the rendezvous warned against a proposed law that would limit the freedom to own and carry a handgun. A pickup carried a bumper sticker proclaiming: "It takes balls to shoot a musket loader." Contemporary men and women were clothed and armed in the image of imagined history.

Instead of walking north to the fort my path on that fine day veered off to the east, and I began the ascent toward Red Knob Pass, the next crest in this mountain sea. The trail, marked by rock cairns, crossed a quiet meadow through the lush grass that refused to accept a beaten track and then forded an unnamed stream, whose banks were dotted with late-summer wildflowers.

I paused in the peacefulness of the scene to consider the frenzy that I had witnessed another time at the end of the other route, then continued to climb in a long, gently ascending arc that took me under the rust-colored knob and deposited me at the pass. I looked below and saw three minute figures and a pack horse inching across the meadow. The trail crew had got a late start. Their jurisdiction ended at the pass, where, once again, the Ashley National Forest took over from the Wasatch. But administrative boundaries did not interfere with my progress.

The Mormons came for different reasons than the mountain men and other emigrants and, except for Bridger and his entourage, were the only ones to settle in the region. They made a commitment to the place rather than taking what they needed and moving on. Of course, they had little choice, having been hounded from other places. So they chose an empty, isolated benchland that was actually in Mexican territory. In those days land belonged to whoever settled upon it.

The best-organized mass movement of civilians in the history of the United States got under way inauspiciously in April of 1847, when the Mormon leader Brigham Young and a party of nearly 150 men, women, and children and 73 wagons left Winter Quarters in Nebraska to scout out the route that the persecuted sect would follow to the promised land in the Salt Lake Valley. The site was selected because of its isolation and farming potential, Frémont's 1845 report being a factor in this decision. By the end of June the party of Mormons had made its way over South Pass and were fording the Little Sandy River, a tributary of the Green, when one of the advance scouts rode back with three strangers, two men being led by Jim Bridger to Fort Laramie.

There were differences in style between the two parties. The trapper and his friends stayed for dinner, and the Saints, who were hungry for information, pumped Bridger for all he was worth. There were some problems with Bridger's circular manner of speech, the more linear Mormons finding the "imperfect and irregular" way he talked confusing. There was some doubt about his veracity, less doubt about his self-aggrandizement, and general confirmation from Bridger's scattered information that the Salt Lake region would serve their purposes. Then Bridger supposedly laid down a challenge to the enterprising Mormons that they could not refuse: $1,000 for a bushel [variously reported as an ear] of corn raised in the Great Basin. It was probably an offhand remark for the trapper, but the Mormons never forgot it. There is no record of their attempting to collect that particular sum, but they did return to cause Bridger trouble and claim his fort. The way Bridger and others around him lived was not the Mormon way of life. The moral element was a new factor in the western equation.

Bridger and the other two men continued to the east while the Mormons proceeded toward the southwest over the dusty road to the fort. Before reaching the gentile-owned fort on July 7, President Young lectured the Mormons on how to be thrifty traders. For the Mormon emigrants, as for others, the fort and its immediate surroundings were a cool oasis after crossing the hot desert. One of them remarked: "The whole region seems filled with rapid streams all bending their way to the principal fork. They doubtless originate from the melting of the snow on the mountains and roar down their cobbly beds till they join Blacks Fork." This observer carefully considered the ice forming overnight on water in early July and concluded, "It is doubtless a very cold region and little calculated for farming purposes." Had the Mormons acted on this intuitive observation, they would have been spared later grief on the north slope.

One of the brethren, Wilford Woodruff, got out the fly rod that he had brought back from England while on mission there and cast an artificial fly into the waters. The traders at the fort said there were few fish in the streams, and his fellow Mormons were having no luck using meat and grasshoppers for bait. But Woodruff had a superior instrument of European origin. In a couple of hours he caught a dozen fish, thus proving the superiority of the artificial fly and introducing that ever-present sport to the region. Later that day Woodruff went up to the fort, the Mormons having camped a half mile distant, and traded a flintlock rifle for four buffalo robes. He found the prices one-third higher than at any previous trading post he had visited.

During the two-day layover, the Mormon blacksmiths repaired wagon wheels and shod horses, and all prepared for the last and most difficult one hundred miles of the historic trek. The mosquitoes were bothersome, and there were some disparaging comments about the squaws and half-breed children. Then they were off, bumping down an indistinct track that veered from the main trail and eventually delivered them to the promised land. The trickle of Mormon emigrants turned into a flood in 1848; but because a shortened road now bypassed Fort Bridger and relief parties were sent out from Salt Lake with supplies, it no longer was an important stop on the Mormon Trail.

The fall-off in Mormon trade was more than compensated for by the gold-rush traffic in 1849, although the bonanza—some forty thousand emigrants moving westward—that might have been expected did not materialize at the fort because a cutoff on the main trail deflected two-thirds of the prospective customers to the north. To intercept this potential business, the partners sent traders north to establish a temporary post along Sublette's Cutoff. They offered skins, robes, horses, mules, and Indian women to the emigrants and took bacon and whiskey, among other goods, in return. The emigrants referred to them as "old mountaineers" and remarked upon their craze for alcohol, card playing, Indian habits, and horsemanship.

The Shoshoni began to show the effects of the heavy traffic that year. They were drawn by the excitement and the hard goods to the dusty trails, where the emigrants noted their rudimentary command of the English language and their clean, handsome appearance. "The finest looking redskins I ever saw," said one forty-niner. One traveler remarked upon their begging for "powdree," "balle," and food scraps. An Indian traded a trout for a cotton shirt. There were many more shirts where that one came from, but not that many more fish. The Indians tended to look ridiculous in the castoff clothes of another culture.

The deluge of emigrants kept coming along the trail, where the thick dust that clogged throats and obscured the way, not the Indians, were the greatest inconveniences. Vasquez stationed himself at the junction of the trails to Fort Bridger and Salt Lake City and "plied argument upon argument" to induce the emigrants, with some success, to use his facilities. About one-third of the traffic took the left fork toward the fort, but some, from ten thousand to fifteen thousand, bypassed the primitive facility and went directly to Salt Lake, where the supplies were cheaper and the food fresher.

For the new colony, the gold rush was an economic boon. The thrifty Mormons from Salt Lake drove wagons back along the trail to pick up items that the forty-niners had abandoned. Even the Indians began patronizing the Mormon settlement. Bridger did not think the Saints had treated him well. His enterprise could be considered the first mercantile establishment in the Interior West that fell victim to the vagaries of passing traffic.

Bridger then became a guide as the emigrant era began to shade into the next explosion of activity in the West. In the year of the gold rush, the trapper led Captain Howard Stansbury of the Topographical Corps on a trip to the west to search out a possible railroad route. Stansbury's conclusion was that the Wasatch Range could not be pierced and that a railroad would have to round those mountains on the north. Then the following year Bridger led Stansbury east along a more direct route than South Pass, which came to be known as Bridger's Pass.

Thus was the general route of the transcontinental railroad determined. Fifteen years later, when Bridger was a guide and consultant on routes for the Union Pacific Railroad, this knowledge was passed on to the railroad builders. One of the mysteries of western emigration was why South Pass was used for so long when an easier, more direct route—now used by the railroad and interstate— lay to the south.

Meanwhile, Bridger was about to lose the fort as the Mormons sought to consolidate their position by seeking control over the gates to the Territory of Utah in the early 1850s. The fort and its surrounding lands, which were in Mexican Territory when Bridger first squatted there, had passed into the hands of the United States upon conclusion of the 1848 war. As head of the dominant religion, governor of the territory, and superintendent of Indian affairs within it, Brigham Young chose to oust Bridger and make what became known as Bridger Valley a Mormon enclave. Bridger's biographer, J. Cecil Alter, wrote: "The Mormon leaders greatly feared that the image of James Bridger meant as much to the Indians as that of Brigham Young meant to the Mormons. Such a domination could be dangerous." Little love was lost between two such different men, the one being the epitome of the wandering hunter and the other the leader of a stable agricultural society.

The immediate pretext for the ouster was Indian troubles. Young thought Bridger was plotting against the Mormons by inciting the Indians. Bridger had actually warned Young about possible Indian troubles. The Mormon leader wrote: "I believe that I know that Old Bridger is death on us, and if he knew 400,000 Indians were coming against us, and any man were to let us know, he would cut his throat." These were tenuous times for the Mormons, who may not have seen everything with absolute clarity.

A posse of 150 men was dispatched from Salt Lake to arrest Bridger and bring him back to that settlement on charges of selling guns and liquor to the Indians. Forewarned, Old Gabe hid in a nearby thicket, where he could watch the Mormons and to which his Indian wife could surreptitiously deliver food and news. The large posse searched but could not find the crafty mountaineer. Whiskey and rum were poured onto the ground and livestock and trade goods were inventoried by the Mormons and carted back to

Salt Lake. Bridger and his heirs were later partially compensated for the loss, which, at the time, amounted to a simple land grab for strategic purposes.

The basin, whose further distances were softened by a blue haze on this day, was the usual Y shape. The Lake Fork River bisected the western branch and Oweep Creek was the dominant stream on the eastern fork. By now I knew the pattern; down the Lake Fork to the junction, then up the Oweep to the next pass, where I would be dumped into the adjacent amphitheater.

On my way down through the upper basin I met three hikers ascending the trail. We stopped for some trail chitchat. Where are you coming from? How many days out? Are you soloing? We exchanged some information on what each of us could expect in the directions that we were proceeding, then passed on to our respective destinations.

They did not mention the sheep droppings that suddenly littered the ground near a running stream where I stopped to get a drink. Survival in the mountains these days takes into account factors that did not exist in earlier times, such as the possibility of being poisoned by what may be lurking in those supposedly pristine mountain streams.

Giardia is a particularly virulent parasite increasingly found in western wilderness streams that year. In the last six years *giardia* has become the most frequently reported waterborne affliction in the nation. The disease, with all the prolonged, debilitating symptoms of Montezuma's Revenge plus some, originates in the fecal wastes of humans and animals. One person or animal is able to shed millions of *giardia* cysts in a day. Animals can infect humans, and vice versa. The ultimate wilderness nightmare encompasses all of us, animals and humans, writhing together in the high country after having poisoned each other.

The sheep droppings that covered the landscape in the upper Lake Fork basin put me on guard. I recalled what I had heard around the campfire the previous night. The Forest Service crew, who ought to know, were unanimous in recommending pills and the boiling for one minute of all drinking and cooking water. They told some horror stories and ended the conversation on an inconclusive note: some get it, some don't.

I fervently hoped that I would be in the latter group, since the precautions seemed too burdensome to follow. I walked a short distance above the main sheep dumping grounds, dipped my aluminum cup into the stream, and drank with some trepidation.

Lunch, followed by a short catnap, was at the junction of the trail that headed up Oweep Creek to Porcupine Pass. No symptoms yet. It was only after I had left the mountains that I learned such symptoms take time to develop.

Had I chosen at the junction to proceed down the Lake Fork trail I would eventually have come to Moon Lake, a reservoir that I had previously used as a departure point for the Brown Duck Basin. The lakes in this basin have been raised by low rock and concrete structures; an early form of water retention. They are periodically bled in the summer months to feed the irrigated pasturelands below. What remained along the expanded shorelines were dead, ghost trees. Moon Lake and other dams at the mouths of canyons, such as Meeks Cabin Reservoir on the north slope, are the second level of entrapment. The third and final interruption in the natural stream flow on the south slope is the Central Utah Project, a billion-dollar-plus band of reservoirs, collection systems, and aqueducts that siphon off the remaining water and transport most of it west to the urban areas along the Wasatch Front.

When the first water from the Uinta Mountains was turned upon the lands near Utah Lake, where that mythical Indian tribe supposedly resided, a local publication in the early years of this century rhapsodized: "In this valley where formerly stretched the gray desolation of sage brush the rose is blooming, and all that has been accomplished in the way of putting Nature's bloom on these regions where the moisture has been insufficient, is small compared with what is under way and will come to realization." The sagebrush and the rose: the one represented the greater reality in the West, the other the eternal wish.

*   *   *

After Bridger fled for what he thought was his life, the Mormons moved in and unsuccessfully attempted to colonize the area. Thirty-nine men were selected for the Green River Mission in October of 1853, and they departed from Salt Lake in a hurry in order to establish themselves before winter. The stated purpose of the mission was to pacify the Indians, who were being influenced by "the wicked plots of the white men." Actually the Mormons hoped to maintain a continued presence at that strategic location.

When the party arrived at Fort Bridger in mid-November, they found the inhabitants of the fort, about a dozen or so disheveled mountaineers, "to be very surly and suspicious of us and the spirit of murder and death appeared to be lurking in their minds." The Mormons camped outside the fort that night, and in the morning they took the hint and rode twelve miles south to the junction of Willow Creek Fork and Smiths Fork. There they established Fort Supply, so named because one of its purposes was to raise enough food to support the incoming Mormon emigrants.

A blockhouse was constructed and potato seeds were planted within two weeks; but the Mormons were ill-prepared for the harsh winter. They ran out of flour before Christmas. A few of their number just barely managed to make it through the deep drifts of snow to Salt Lake to summon help. Those who remained wearily guarded their establishment around the clock, fearful of an attack by Indians or trappers or both.

The wind and cold were fearsome. Down plunged the thermometer to 30 degrees below zero. There were cases of frostbite and some cattle died. The trick was to think positively, and one Mormon wrote: "The spirit of the Lord has been with us, and we have enjoyed ourselves much." In this manner the Mormons endured where others would have failed more quickly.

When it eventually warmed up in the spring of 1854, the Mormons went out to do some proselytizing among the natives. One way to gain favor with the Indians, said a Mormon leader, was "to identify our interests with theirs and even to marry among them if we would be permitted to take the young women of the chief and leading men, and have them dress like civilized people and educated."

Sitting down with a council of Shoshoni tribal elders, the Mormons broached their marriage idea, to which the wise chief replied: "I cannot see why a white man wants an Indian girl. They are dirty, ugly, stubborn and cross, and it is a strange idea for white men to want such wives. The white men may look around though; and if any of you could find a girl that would go with him, it would be all right. But the Indian must have the same privilege among the white men." So ended the plan of intermarriage for purposes of alliance.

This mission was not the usual success story. It was planned too hurriedly, achieved no baptisms, and experienced bad morale and discipline problems from the start. "Separation from families, crowded quarters, guard duty in the extreme cold, pressure to take Indian wives and an inadequate food supply, all served to test the faith of the missionaries," stated a history of Fort Supply written by two Brigham Young University professors. Some actually lost their faith, and there were desertions. "Perhaps the fact that the thermometer registered ten degrees above zero on May 30th may have influenced them," stated the history, referring to those who deserted the fort late that month. The official statements at the time were that all was well, but the simple fact was that the mission failed and Fort Supply was abandoned in July of 1854. It was, in the words of those who had been there, a "forbidding and God forsaken place." Cold lands were not made for farming, as that earlier Mormon observer had noted.

The Mormons, as was their habit, did not give up easily. They returned to Fort Supply in the spring of 1855. A few natives were converted, but at the same time they were plagued by the Indians' pilfering and destroying of their crops and livestock. The fear of an Indian attack grew to such proportions that, when the white Indian agent appeared with a band of Indians, the Mormons ran for cover. The cold damaged the crops, and it was a struggle to get through the difficult winters.

Fort Supply could not even support its own inhabitants, let alone the Mormon emigrants; so additional supplies had to be shipped from Salt Lake. Mormon industry and faith were pitted against the climate; and given that contest, the winner was a foregone conclusion. The Mormons had conquered aridity, being the first to irrigate in Wyoming, but they could not overcome the extremes of temperature.

The *coup de grâce* was administered in the fall of 1857 by the invasion of outsiders, and the Bridger Valley was sacrificed for the more defensible positions of the canyons above Salt Lake. With the approach of 2,100 troops sent by President James Buchanan to reestablish the federal presence in the territory, the Mormons abandoned Fort Supply, nearby Supply City, and Fort Bridger, which they had purchased and reoccupied in 1855. They fled to Salt Lake, burning the structures and crops in a scorched-earth policy that denuded the ground in front of the advancing army. One witness to the midnight burning of Fort Supply wrote: "I will mention that owners of property in several places begged the privilege of setting fire to their own, which they freely did, thus destroying at once what they had labored for years to build, and that without a word." What the Mormons built together, they destroyed together.

Harassed by Mormon guerrillas on the plains north of the Uintas and prevented by snow from invading the Salt Lake Valley that fall, the Army staggered into the remnants of Fort Bridger and took refuge that winter from the elements as best it could. Upon the arrival of the weary troops on November 18, having taken twelve days to march thirty-five miles through the snow and cold, Colonel Albert Sidney Johnston, the commanding officer, and later Confederate commander at Shiloh, took possession of the ashes of the old fort, the surviving stone wall that the Mormons had built, and the surrounding lands, and declared them to be a federal military reservation. In such a manner was the concept of federal lands officially trumpeted to the surrounding region.

I rose from the sun-warmed pine needles where I was napping and checked the sign at the trail junction. In two half days and one full day of walking, I had covered about thirty-five miles. Should I want to exit from the mountains in case of a sudden intestinal attack, it would be fourteen miles to the Moon Lake campground. That would be a rather ignoble end to a nobly conceived journey. I had walked eight miles this day, and it was another two or three miles to Lambert Lake, where I planned to take a day off. I continued on my planned course.

By midafternoon I reached the point on the trail where Lambert Lake lay a short distance to the south. I cut across country and struck the lake about midway along its length. From an overlook I saw that I would be the sole inhabitant of that prime piece of mountain real estate. I picked my homesite in the early afternoon, erected and furnished my house in a matter of minutes, and plunged into the frigid lake to wash off the trail dirt and sweat that had accumulated over the last days.

When the washing and other chores were completed, I hauled out the thick book from my pack and read propped up against a tree trunk. Warm afternoon sun slanted down and camp-robber jays squawked in the trees above me. On such journeys I like to bring novels that have nothing to do with the immediate surroundings. *The Jewel and the Crown* transported me from the hard-edged physical clarity of the West and submerged me in ambiguous India, where illusion and reality also existed.

Chapter 5

RAILROADERS

First there was sagebrush, then a thriving settlement and civilization of a sort was hurled upon the landscape. It was every man and a few women for themselves for a brief period, then most passed on to the next place of quick opportunity. A few remained to mold the residue into something more lasting.

Wyoming was an instant creation of the railroad— to be exact, the Union Pacific Railroad, whose financial backing for a transcontinental route came from wealthy New Englanders. They hoped to turn a profit by carrying passengers from one end of the country to the other and transporting minerals out of the Interior West. To easterners the rails were "a long and irresistible arm with which the powerful East embraces the mighty and virgin West."

The West was not exactly an untouched maiden at the time, having been brusquely handled by a number of previous occupants. But, after the traumatic passage of the "hell on wheels" phenomenon across the high Wyoming plains in 1868, the luster had passed from the young body that was available for any commercial caress.

The repeated seduction of the West is described thus in a recent City of Evanston (Wyoming) planning document:

Evanston, historically, has been an impact town, fluctuating with the rises and declines of its leading industries. Beginning in 1868, with the construction of the Union Pacific Railroad and the opening of the timber industry, Evanston's population has been associated with primary industries. Since the time of the decline of the railroad and timber industry and the rise and decline of the coal industry, Evanston has adjusted to a city based on service industries, government, and tourism. With the possible development of oil and coal in the near future, Evanston once again may face a period of expansion [and subsequent decline] based on heavy industry.

The plan predicted a very modest gain of a few hundred residents in the next three years. Instead, the population doubled and then doubled again at the end of the 1970s, when an energy boom, reminiscent of the building of the railroad, washed over the north slope. Then it, too, went bust.

From the very beginning Evanston and other similar western towns, cities, counties, and states always accepted what they were offered by outsiders without questioning its real value for the region, prayed for stability at a high economic level, and were ultimately disappointed when the distant markets for the raw materials that were produced by the docile natives declined for reasons beyond their control. Then the cycle repeated itself after the original players had died or drifted away.

After the waves of emigrants had passed through, leaving the marks of wagon wheels on the floor of the high desert as a reminder of their transience, the railroad laid down iron tracks, strung towns like beads on a metal thread, and left in its wake the memories of where other, less-favored settlements had briefly stood. Then the voracious machine reached out to the sides to grab coal and timber. Soon it brought troops and settlers and departed with cattle and minerals.

In the beginning the railroad was the de facto ruler of the West. General Grenville M. Dodge, the chief engineer of the Union Pacific, said, "There was no law in the country, and no court. We laid out towns, officered them, kept peace, and everything went on smoothly and in harmony." He meant that everything was in harmony with the railroad's wishes, and it was.

Those wishes were national policy following the Civil War. There was a *furor Americanus* to develop the West, and the railroad was the chief means to that end. Railroad fever was abroad in the land. Every city or small town thought it needed to be served by a railroad in order to survive economically. The federal government made all this development possible by supplying the land—the first major giveaway of the public domain.

From 1835 on, Congress granted rights-of-way across the public lands to railroads. In 1852 the lawmakers upped the ante by giving away additional parcels and the natural resources, such as timber and coal, on nearby lands. In 1864 the Union Pacific received a 400-foot right-of-way through public lands and 12,800 acres on each side, which were divided into twenty odd-numbered sections for each mile of rail that it laid along the transcontinental route from the Mississippi River to the border of Nevada. Similar largesse, along with loans, went to the Central Pacific Railroad for its construction of the railroad from west to east.

Lobbyists for communities and railroads went to work on Congress to shake more lands loose from the public domain. General Dodge, a Civil War veteran, told Congress:

> These mountains are underlaid with gold, silver, iron, copper and coal. The timber ranges that these roads pass will develop an immense lumber trade, and the millions upon millions of acres of Government land that they will bring into the market and render feasible for settlement will bring to the Government more money than all the bonds amount to; and this land and these minerals never would have brought this Government one cent if it were not for the builders of these roads.

Altogether 131.5 million acres of public lands were given away by Congress to the states and private corporations for the construction of railroads, an amount far greater than for any other single purpose except homesteading. The railroads sold off the lands as quickly as possible in order to pay off their bonded indebtedness and in the

The north slope of the Uintas from Christmas Meadow

T O P : *The crest at Dead Horse Pass*

A B O V E : *The basic rhythm: amphitheater and ridge*

A high-country lake

Horses near Burntfork, Wyoming

TOP: *Winter in the Uintas*

RIGHT: *Early summer runoff from Hayden Peak*

The Green River slices through the Uintas

A summer storm crosses the badlands

BELOW: *Sagebrush and a ghost town*

T O P : *Lonetree, Wyoming*

A B O V E : *Where Escalante's party crossed the Green River*

TOP: *A plow and log cabin near Fox Lake*

ABOVE: *A forest weakened by beetles,*
then charred by fire

LEFT: *This is dinosaur land*

BELOW: *A summer sheep camp*

Sheep below Smiths Fork Pass

T O P : *Driving cattle across Dinosaur National Monument*

C E N T E R : *Pads on which energy workers once parked
their transient homes near Vernal, Utah*

A B O V E : *The start of the Yampa River trip on a foggy morning*

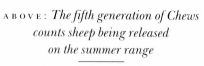

ABOVE: *The fifth generation of Chews counts sheep being released on the summer range*

RIGHT: *Exploration for oil on the north slope*

TOP: *Camping at an abandoned logging camp*

ABOVE: *Older oil production facilities and a new coal-fired electrical generating plant in the Uintah Basin*

Abandoned charcoal kilns on the north slope

TOP: *Sunday traffic in the Uintas*

ABOVE: *Family fishing*

process settled the West with customers. Fifteen years after completion of the transcontinental railroad, only 3.3 million acres out of
the original 11.1-million-acre grant to the Union Pacific remained
to be sold. The railroads dispensed land like kings. "Their management policies in advertising, pricing, credit, classification, withdrawals from sale, development, and leasing all probably affected
the areas of their [the towns'] locations," wrote Paul W. Gates, an
authority on the history of public lands.

Today I remained in one place and savored it. Spruce and fir trees
edged the narrow meadow that was filled with my green tent and
the blue of explorer's gentian. The effervescent blue of the lake,
pierced by trout on occasion, was backed by the dark green of
the trees just below timberline. Millions of intense white sparkles
reflected off the surface when a breeze fluttered across the water
and then advanced over the meadow, causing the blue gentian to
sway in the light green grass. The movements of water and vegetation were gentle, and I felt caressed by them. A jay checked for stray
food in my sheltered dell, then gave me a quizzical look. I kept a
clean camp.

The seven-acre lake was a sheltered place. Here the trees grew
straight and true. Above 11,000 feet there was a different story. In
mute testimony to stormier days and their exposed position, the
dwarf trees were permanently bowed toward the east. They huddled
in protective clumps, their branches streaming out from the main
stem like so many tattered pennants on an exposed landscape.

First I did the laundry, then I undertook a reconnaissance of my
immediate surroundings. I passed slowly around the lake with
constant reference to my campsite. It was an axial progression.
I pictured myself as a satellite absorbing the images of one place
from different perspectives. The real satellites were easily seen here
at night, arching across the clear sky, a telltale blinking light marking their progression.

After completing a slow circle of the lake, I headed up past
timberline to gain a modest height and a view of the Lake Fork
Basin. On another fine morning, not far to the north of the Uinta

Mountains, I had hiked to the top of the Oregon Buttes to gain a perspective over the region as a whole.

It was the sight of these buttes that told the emigrants, as they topped South Pass and began the descent down the western slope of the Continental Divide, that they had traveled halfway from the Missouri River to the Pacific Ocean. The interstate highway and the transcontinental railroad now passed to the south of the Oregon Buttes. Surrounding the buttes were all the realities and abandoned hopes of King Bonanza that were so typical of the Sagebrush West.

When I first came into this basin in the early seventies, the Atomic Energy Commission was pushing hard to set off a string of five nuclear explosions to unlock natural-gas supplies. There were fierce objections. Ranchers worried about their water supplies, urban refugees were concerned that the peaceful rural existence they sought was going to disappear in a mushroom cloud, and the oil industry feared what such an underground disturbance might do to its production. Common sense prevailed, and the AEC withdrew from the scene.

A few years later, during the uranium rush of the mid-seventies, the Great Divide Basin was covered with newly cut wooden stakes that marked numerous mining claims. Now those yellow stakes have weathered to gray or disappeared entirely (as did the stakes planted twenty years earlier during a previous mining boom) with the crash of the market for uranium. Exploration and production of uranium plummeted when the construction of nuclear power plants outside the region was drastically cut back because of high prices and safety concerns.

Other aspects of the western syndrome had been visited upon this land. During the energy crisis of the seventies, oil exploration and production rocketed upward then dropped when the price of oil lessened in the eighties. Some of the edge of that bust was softened by plans for increased production of sour gas, which would be converted to natural gas, with the by-product, sulphur, to be used in combination with phosphate mined in the Uinta Mountains to make fertilizer.

A map of the existing and proposed gas transmission lines across southwestern Wyoming in the mid-eighties resembled a plate of spaghetti. The serpentine lines fed into other lines, which eventually led out of the region toward faraway consumers.

There was an atmosphere of madness abroad in the region, which seemed to be hooked on following one unsustainable high after another. In recent years it was uranium, oil, and sour gas. Before, it was beaver, railroad construction, livestock, logging, and mining. One day on the drive across the western end of the Uintas from Evanston to Kamas I had passed signs that displayed a skull and crossbones above a warning against trespassing.

I had stopped at a café and asked if a secret society or a paramilitary group was about. No, I was assured, it was only a warning for the deadly hydrogen-sulfide gas that was leaking from nearby test wells.

All the frenzied activity of the last decade had been reduced to the bland language of a federal planning document. It read:

> Western Wyoming is currently undergoing a change from an area characterized by rangeland and wilderness to one experiencing industrial growth and active exploration and development of oil and gas reserves. This trend is having many beneficial and adverse effects on the human and natural environments of the area.

On that clear day I parked my vehicle on the ridge that led to the buttes and walked up a track that gave out midway up the first butte. From there it was a short but steep bushwhack to the flat top of the butte and a magnificent view in all directions.

The Red Desert, to the east, is not an area to enter lightly. I have always had to push myself to penetrate what I considered the most lonesome space in the West. The desert is within the Great Divide Basin, a 3,916-square-mile anomaly lying astride the Continental Divide. The streams flow neither to the Atlantic nor to the Pacific but rather disappear into the sagebrush flats of the self-contained basin. This is typical public-domain land, managed—in a manner of speaking—by the Bureau of Land Management.

Vast ordinariness and small wonders are juxtaposed in the basin. There are nearly two hundred square miles of shifting sand dunes that reach heights of one hundred feet and contain year-round ice buried underneath their insulating surface. The extremely rare

black-footed ferret and the world's largest herd of migrating prong-
horn antelope share the range with cattle, sheep, and wild horses.
There are a few oil wells of ancient vintage. The Honeycomb Buttes
are an eroded badlands containing an immense gradation of subtle
colors. The clouds seem to touch the undulating landscape. There
is no place to hide in this large blank spot depicted on road maps.
Exposure is total.

When I drove across the basin a mountain lion was stalking a
herd of antelope a short distance off the dirt road and a golden
eagle sat atop the entrance gate to the Sweetwater Uranium Project,
through which few cars had passed that year. There was a caretaker
superintendent who gave me a desultory tour. The mine and mill
were closed, the victims of lessening needs and changing economics.
A half-dozen years earlier an enthusiastic superintendent told me
what great things were planned; the contrast was startling. At that
time there were a test pit, a temporary trailer, and plenty of activity.
Now there were permanent buildings, but only a handful of
occupants. Huge, expectant excavations—with only some slight
attempts at reclamation—stared open-mouthed at the sky.

In nearby Jeffrey City, once totally dependent upon the same
industry, there was the same sense of quick departure. The bar I
visited last time was closed, the sprouting subdivisions were now
almost entirely deserted, and the sagebrush was encroaching upon
dry, lifeless lawns. You could hear the wind.

But wild swings in economic fortunes were the norm. Jeffrey City
boomed during the fifties when the AEC stockpiled domestic
uranium supplies, declined in the sixties, then roared back in the
seventies, at which time a worried newspaper editor with a sense of
history wrote: "Progress has brought industry once again to the
Sweetwater Valley, but will the pattern some day come full circle?
Will the buildings and trailer town disappear as others have before
them?" Yes, they would. Such structures were but a passing chimera
upon this landscape.

On this intensely clear morning atop the Oregon Buttes, when a
red-tailed hawk wheeled in an updraft, I would have liked to say
that I could see the snow-capped Uinta Mountains some 120 miles
to the southwest. There was every reason why I should have been

able to spot those high peaks, except for the band of yellow-brown smog that hung over the southern horizon.

Whether the smog was from the heavy traffic on the interstate, the Jim Bridger Power Plant, various trona plants, or other assorted industrial facilities, I did not know. But not being able to see the mountains struck a discordant note.

When "the hell on wheels" phenomenon came screeching through those quiet spaces with all its raucous noise, the movement of land, people, and machinery abounded. As the construction crews, their bulky paraphernalia, and the camp followers, described as the "fungi indigenous to American railways," pushed their way across the Wyoming steppe in the summer of 1868, what was to become the state was being detached from the Dakota Territory. "Dakota is a slow coach; we travel by steam," boasted a Wyoming newspaper. Those were unusual times, and the inexorable quality of the movement was caught by Robert G. Athearn in *Union Pacific Country:* "Meanwhile, the work trains continued westward, and the iron tendrils that carried them probed through arid country that sported only sagebrush, edging toward Zion and the completion of the nation's most exciting engineering project since the Erie Canal."

Up popped white canvas tents or more substantial yet portable structures made of painted pine, which were shipped from Chicago and erected in a day with a screwdriver. There was a jarring quality to these instant towns, consisting of rectangular structures on a bare, open plain that lacked vegetation of any significant height.

One of the camp followers was the *Frontier Index,* a weekly newspaper known as "the press on wheels." The *Index* and its two proprietors, Legh and Fred Freeman, kept pace with the construction of the railroad through Nebraska, Colorado, and Wyoming. They speculated on the side in real estate and coal, and in the process built up the circulation of the newspaper and enriched themselves. Like the newspapers that were to follow in this region, they were boosters, not questioners.

Legh Freeman moved the portable newspaper first to Green River and then to Bear River City in the shadow of the Uinta Mountains that summer and fall of 1868. His brother remained in more-civilized Cheyenne. Bear River City sprang from the sagebrush alongside the river of the same name in September with a population of some 2,000 persons in 140 structures of one type or another. Set against a low bluff, the rutted main thoroughfare was named Uintah Street. There were pine-planked and log buildings, the ubiquitous canvas tents, men lounging about in doorways, and horses and wagons hitched to the railings. Above all, there was an air of expectancy and tension.

The action swirled around Legh Freeman, who had cast his fate with the more or less stable elements of the community. Freeman was a bombastic, flamboyant, cruel, vituperative promoter of the frontier and his own well-being. Grab it and keep it for as long as you can could have been his motto, and his newspaper was the vehicle whereby he promoted his self-interest.

A Virginia native, Freeman served with the South in the Civil War. The editor told his readers that the newly-elected President, Ulysses S. Grant, was a "whiskey-bloated, squaw-ravishing adulterer, monkey-ridden, nigger-worshipping mogul." Freeman ended that little blast with the warning, "Booth still lives." The paper was anti-Republican, anti-Chinese, anti-Indian, anti-Mormon, and pro-Freeman. His brand of racism was prevalent on the north slope. Freeman blasted the postal service, and was subsequently named postmaster of Bear River City. A newspaper editor, if he played his cards right, received certain perks.

In that temporary community, which had hopes of becoming permanent, Freeman housed his operation in a tent located next to a slaughterhouse. From that vantage point he had an unobstructed view of the happenings on Uintah Street. He wrote that he had cast his lot with "a brotherhood which has converted a savage desert into the happiest community in America." That overstatement of fact fell within the bounds of western boosterism.

This brotherhood's interests lay in making money off those who were building the railroad. They could be called merchants or speculators. Their nemesis, indeed their only competitors, were those who were even further outside the recognized law. The brotherhood's interests were protected by vigilante action. Freeman denied that he was "the chief of the vigilantes," as some said he was; but the editor openly endorsed their activities. He wrote: "It is well known that wherever we have sojourned in the Territories, we have opposed violence in any form and given the common law priority, but when very fiends assume to run our place of publication, there are plenty of men who rather delight in doing the dirty work of hanging without us, as was evidenced Tuesday night, and as will be witnessed again if the ring leaders are found in town by midnight of this Friday, November the 13th."

The editor was referring to the hanging of three young men from the beam of an unfinished building by "parties unknown." Attached to their coats were tags stating, "Warning to the road agents." One of the men, Little Jack O'Neill, had been involved in an earlier scuffle with Freeman in Green River.

The outspoken editor did not lack for enemies. Many of the railroad graders were Union veterans, others had been personally scourged by his vitriolic pen, and the overt lawless element was told by Freeman that they had "the mark of the beast in their foreheads." The town was ready to explode.

Following the arrest of three graders for drunkenness and Freeman's usual overreaction, a mob formed. It marched to the jail and released the prisoners, then went after the editor, who just managed to escape in time out the back of the tent. A doctor saw Freeman's hasty departure for Fort Bridger and later commented, "He was traveling so fast that you could have played checkers on his coattails." Violence ensued, the newspaper office was wrecked, and anywhere from none to forty persons were killed, depending on the account. The troops arrived from the fort the next morning and found everything peaceful.

Freeman blamed his troubles on the Union Pacific, which, he claimed, had hired "cut throats" to get him because he had exposed "the frauds of that hydra-headed monster." Fraud was not absent from building the railroad, but Freeman had not written about it in his newspaper. He established another newspaper in Ogden, Utah, where he was remembered as being "in constant hot water during the time he remained here in consequence of his malignity and abuse of the citizens."

By the end of December, 1868, Bear River City was deserted. Evanston, fifteen miles to the northwest, had been named the next division point, and the scene of so much brief hate and violence faded back into the obscurity of an eventual roadside historical marker.

If Wyoming was a creation of the railroad, then Evanston was its very embodiment. Named after the Union Pacific surveyor who laid out the townsite, the community existed at the whim of the railroad, which was enriched by the sale of the lots. The streets were laid out parallel and at right angles to the tracks. When the town grew it was eventually split in half by the iron rails. Those who lived on the heights to the south were better off than those who lived on the flats to the north. The split was economic, social, and racial, the Chinese community being confined to the flats.

And the railroad profited. As John W. Reps noted in *Cities of the American West:*

> The total profits realized from townsite development by the Union Pacific have apparently never been calculated. They were, of course, enormous when one remembers that the land cost nothing, surveying costs were kept to a minimum, and land sales were handled by agents who also performed other duties. In these early years of construction, revenues from land sales, in which town lots bulked large, must have exceeded those derived from freight charges.

A French engineer arrived in Wyoming at this time and described the frenetic activity of town building:

> Everywhere I hear the sound of the saw and the hammer; everywhere wooden houses are going up; everywhere streets are being laid out, cut on the square, and not at oblique angles as in Europe. There is no time to hunt for names for these streets. There are streets numbered 1, 2, 3, 4, or A, B, C, D etc. Already stores are everywhere, especially of ready-made clothing, restaurants, hotels, saloons. To clothe oneself, eat, drink, and sleep, says the American, such are the four necessities which must be provided for in all newborn settlements.

The railroad cars reached Evanston in December of 1868, and within a few weeks there were six to seven hundred persons living in the hastily constructed town. Then next year those persons in power in the distant offices of the Union Pacific decided to move the division point twelve miles west to another instant town named Wasatch. Within three days Evanston's population consisted of the two owners of a saloon. They remained to cater "to the wants of such travelers as chanced to pass this way."

Minds changed again, and Evanston once more became the division point. Back came the railroad workers and their followers to live on the banks of the Bear River. The first years for Evanston were economically shaky. A pharmacist and his wife arrived. A bank opened in 1873, the year Evanston incorporated as a city, only to disincorporate three years later because of lack of revenues. The town eventually survived to become the county seat. The winters were fearsome. The summers were pleasant, with the chief diversion being hunting for grouse and sage hen.

The railroad did not live up to those wishful dreams that projected instant, sustainable wealth. The Union Pacific invested limited resources and took a great deal more out, a policy that angered residents. "Citizens often abused the management of the Union Pacific for its town-lot policies, high freight and passenger rates, high coal prices, introduction of Chinese labor, resistance to local taxation and failure to build and improve shops and passenger stations," wrote Wyoming historian T. A. Larson. But the railroad was the only act in town.

Gradually it became possible to make a relatively stable if unspectacular living in the town and the surrounding countryside. Railroad engineers, the aristocracy of the workers, earned between $100 and $130 a month, while cowboys were paid $30 to $35, room and board included. In between were the white-collar workers, such as J. C. Penney, who got his start as a $50-a-month clerk at the Golden Rule Mercantile Company. The Wyoming railroad towns divided up the spoils. Cheyenne got the state capitol, Laramie the university, and Evanston the insane asylum.

The Indians were given what remained. A familiar figure on the streets of Evanston in the latter quarter of the nineteenth century was Chief Washakie of the eastern Shoshoni, a tribe mistakenly thought by a local historian to be of Hindu origin. Washakie and his band camped in a vacant lot in town. The chief favored exotic headgear, such as a stovepipe hat given to him by President Chester A. Arthur and a wide-brimmed hat to which a silver plate inscribed with the phrase "Our Baby" had been affixed. The plate was the result of the trade of a bow and arrows to a local furniture dealer who carried a supply of coffins. When a train carrying the famous actress Sarah Bernhardt was delayed in Evanston, the Indians were hastily rounded up to give a demonstration of their riding skills.

It had taken only a few years for Washakie and the Shoshoni to be reduced to vaudeville actors on the white man's stage. Their fall from grace came when they surrendered their land to the juggernaut that overwhelmed them. Actually, there was nothing else they could have done. The chief chose to cooperate rather than indulge in futile resistance.

Washakie, who became the epitome of the noble savage, was born at the turn of the century in Montana. His parents were of mixed Indian blood. Journeying south as a young man, he joined the Shoshoni in Bridger Valley around 1830. At times he traveled with white trappers, such as Jim Bridger. In 1843, at the beginning of the emigration era, Washakie assumed the leadership of the eastern Shoshoni, who roamed from the Wind River Range to the Uinta Mountains and from Browns Hole to the Great Salt Lake. As an Indian leader, Washakie maintained an unusual amount of control over his band, estimated at about three thousand persons. They were well mounted, armed, and disciplined. He acted decisively. A little wife beating was common among the Shoshoni, but a particularly cruel, repeat offender was killed on the chief's orders.

A picture of Washakie at the height of his powers showed him in a cotton shirt, with a feathered bonnet on his head. In one hand was a rifle, in the other a peace pipe. The rounded features on his face seemed carved out of dark, glistening marble. The adjectives that were applied to Washakie by contemporary white men were "bold," "noble," "hospitable," "honorable," and "intelligent."

Had he chosen to, the chief and his tribe could have been formidable adversaries to the invaders. Instead they aided the emigrants, who sometimes fired their guns at them. The Mormons brought a wagon driver with frozen feet into Washakie's camp, and the chief had the man place them against the breasts of his wife. In his later years Washakie cherished a paper signed with the names of nine thousand emigrants thanking him for his help. Grace Raymond Hebard, a University of Wyoming historian, wrote, "Peacefully and without noted incident he brought his reluctant people into the new era."

The chief explained his policy of peaceful coexistence by picking up a Colt revolver and stating:

> The white man can make this, and a little thing that he carries in his pocket, so that he can tell where the sun is on a dark day, and when it is right he can tell when it will come daylight. This is because the face of the Father is toward him, and His back is toward us. But after a while the Great Father will quit being mad and will turn his face toward us. Then our skin will be light, then our mind will be strong like the white man's, and we can make and use things like he does.

The greatest orator he had ever heard, said a Mormon emissary who listened to the speech.

The eastern Shoshoni had joined the trappers at their rendezvous and helped the emigrants find their way across the high plains; but now, with the coming of the railroad that would bring permanent settlers, they had to be relegated to one place. Washakie wanted a reservation, first suggesting the Henrys Fork Valley, then Bridger Valley, and finally the Wind River Valley near present-day Lander. The latter place was set aside for the Indians. It was far enough from the railroad so as not to be immediately desirable to the white man and located so that the friendly Shoshoni could serve as a buffer between the gold miners at South Pass and the marauding Sioux to the east. Treaties were signed in 1863 and 1868. The government did not honor them by sending the agreed-upon provisions. With their hunting grounds depleted, the Shoshoni, once known as the buffalo-eating people, were reduced to begging. Agriculture was never their forte, and the growing season was extremely short on the Wind River Reservation, which, over the years, shrank to one-fifth its original size because of the continuing demands of the white men. Washakie, whose life spanned the complete ascension of the white man in the West, died in 1900 after losing his eyesight.

Meanwhile, the railroad and the people of Evanston cast their eyes upon the land surrounding them. To the west was a gentle grade downward and out of the territory through the canyons to Salt Lake and Ogden. Across the high plains to the east were a series of wavelike ridges extending down from the flanks of the Uinta Mountains, like roots from a tree. The streams that flowed north between the ridges eventually bent to the west, in the case of the Bear River, or toward the east, as did Blacks and Henrys forks; then flowed south, thus doubling back upon their origins. The Bear River emptied into the Great Salt Lake and the two easternmost forks became part of the Green River, which eventually merged with the Colorado River.

There were cottonwood trees along the streambanks, but leave the water and gain just a little height and the vegetation became rabbitbrush and sagebrush, known locally as black sage. The wind can roar eastward across this unobstructed dry plain, bringing with it some fourteen inches of rain in an average year. Those first years hay and some grain crops were grown, the land first being cleared of the native bushes. The settlers found that hardy grains, grasses, alfalfa, and a few vegetables were the only crops that would grow where frost-free days averaged three summer months.

Besides cattle and sheep grazing on the open range, there were logging and mineral production. The first log drive down the Bear River was held in 1867 as preparation for the arrival of the railroad. The timber was used for railroad ties, mine props, and charcoal, "all of which were produced with relatively little overhead to meet short term demands," according to a history of the Wasatch National Forest. The props went to gold, silver, and coal mines, while the charcoal was used in an emerging smelter industry. The railroad made all these activities possible, being the dominant user of wood products for ties and trestles along the right-of-way and props in its nearby coal mines. Once the initial rush to build the railroad was over, wood was purchased from independent contractors at a low price. The railroad transported logs or finished wood products out of the region at a high price.

The stripping of the Douglas fir and pine forests on the north slope of the Uintas followed the decline of the beaver. The difference between that first splurge of timber harvesting and subsequent cuttings was that it was unrestrained by any regulations. Several hundred men were in the mountains cutting timber wherever and whenever they pleased. Seventy-five tie hackers worked in the mid-1870s along one stretch of riverbank, where the ties were stacked for a distance of two to three miles, twenty feet separating the work of different crews. Each outfit marked its ties differently, much as livestock was branded. Evanston Lumber Company branded its logs with a circle, Coe and Carter with a C, and Burris and Bennett with a B or BB.

A snapshot shows a group of men, flanked by two dogs, lined up to be photographed with mallets and peavys in their hands before a huge stack of logs. They look pleased with their work. Hungry men would descend like a swarm of Mormon crickets on huge piles of food placed on outdoor tables in front of the log commissaries. In winter the horses labored chest high in snow to pull sleds laden with logs to the bank of a nearby stream. With the spring thaw the drive crews, looking strong and agile, with long poles in their hands, rode the logs down to Evanston. Some lost their lives along the way in the grinding, churning mass that choked the river.

A feeling of well-being and exuberance was abroad in the land. From 856 persons in 1870, Uinta County's population grew to 2,859 ten years later, 7,414 in 1890, and 12,223 in 1900. A writer for *Leslie's Weekly* described the Mountain Trout House in Evanston, later to become the Union Pacific Hotel: "In the little office of the hotel there is a good deal of decoration in the way of Chinese and Japanese pictures and some fine stuffed heads of Buffalo and lesser game. These trophies, together with the large dish of fresh trout which adorns one of the windows, are evidences of the pleasures of the chase that can be indulged in around Evanston."

An opera house was built on Front Street in 1885; and to mark Evanston's emergence and the turn of the century, the Union

Pacific built a granite, gothic-style passenger depot, complete with
two octagonal turrets, that resembled a mini-castle. The depot was
meant to symbolize the railroad company's permanence, yet Amtrak
became the eventual occupant.

While the railroad prospered, human beings suffered or lost
their lives. The Almy coal mines became known as the most dangerous in the world. Explosion after explosion rocked the mines and
the surrounding countryside, killing hundreds of miners. Sixty
white men, about half of whom were Mormons, and "an undetermined number of Chinese" were killed by an 1895 explosion within
a mine, while seven others died as a result of flying timbers on the
surface. Eight years later 171 miners were killed in another Union
Pacific mine, causing a Denver newspaper to editorialize: "Martyrs
not to our civilization, but to our ignorance, thoughtlessness and
greed!"

It is possible that the Indians burned coal before the coming of
the white man. Frémont commented on the appearance of coal
near Evanston, and the trappers knew about it. In the summer of
1868, when the railroad spurred the first economic activity of an
industrial nature in the region, coal was "found" three miles north
of Evanston at what became the mining town of Almy. With completion of the railroad, coal mining became the state's leading industry,
and the salvation of the economically troubled Union Pacific.
Larson wrote: "No doubt the Union Pacific profited handsomely
from its coal, using it as fuel, selling it at high prices, and preventing
competition by charging outrageous freight rates." The president of
the company testified before Congress in 1887 that its coal mines
were "the salvation of the Union Pacific."

In its heyday, Almy was a boom town. There were two major
mining companies and a total of seven mines to support a population of five thousand. Both of the major mining concerns, the
Union Pacific and the Rocky Mountain Coal and Iron Company,
maintained company stores and lodging facilities, thus increasing
their profits and the indentured status of their employees. The first
miners were from the British Isles; but many of the whites were
replaced by Chinese workers when the "Celestials," who worked
harder for less money, were chased out of Rock Springs.

Other than the Indians, the Chinese were the only minority group to live in the region; and they fared even worse than the natives because they had no landed status. Chinese were originally imported to work on the construction of the railroad, then imported again in 1885 to work as strikebreakers in the Union Pacific's Rock Springs coal mines. The displaced white miners and their allies went on a rampage in early September of that year and killed twenty-eight Chinese, wounded fifteen more, set fire to their ramshackle community, and chased the remaining Orientals out of Rock Springs. The Chinese, with the help of the railroad, took refuge in Evanston and nearby Almy, where they went to work in the mines.

The attitude of Wyoming, as expressed by Governor Francis E. Warren in 1887, was that, since the Chinese had failed to assimilate, they "therefore are not to be regarded as a desirable element in our civilization." The Chinese in Evanston held themselves apart and were relegated by the whites to a separate place and status. They lived on flatlands to the north of the tracks in shanties constructed of packing boxes with roofs of flattened oil cans. But they managed to build a splendid Joss House, one of the few such temples in the country, along with the standard opium and gambling dens. A few operated laundries and small shops or cultivated vegetables that they sold door to door.

With the last coal mine closing in 1920, there was only a scant chance of employment; and most of the Chinese community melted away after fifty hard years in southwestern Wyoming. In 1922, forty-five minutes after the Union Pacific evicted the Chinese from the Joss House, which was on railroad property, the elaborate structure burned to the ground. It is interesting to speculate who may have set the fire, since the motivations were multiple. The Chinese could have done it in order to deprive the railroad of something that was of religious and cultural significance to them. The railroad might have wanted to raze the structure, or white hooligans could have done it for racial reasons.

Oil followed coal, and again the railroad profited. In Spring Valley, near Evanston, the migrating Mormons were aware of a small tar spring that could be used for lubricating wagon wheels, polishing wooden gun stocks, or to doctor the sores of horses. They called it the Brigham Young Oil Spring. Twenty years later a Salt Lake newspaper editor, traveling from Fort Bridger to Evanston, wrote about what was then called Tar Spring. In that same year of 1868 the fort's sutler, William Carter, who was widening his commercial empire, developed an oil well at the spring and produced lubricating oil, which he sold to the Union Pacific. Geologists and government surveyors noted the oil springs in their reports for the balance of the century.

Then the Union Pacific went looking for water in 1900 and the drillers instead found oil at shallow levels. The rush was on. The Evanston newspaper, ever the booster, proclaimed: "The oil excitement continues unabated and the people here are at least awakening to the fact that Uinta County is to become one of the greatest oil fields the world has ever seen." (Eighty years later the Evanston newspaper—different name, different owner, but with the same shallow perspective on history—announced prematurely that the true oil and gas age had arrived.) With the news of the oil strike, workers flocked to Evanston, where the few hotels and rooming houses at the turn of the century were overflowing.

One year later, when the first strike was made in commercial quantities of oil, the town's residents lit a bonfire on Main Street. Thirty-one oil companies had located in Evanston, along with equipment suppliers and the usual company of thieves and swindlers. Some of the companies made honest efforts, while others were intent on fraud. Local businesses prospered and new ones located in town, replacing older stores. The Evanston Lumber Company sold timber from the Uintas for use in oil rigs and instant housing.

Out in the oil fields more than one thousand placer claims were filed on federal lands. There were problems with claim jumpers, and the Association for the Protection of Locations was formed to prevent the theft of claims. Speculation was rampant. A report by the United States Geological Survey noted: "Intensive excitement followed this [1900] find and as the greater part of the land in this section was unoccupied Government land the whole region was soon staked out as petroleum claims under the placer-mining laws. A large part of these were purely speculative claims, which the owners had no intention of developing."

The hopes for quick riches from oil were dashed by economic reality, which, originating elsewhere, swept over the high plains a few years later. A fair amount of oil was being produced elsewhere in Wyoming and in California, and there was no market, as yet, for what the Evanston fields were producing. A history of the early oil rush stated: "The county's complex geology, harsh winters and scarcity of water retarded oil development during the early 1900s to the point that after ten years of drilling Uinta County had barely progressed beyond infancy." So ended the region's belated introduction to the industrial age.

Chapter 6

SETTLERS
(NORTH SLOPE)

Along with the troops of Colonel Johnston that stumbled in a benumbed condition into the charred remains of Fort Bridger in November of 1857, there was a civilian by the name of William A. Carter. On the verge of forty, the peripatetic Carter had tried his hand at teaching, the law, the army, business, gold mining, and farming in his native Virginia, and in Florida, California, and Missouri. None of the occupations or places had taken hold of or fit him, and the ambitious yet thwarted Carter had gambled everything he had on being appointed sutler at Fort Bridger. The odds of getting the job were in Carter's favor, as he had good connections with Army personnel.

A sutler was a civilian merchant who was appointed by the military to operate a post store. By separate contract he could supply the military with surrounding natural resources—such as lumber, firewood, hay, and grain from the public lands. Since at Fort Bridger the nearest competition was in Salt Lake, and the Mormons were regarded as aliens and a potential enemy in the early years of military tenancy, the monopoly position could be quite lucrative.

Shortly after the exhausted troops reached the fort, Carter wrote his wife and described "the great length and severity of the march, and the almost desert country through which we passed." He met Jim Bridger at the fort, and the two did not get along. The educated Carter noted his fellow Virginian's illiteracy and his "excessive egotism." In a rather nasty manner, which was not his usual style, Carter said that Bridger had gotten his start in the fur trade as "Ashley's valet." Carter had been the victim of Bridger's telling a patently false story when pressed by the newcomer to recount his exploits, which was the usual way Bridger made such questioners feel like a fool.

Their differences were multiple and symbolic, representing different eras. One was the trailblazer, the other the settler. Bridger and Carter came from opposite ends of the social scale in Virginia, their manners and outlooks differed, and one man was on his way out of Fort Bridger, which he had founded, while the other had just arrived for a twenty-four-year stay. Bridger eventually left Sagebrush Country to die in Missouri. Carter had departed from Missouri to make his fortune at Fort Bridger, where he was eventually buried. The sutler who remained to become a regional autocrat left a more lasting impression on the place than the transient trapper-trader.

The first years were difficult. That winter Carter and the troops "feasted off the fruits of Mormon labor," meaning caches of potatoes they found at the ruined Fort Supply. Carter ordered $100,000 worth of goods and had to assign three-fourths of his expected business to his creditors. But he predicted to his wife that, when he was named sutler, "I will be able to secure all the Indian trade this side of the Mountains, all the emigrant trade and the trade of the mountaineers which is very considerable."

When the expected appointment materialized, he assured his wife back in Missouri that "I am striving for the best." The best, as he frequently defined it, was the well-being of his family.

In the summer of 1858, with sixteen companies of troops at Fort Bridger, plus teamsters and other civilians milling about, Carter started a land-office business. He crowed, "I have the best location from the states to Salt Lake City," and added, "I am called upon by everybody for everything and thousands of dollars pass through my hands daily." He felt he could sell $150,000 worth of goods a year.

The trade was varied and the activity frenzied. Deerskins were bought from the Indians for 50 cents apiece and sold for $2.50. Elk skins went for $4. Carter bought twenty-two wagons for $8 apiece and fifteen minutes later was offered three times that amount for just the iron that held them together. At the same time thirty men worked on building the store, which needed to be completed before winter set in with its "shivering terrors." The sutler, his assistant, and two clerks frequently labored into the early-morning hours. They were exhausted. Carter himself became ill from overwork.

When the store was completed, Carter bounced back. "I have a great many irons in the fire," he wrote his wife. Besides being the post sutler, a position that could easily have occupied all the energies of one man, Carter was the postmaster, special agent for the post office, justice of the peace, probate judge, jailer, district clerk, and president of the selectmen.

In effect, all of these positions made Carter the reigning civilian presence in western Wyoming. As special agent for the Post Office, he was responsible for postal appointments and deliveries and payments by other postmasters in portions of Wyoming, Utah, and Idaho. Robberies by white men and raids by Indians upon the postal routes concerned him. Under the peculiarities of the law at the time, the probate judge handled federal and state cases involving both civil and criminal complaints. In an era when the law was a tenuous factor in daily affairs and those who administered it were sometimes incompetent, if not crooked, Judge Carter, as he came to be called, "kept faith with high principle to place the priceless stamp of integrity on the law and justice of his locale," as one flowery examiner of his judicial record wrote.

Most of the cases involved the theft of livestock, since the riding and raising of four-legged animals was the principal activity in the territory. Judge Carter sentenced two mule thieves to two years' imprisonment in the territorial jail and ordered the deputy sheriff to deliver "the bodies," as it was customary to word the sentence, to the warden. One of the thieves tried to escape while on the way to prison and was killed by the literal-minded lawman, who then delivered the corpse as well as the live thief to the designated place.

The judge dominated the commercial, judicial, and political life of the territory so completely that the first county that was carved out of western Wyoming, then in the Dakota territory, was named Carter County. President Grant offered Carter the appointment as first territorial governor of Wyoming in 1868, but the judge turned it down, preferring to remain home with his family. His wife and six children had joined him at Fort Bridger in 1859, and remained there during the Civil War, when, upon the withdrawal of the Army troops, Carter was faced with the loss "to desperadoes" of his empire. With customary Carter verve, the sutler armed his own militia, who deterred threats until the return of the military.

A tall, spare man who later sported the long, snow-white beard of a patriarch, Carter was a benevolent autocrat. The English traveler and author Sir Richard F. Burton wrote: "We were conducted by Judge Carter to a building which combined the function of post-office and sutler's store, the judge being also sutler, and performing both parts, I believe, to the satisfaction of every one." Carter was known for his hospitality. He would meet the morning stage from the east (there being no mention of meeting the stage from the west) and bring back the most interesting of the weary travelers to his home for a breakfast of steak, mountain trout, desert sage hen, waffles, hot biscuits, and muffins. Along with the store clerks, who regularly ate at the Carter home, and the large family, there were usually anywhere from two to six extra persons at the table. "Mother was a very busy woman," a daughter recalled.

The judge's home was a cultural beacon in a vast sea of sagebrush. With a fine library, subscriptions to New York newspapers and magazines, the first piano in the territory, and four daughters, the roomy log house carpeted with animal skins was a natural gathering place for Army officers, travelers, and the more distinguished local citizenry. Some accounts state that the small schoolhouse erected at the fort was the first in the territory; others claim that honor belongs to Fort Laramie. Whatever the case, there was no doubt that the Fort Bridger school, which the judge furnished with the best teachers he could find, had the best college admissions record. One of Carter's sons went directly to Cornell University and a daughter attended Vassar College.

Carter wielded his considerable powers in an unobtrusive manner. William N. Davis, Jr., a history professor and former California State

Archivist, wrote: "A willingness to serve the public was always characteristic of him, but doubtless he would have been frank to admit
that the value of the office to his business operations also counted
in his decision [to accept the judgeship]." Carter was not above
writing a senator or congressman from his state to let them know his
position on pending legislation that would affect his many interests,
and occasionally he traveled back East to protect these interests in
person. On several such trips Carter, who wanted to keep the
Bridger area free from Mormon influence, lobbied hard for a
"square" Wyoming, meaning that Utah would have to give up a
chunk of its northeastern territory, which it did. Thus Fort Bridger
wound up in Wyoming.

In the commercial sphere Carter served the Army in a variety of
capacities and drew heavily on the natural resources of the region.
In addition to being the storekeeper, Carter was the owner of the
only saloon on the reservation, agent for the Pony Express, paymaster,
lender, creditor, banker, and general all-around consultant and
confidant to the constantly rotating officers. He supplied the Army
and later the Union Pacific and other civilian accounts with lubricating oil, coal, firewood, lumber, shingles, railroad ties, charcoal,
lime, hay, grain, and cattle. He gave good weight, being known for
selling fine whiskey that was not diluted. He also served it liberally,
the post saloon having to be closed down at least once by the
commander because of too much drunkenness. A few sniped at the
sutler's high prices and "special monopoly."

In his most active years, Carter employed about one hundred
persons as clerks, bookkeepers, herders, farmworkers, teamsters,
blacksmiths, woodcutters, mill workers, and carpenters. The railroad stop ten miles north of the post was named Carter Station. The
sawmills were located in the Uintas and on the military reservation.
The judge had an unsuccessful bill introduced in Congress that
would have allowed him the customary land grants to build a
railroad from the station to the mountain timberlands. Carter's
activities "touched almost every phase of the economic development of the Rocky Mountain and Great Basin country in that
period," wrote Davis.

The judge's most significant and long-lasting contribution was to bring cows and agriculture to the north slope on a permanent basis. He not only imported cattle and raised them for his own profit; but also, inadvertently, for the benefit of others. A local historian wrote: "Judge Carter was the first to build up a considerable spread in the area in which we are interested. And such were the free and easy ways of that era, it can be said without exaggeration that almost every subsequent settler on Henrys Fork or Blacks Fork made use of a running iron to set himself up in the cattle business at Carter's expense."

Livestock were first introduced by Francisco Vásquez de Coronado during his journey through the Southwest in 1540, and were subsequently imported from Mexico. The emigrants passed through with the first cattle to be seen on the northern ranges in the 1840s. Bridger traded fat cows for the lean, trail-worn beasts that arrived with the emigrants and fed them on the lush grasses of Blacks Fork to complete the cycle. But cattle were a very limited commodity in this region until the 1870s, when huge herds began arriving from Texas. In 1870 the assessment rolls for the Wyoming territory listed a bare 8,143 cattle. Fifteen years later, at the height of the cattle boom, those same rolls recorded 894,788, while the actual number of cows in Wyoming was thought to be closer to 1.5 million.

Some cattle came from Oregon via Fort Bridger, but most were driven from Texas. The Texans soon taught the lore and practices of the open-range system to the Wyoming ranchers. What the practice of running cattle on the open range meant was free, unrestricted use of the public lands by those who got there first and could hold on to them by fair means or foul. When it was discovered by accident that cattle could survive untended during Wyoming winters, an assumption that later proved false, they were simply let go to drift over the range until it was time to round them up. The advantage of the system was obvious. Little privately-owned land, manpower or overhead was involved. A $5 calf, after running free for three years on the open range, could be fattened up at little expense to become a 1,200-pound steer that would bring $35 or $40 on the eastern markets. Such an animal needed approximately forty acres in order to survive, since on the Wyoming steppe grass was sparse. The increasing numbers of cattle meant that soon most of Wyoming was given over to grazing.

The cattle bonanza, as booms and firestorms tend to do, fed upon itself. Glowing accounts of the wealth that could be made by raising cattle appeared in eastern publications and spread across the Atlantic to England and Scotland, where foreign investors were attracted to western lands. Soon, with the aid of the railroad, a different type of emigrant was traveling West for a short visit. "On the basis of such accounts eastern money poured into the West like water, and the capitalists came west not on horseback but in their Pullman cars decorated in plush red velvet and stocked with wine, Havana cigars, and other trappings of the wealthy easterner," wrote David Dary in *Cowboy Culture*. In a single year twenty cattle corporations, worth more than $12 million, were organized under Wyoming laws. Fraud was rampant, as it usually is during such boom conditions. Fortunes were made and lost.

The few public land laws on the books did little to alleviate the situation. The Homestead Act of 1862, the Timber Culture Act of 1873, and the Desert Land Act of 1877 were all loosely drawn without the reality of arid lands in mind. The reality was that it took much more land to produce less than what was raised on an equivalent piece of property in a humid region; and the land was virtually useless without water being transported from elsewhere. John Wesley Powell, in his 1878 report on the arid lands of the West, recommended enlarging the basic homestead from 160 acres to a minimum 2,560 acres, a figure his western friends thought was too low. Cowboys filed on adjacent homestead tracts for their bosses in order to circumvent the acreage restriction. Filings on land were made under the timber act by persons who had no intention of planting the required number of trees, and these 160-acre tracts were often combined with an adjacent homestead tract. The desert act proved to be a farce, since the lands had not been classified and a land-office clerk was not likely to know what was lush meadow or hard ground.

Respect, or even tolerance, for the laws broke down in the rush for land. A report by the land commissioner A. J. Sparks stated, "Men who would scorn to commit a dishonest act toward an individual, though he were a total stranger, eagerly listen to every scheme for evading the letter and spirit of the settlement laws, and in a majority of instances I believe avail themselves of them." Sparks added that the federal land officers "partake of this feeling in many instances and if they do not corruptly connive at fraudulent entries, modify their discretionary powers in examination of final proof."

The Wyoming stockmen turned down a proposal to lease cheaply or buy public land at five cents an acre. Why buy or lease when use was free and the existing laws allowed such painless acquisition? The United States Public Land Commission held extensive hearings throughout the West in 1879 and 1880 and concluded that most of the arable lands were already spoken for and more equitable and effective laws were needed. Little attention was paid to the commission's findings. Paul Gates wrote: "The West was enjoying its greatest land boom—financed largely by a huge outpouring of funds from the East—and until the late eighties there were few who favored any action that might slow down the boom and the transfer of public lands to private ownership."

With more people and more cows came more problems. Overcrowding on the range and cattle diseases were dealt with, for a time, by fencing. With the invention of barbed wire in 1873 a cheap, effective method became available to enclose large areas. Barbed wire did not come into general use until around 1880, and then it began to be stretched in increasing amounts across the public domain in an effort by the large cattle companies to keep out smaller settlers. The wire stretchers went berserk with their new material. It was not only stretched across grazing lands but also railroad sections, school grant lands, and timberlands.

In 1884 the General Land Office, which had overall charge of the public domain, reported that 125 large cattle companies in Wyoming had fences on public lands. The federal government moved against the offenders with indifferent success. The same story concerning inept federal enforcement actions against infractions of land laws would be repeated in future years—there were too little funds and too few enforcement officials, and the latter were too timid, too beholden to local interests, and their methods were too ponderous to outmaneuver those same interests, who had, like William Carter, effective lines of communication to Congress and sharp lawyers. The federal government was defeated by the sheer weight of the offenses and by courts favorably inclined toward the local viewpoint. Wyoming historian Larson wrote of Sparks, the crusading commissioner of the General Land Office, who attempted to prosecute the offenders: "Despite the best efforts of Sparks and his special agents, government land remained under fence in Wyoming for many years."

Sparks then sealed his own fate, as would other overdiligent and outspoken federal land managers in the future. He lashed out at the broad spectrum of misuse and fraud on public lands and in the process alienated every major interest in the West. The cattlemen and others, through their representatives in Congress, went after the commissioner, and he resigned—the victim of his own lack of political astuteness, and of history. The western precedent was one of free and unrestricted use of land, and such habits were not easily discarded.

Judge Carter had the free and exclusive use of the five-hundred-square-mile military reservation and most of the desert and forest lands surrounding it. As time went on, he centered more of his efforts on cattle raising. Supplying the military was a fickle business, since they came and went in varying numbers and sometimes disappeared entirely from the fort. With the coming of the railroad and the growth of Evanston, goods could be shipped directly to purchasers, and competitors vied for the military contracts. In a study of Carter's commercial activities, William Davis wrote:

Carter's ventures in livestock production reflected many of the elements in the rise and climax of the range cattle industry. There was the studied progression through the evolving phases: building the herd, first to numbers sufficient to support his own and local needs; entry into the market; acquisition of Texas cattle, improvement by Oregon stock, and then importation of blooded bulls from Missouri; vision of the brightness of the prospect—in Carter's case in 1868, when he turned to the beef cattle industry as the field of his chief endeavor; reaching out for new range land—Big Horn Basin, one of the last of the unoccupied sections of the free range, was opened primarily by the herd of 2,500 head that Carter sent there in 1879; and the annual sales to the brokers at Cheyenne on the Union Pacific. When, in his last years, he was being pressed on all sides by the new economic forces at work in the West, Carter came to the conclusion that of all the old enterprises he had engaged in, the cattle business alone offered any hope in the future.

When Carter arrived with the Army troops at Fort Bridger he brought with him a number of mules and cows, along with such farming implements as plows, a thresher, and a reaper. Three years later he reported that his cattle and grain crop were doing well, but then came a setback. The winter of 1865 was severe, and the judge lost $6,000 worth of cattle. He gradually built his herd back up to the point where 1,000 head of cattle were assessed at $15,000 in 1873. Cows were his single largest reported holding, the sawmills and other machinery being less than half that amount. At approximately the same time an English correspondent reported that Judge Carter had 2,000 head of cattle roaming the range and was "the great man" of western Wyoming.

One measure of Carter's increasing status as a stockman was his election to the board of the powerful Wyoming Stock and Wool Growers Association. The association kept a special fund "to be expended in the detection, arrest, and conviction of stock thieves, and in the purchase of rope with which to hang them." Such associations were formed to protect the interests of the larger stockmen; and their vigilante activities were directed not only against rustlers but also against small settlers, as the residents of Browns Park were to find out.

The War Department gave Carter a lease for the free and exclusive use of the five-hundred-square-mile military reservation for agricultural purposes. The judge's monopoly over the land enabled him to stifle local competition and to charge Salt Lake prices for commodities raised in the Bridger Valley. Davis wrote: "The arrangement and the conditions underlying it, and they were in no way extraordinary, are perhaps symbolic of the day in which the authority of the army was broad over the West. It was a good time to be a sutler."

Memories are selective and would dim; but the myth of early western independence is punctured by its dependence on the military. The federal government, through its military presence,

became the second-largest economic prop in Wyoming during the
1870s. The railroad was usually first, although they sometimes
traded places. (The government has remained a major contributor
to the state's economy up to the present air bases and missile-
launching sites.)

Carter's control over forest and desert lands beyond the confines
of the reservations was not absolute, but it was dominant. Eight
miles south of Fort Bridger, on the banks of Smiths Fork, a summer
dormitory for herders was built with lumber from the judge's
sawmill on Poison Creek. The Herd House, as it was called, had a
large bunkroom, a smaller bedroom for the cook, a large kitchen,
and a storeroom.

There was this contemporary account of open-range ranching
procedures:

> All cattle on the Smiths Fork range belonged to Judge Carter and
> Uncle Jack Robertson [a former trapper and the area's first perma-
> nent white resident]. The cattle with other brands were property
> of ranchers on the Henrys Fork range. Due to the fact that
> the two ranges were connected, the cattle soon became mixed,
> causing a difficulty in separating them. To overcome this dif-
> ficulty, Judge Carter built a large chute. The cattle were brought
> to this location, all put in one bunch in a large corral con-
> nected with the chute, and then they began their work. Each
> animal was put through the chute and its owner identified it
> according to the brand. If the cows claimed a small calf, it was
> branded in the chute with the same brand of its mother. To
> eliminate counting one animal twice, the bushy part of each tail
> was cut off while in the chute. Each rancher counted his own
> cattle and kept an account of the number. In this manner all the
> ranchers had their cattle branded, counted, and separated in one
> procedure.

The judge made his bid in the late 1870s to control the livestock
trade in the surrounding states. Ten miles east of Carter Station, off
on a spur track that could hold forty cattle cars, Carter built
"commodious lots and extensive enclosures" to hold cattle driven

down from Idaho and Montana for shipment on the railroad. In the printed brochure that he used as an advertisement for these services, Carter advised that it would be best to ship livestock immediately because they "are now bearing excellent prices east."

In an economic venture and a personal act of hubris, the judge undertook the construction of a log road across the Uinta Mountains so that he could supply the newly established Fort Thornburgh on the south slope. The corduroy wagon road followed a path, known as the Lodgepole Trail, that was used by the Ute Indians to cross the Uinta Mountains from near Vernal to Burntfork. The white men had no concept of what a bog those wet mountain lands could become. Carter caught pneumonia while helping to build the road and died in 1881 before the cattle market went bust for the first time.

Overgrazing, deep snow, severe cold, and drought drastically reduced the herds throughout the Interior West during the winter and spring of 1886–87. Half the cattle froze to death, some in a standing position, in the Bridger Valley and along Henrys Fork; and wolves and coyotes invaded the area. The governor said, "This was the turning point in the history of Wyoming."

But the territory had a history of barely twenty years, and there would be many more turning points. The cattle disaster was the first reminder for the newest emigrants that the Sagebrush West was not a lush Garden of Eden; that inflated expectations would inevitably be punctured by the harsh climate or the fortuitous decline of outside markets; and that what went up would inevitably come down in the West. Of those speculators, Larson wrote: "In their desire to make money fast, they pushed things too hard, took too long chances, and became inextricably entangled in the age-old cycle of boom and bust."

A day of rest did wonders. I felt clean and revitalized as I clambered up the boulder slope behind my former campsite at 7:15 a.m. Soon I was steaming up the gently inclining trail, thinking what a great day to be alone and alive, when I was startled by animals snorting and stomping. Tethered horses and two large tents stood below the trail to the right. The unexpected nearness of others constantly surprised me in the mountains.

Although the clouds had built up the previous afternoon, this morning was cold and clear. It was now mid-August, and I felt a hint of autumn in the air and on the ground. The miniature plants of the tundra community through which I made my way in the Oweep Basin seemed to have an extra dash of red in them this morning.

After one hour, my customary length of time on the trail before taking a break, I stopped to drink at an unnamed stream flowing into Oweep Creek. No sheep here, I thought. I deluded myself. A few steps beyond the sound of rushing water I heard the bleat of sheep. At the upper limits of the meadow a dense flock stood out against the dark rock. The herder was a lone figure on horseback.

A few hundred yards further along the Highline Trail and I crossed the swath those four-legged locusts had chomped through the lush carpet of the high-country meadow. The earth was punctured by cloven hooves and the grass decapitated by clacking teeth. What had been ingested elsewhere was deposited in the form of curly droppings.

The herder's spare horses were grazing near his campsite. They had contributed their own distinctive hoof marks and grass-mowing capabilities to the general turbulence of the scene.

The meadow was wet, and it was difficult to escape the mire. My boots emitted a sucking noise as I forcefully extracted them with each step through the thick goo of the mountain pig pen.

The trail passed the white canvas tent that served as a summer residence for the herder. All the well-used implements of the cowboy culture lay scattered about. There were ropes, harnesses, cans of food, cast-iron pans and pots, laundry hung out to dry on a line, and a neat stack of firewood.

What was happening here differed little from what occurred in and around these mountains some hundred years ago when the first settlers brought livestock into the region. While the home ranges at lower elevations repaired themselves in the summer, the livestock were driven into the mountains. With the proper permit from the Forest Service, grazing was legal in a wilderness area. The livestock descended in the fall to eat the harvested grasses over the winter months. It was the basic, rhythmic activity of the West.

The scattered trees dropped back after this last rather sordid evidence of human activity, and the rising grass-covered ground was studded with boulders. To the north a trail passed over Squaw Pass, a noticeable depression in the crest, while Porcupine Pass, my immediate destination, loomed to the east. As I approached the steep half-mile climb to the 12,236-foot summit of the pass, I saw three figures with backpacks huddled behind a boulder about a quarter mile away. My guess was that they were taking refuge against the piercing, cold wind that blew down from the pass.

Two women of vastly different temperaments reflected the settler era on the north slope. One of them, Elinore Pruitt Stewart, was in harmony with her surroundings. The other, Ann Bassett, who came to be known as Queen Ann, was born with a burr under her saddle. As a woman in a man's world, she fought to be accepted as an equal. She also battled the large cattle companies. The sharp-edged West was a place you either accepted or you fought; and these two women—in their separate, independent ways—reflected that stark choice. There was a third choice, however, and that was to depart.

The Bassett family represented the hierarchy in Browns Park. Indians, Spanish traders, trappers, and a few miscellaneous passersby had walked or ridden the trail from Fort Bridger to Browns Park before the Army opened a road in 1865. From Blacks Fork the road made its sinuous way across the crusty badlands to Henrys Fork; then, after crossing that stream seven times, it reached the Green River, jogged north for two or three miles, and crossed the river at a shallow point. The dirt track followed Spring Creek to Minnie's Gap and the Clay Basin, then dropped down to the upper end of Browns Park.

Here was a refuge in the midst of the Uinta Mountains. The land was flat and well watered, and the grasses grew thick and tall. The climate at the lower, eastern end of the mountains was warmer than either slope in the winter. When Sam Bassett wandered into the basin on "Spanish Joe's Trail" in 1852, the miner found lush grass for his mules. His journal entry read: "Mountains to the right of us, mountains to the left of us, not in formation but highly mineralized. To the South, a range in uncontested beauty of contour, its great stone mouth drinking a river." The miner with the gift of imagery was referring to the Gates of Lodore, through which the Green River leaves the park.

Park residents had closer economic and cultural ties to the north slope than to the south slope. The railroad passed by to the north, and people and goods tended to come and go in that direction, once it was completed. The Mormons did not attempt to colonize the small basin. Indeed, the park was the gathering place for all the disparate elements in the West who were attracted by its central location, inaccessibility, benign climate, and the nearby borders of three states, any one of which could be easily crossed when the lawmen from another state ventured into the park.

Browns Park was essentially a peaceful place. But it was also the scene of those brief spurts of cowardly violence that were the hall-mark of the West. The bloody incidents that took place there were, in the abstract, chiefly over the use of land and the most valuable resource that trod upon it—livestock. Queen Ann was either a witness to most of these events or at or near the center of them.

A band of Cherokee Indians from the South were the first known persons to bring cattle into the park. The Indians, who were unhappy with the reservation they had been given, were on their way to the California gold fields in 1849 when they wintered their herd of horses and cattle in the park and then continued on their way in the spring of 1850. In 1869 two Englishmen and a Boston gentle-man brought their large herd into the park; and by the early 1870s it was common for cattle either to be wintering in the park or passing through from Texas to the northern ranges, such as those controlled by Judge Carter. Over the winter of 1871–72, at least 4,500 head of cattle were in the park and things were starting to get a bit crowded. Also spending the winter in the park were an uncounted number of Ute Indians, eleven Anglo men, and an equal number of Mexicans.

The Bassett family arrived in 1877. Herbert Bassett, a native of the Mohawk Valley in New York State, was guided to the park by his brother. Sam's college-educated and asthmatic brother was seeking a dry climate when he brought his Virginia-born wife, Elizabeth, and two children into the park. Up to a point, there were parallels between Judge Carter and Herb Bassett. Both came into the wilderness from the East with trained minds. The Bassetts brought with them a small library and an organ. Their home became the natural gathering place in the park. Herb became the postmaster and the justice of the peace, but he was not an empire builder like the judge. His wife, an ardent feminist, possessed those capabilities; but she died of appendicitis at the age of thirty-seven.

Elizabeth Bassett gave birth to a daughter the second year the family was in Browns Park; and the exhausted mother, who had no milk, surrendered the baby to a Ute woman, who nursed the child. Ann Bassett grew up with a streak of wildness and an imperious quality, thus her nickname.

Other families headed toward the park to carve homesteads from the public domain. All were squatters until the survey of the park was completed in the summer of 1884 and they recorded their claims. Two of the earliest settlers, Jesse and Valentine Hoy, hired outsiders to file claims adjacent to theirs and then bought them out once they had acquired title to the 160-acre parcels of prime river-bottom lands. The Hoys were thought to be "land grabbers" by their neighbors, the Bassetts, who had nothing to do with them after Valentine attempted to "swift" the Bassett place. Herb beat him to the Colorado courthouse, which was more than one hundred miles distant.

In the last half of the nineteenth century many trips were being made to courthouses throughout the West for the purpose of filing on virtually free land. Except for a catchall category, more public land was given away or purchased at nominal cost for the stated purpose of homesteading than for any other single use. Over the years 287.5 million acres would be carved up into small pieces for homesteads. These lands were not necessarily choice; in fact they were quite poor and too small in most cases. The railroads, states, Indian tribes, private landowners, and speculators had already made their selections by the time the big land rushes got underway.

The basic legislation, the Homestead Act of 1862, was the result of a land-reform movement that had its roots in the works of such thinkers as Thomas Jefferson and Tom Paine, easterners who thought that every man had a natural right to a small tract of land that he could farm in some sort of bucolic fashion. Free land for all became a national issue and Congress was besieged with petitions—westerners seeing it as an opportunity for growth and some easterners envisioning a western dumping ground for undesirables. The safeguards against fraud were minimal. A person had to swear that the land was going to be used for actual settlement and cultivation and that the filing was not being made for another person. Easy enough. Perjury was not unknown. Paul Gates wrote of the smaller, more numerous cheaters: "When he swore that he was not making the extra entry for others he was committing perjury but his crime, if crime it was, was commonly done and was not as harmful as if he were making his entries for a cattleman, a timber baron, or a large capitalist estate builder." Despite their drawbacks, the homestead laws and the related statutes prevented the conditions of tenancy prevalent in older states and nations to the east.

The influx of settlers continued into the park. In 1879 a school was established and three years later a killing was recorded at the Bassett home.

Three men rode up to the Bassett ranch in 1882 and shot one of the hired hands in the back as he was reaching for his bridle. The children were gathered up, and the men and women at the ranch, including Elizabeth Bassett, got the drop on the killer and his two friends. The friends said the hired hand had shot the killer's brother; and this was how they settled scores in Texas, where they came from. Word circulated throughout the park, and a lynching was in the making. Herb Bassett, a mild, unrealistic man, let the three men go with instructions for them to turn themselves in to the distant sheriff. Needless to say, they were never seen again.

Killings were common in the park. Of the death of the only doctor, an oldtimer wrote that it was the first natural death to occur in the park. Elizabeth Bassett, who was made of stronger stuff than her husband, then took over as the community surgeon. The Bassett ranch was the center of the community, so it attracted more than its share of western-style violence.

Some years later a suspected killer of two park residents, who was being held at the ranch for the arrival of the sheriff, was lynched by seven masked men. None of the men knew how to tie the hangman's knot so they recruited Herb, who somehow possessed that skill. Bassett wanted no part of the actual hanging, so he returned to his small post office building after tying the knot. The drop from the buckboard was too short, and the man's neck failed to break. It took him three minutes of grotesque jerking about before he strangled to death. The vigilante neighbors took off their masks, washed their hands, and entered the house to eat a peaceful meal with the Bassett family.

Ann Bassett grew up as a tomboy in this environment. She rode and roped and hung out with the cowboys, discarding the dresses of the period for buckskin pants to the horror of her mother. She was sent to an exclusive girls' school outside Boston, which was an unhappy experience. "Endless months dragged past in a restricted social atmosphere of quaint gentility and baked beans," she later wrote. Bassett lasted one term at the school, having offended the authorities by giving an impromptu demonstration of western riding skills in front of the riding "Mawstah" and her fellow students, all of whom were sitting sidesaddle. She returned to Colorado with the veneer of a young lady wrapped around the core of a cowboy. In a picture of the period she looks properly wistful, but her actions spoke otherwise. There was always that duality about her.

Herds of Texas longhorns were on the move north and the country around Browns Park began filling up with large cattle companies that coveted the park's grazing lands and regarded the small homesteaders as an obstruction to their growth. To the south and west Lodore Canyon, the high plateaus, and the monolithic Mormons, who were also small ranchers, formed barriers to the large cattlemen. The park's residents banded together and encouraged the planting of sheep herds on the periphery of their natural boundaries to the north and east. Thus the cattle, which did not like to cross lands grazed by sheep, were discouraged from wandering into the park from those more accessible directions. A few did. The strays were gathered up, the brands changed, and the animals were incorporated into new herds. This was one way to increase holdings, and as a young woman Ann Bassett, along with other amateur rustlers in the park, altered a brand or two.

Then there were the professional outlaws who passed through or made the park their home for brief periods of time. They were divided into two categories—the good bad guys and the bad bad guys. Queen Ann remembered a shy, well-mannered cowboy who spent a short time at the Bassett Ranch, where he and Josie, her sister, became good friends, and then went to work elsewhere in the park. He was known as Ed Cassidy to the residents, and later as Butch Cassidy to detectives. The ranchers had their own concerns, and the outlaws were not part of them unless they actively infringed on the inhabitants' lives. Bassett recalled, "Cassidy had not harmed nor otherwise bothered the people of our neighborhood. If the law officers wanted him, it was their place to take him, not ours." And so the park's residents sat down to Thanksgiving dinner with Cassidy and his wild bunch.

A different type of outlaw rode into the valley in April of 1900, a dark stranger who posed variously as a buyer of horses or ranches, two guises that would give him the information he sought. He said his name was James Hicks; but he really was Tom Horn, a paid gunman for the large stockmen's associations in Wyoming and Colorado, which were concerned about losses to rustlers. Ann Bassett wrote, "There was hired secretly one who would strike, kill, and leave no sign. One who would not hesitate to shoot down friend or foe, man, woman, or child for pay. In Tom Horn was found this killer, a murderer, lusting for blood money." She came to feel a special animosity toward the killer and the man she suspected of hiring him, Ora Haley, the owner of a large cattle operation in southern Wyoming and northwestern Colorado.

Hicks was given the usual hospitality and a job at the Bassett homestead. With the benefit of hindsight, Ann Bassett could say that she "did not take kindly to the new cook" because of his boastfulness about killing Indians when he served as an Army scout during the Apache wars. The swarthy Hicks moved on after making some observations about the local ranching practices.

Not long after Hicks-Horn departed several ranchers found notes outside their homes warning them to leave the park within thirty days or suffer the consequences. Matt Rash and Isom Dart were among the recipients of the warning. Both ignored it. Both were shot and killed a few months later, Rash from behind while he sat in his cabin and Dart while walking outside a cabin he was sharing with several other men in the mistaken belief that there was safety in numbers. Two shots fired through a hole in the front door narrowly missed Ann Bassett while she sat surrounded by friends and family one rainy night in her home. She was particularly aggrieved by the killings, having been very close if not actually engaged to Rash, who was head of the Browns Park cattleman's association.

Immediately after the shootings some Browns Park cowboys hastily fled the scene, but not Bassett. In her early twenties she embarked upon a personal vendetta against Haley and his Two Bar ranch crew, who were headquartered near Craig, Colorado. She married and divorced Haley's extremely capable ranch manager and wreaked limited havoc on the Two Bar herds, eventually being arrested with a cowboy friend for cattle rustling. The first trial resulted in a hung jury, but the second brought acquittal, following which shots were fired in the air, Queen Ann was paraded through town with a brass band, and a banquet and ball were held in her honor.

Meanwhile, Tom Horn had left Colorado without legally being implicated in the killings. He was hanged in Wyoming in 1903 for the shooting of a teenage boy he had mistaken for the youth's father, a sheepman. Bassett's second husband, Frank Willis, later wrote: "It all sums up to the question of ground, the question that started when the first white man advanced westward. First, we killed the Indians to get it, now we kill each other for the same reason, and will continue to kill until the public land problem is permanently settled."

Ann Bassett Willis died at the age of seventy-nine after moving to California, Arizona, and finally Utah, with frequent visits back to Browns Park. She was convinced, after completion of a course in forestry at the University of Arizona, that she had been turned down for a job in the Forest Service because the law read "male applicant." In her typical way, she added: "For the slapdash reason that I happened to be a female, I was forced to withdraw my application. I am still protesting the law."

* * *

Very soon the mountains took on a desolate, forlorn quality. The softness of summer vanished, to be replaced by the edge of the next season. I was faced with an option. My destination was the Red Castle area, just a quick jump across the crest from the head of Oweep Basin. I was carrying an overall topographical map of the former primitive area, not the numerous, more detailed quadrangle maps that would have taken up more room in my pack. From the few lines of elevation on the map and from what I could see on this side of the crest, the jump looked possible. But there might be a ledge or another unknown obstacle on the other side that would put me in a perilous position or force me to return to the more established route and lose a day in the process.

I was in no hurry and could afford the extra day, and there was a challenge to the cross-country route. It represented the unrestricted path, the route one imagined a mountain man would have forged. But I was not that person. The huddled figures, the unseasonable chill, and the story of the fool decided me.

The fool was a black-clad figure who had arrived at the small campground where I was staying earlier that year in Organ Pipe Cactus National Monument. I had gone to the southern Arizona desert to purify myself after a personal defeat, and during the process I discovered the dark side of a wild place.

Organ Pipe, at the southern extremity of Sagebrush Country, is within the prickly Sonoran desert. The Park Service, which administers the monument, has been unable to stem the tides of shadowy people who have historically migrated across those hot lands.

The Papago Indians padded by on their way to the Gulf of California on their annual pilgrimage for salt. During the gold rush, the main route from northern Mexico to California passed through the southern boundary of what was to become the monument. The Mexicans called the trail El Camino del Diablo. To the Americans it was the Trail of Graves because of those who died of thirst in the burning sun. An Army lieutenant who accompanied the international boundary survey in 1855 reported: "All traces of the road are sometimes erased by the high winds sweeping the unstable soil before them, but death has strewn a continuous line of bleached bones and withered carcasses of horses and cattle, as monuments to mark the way."

At the turn of the century ill-equipped Japanese and Chinese immigrants illegally crossed the border at this point, the fate of some being to perish in a hostile environment far removed from their origins. Within Park Service times rum and mescal, a gallon jug tied to each side of a horse, were smuggled across the border to the nearby Papago Indian Reservation, which was supposedly dry; and during Prohibition liquor was smuggled across the border.

Lately most of the traffic has been drugs or illegal Mexican aliens and Central American refugees, who easily slip under the three strands of taut barbed wire that mark the border. A few years ago about a dozen Salvadorans died of thirst in the monument after they had been robbed and abandoned by their Mexican guides, called "coyotes."

It was into this past history that the fool rode in a new pickup truck with a camper shell to almost become part of that destiny. I saw him puttering about his campsite for a day. It seemed to take him a very long time to put up his tent, but I didn't pay close attention to his activities. The next morning I looked up from eating breakfast and was momentarily startled to see a warlike apparition pass by on its way into the nearby Ajo Mountains. It was the fool complete with black beret, long hunting knife, and rifle. I give him a desultory wave that would discourage conversation and resumed eating.

After a gorgeous climb up the flanks of Mount Ajo, I returned late that afternoon to the primitive campground at the mouth of Alamo Canyon. Another camper knocked on my van as I was eating dinner and asked if I had heard any faint yells. No, I hadn't, since I was inside; but outside we could hear them and see a light blink occasionally from a nearby peak. I looked about. The fool had not returned to the campground. I knew it must be he.

His keys were in the ignition of the pickup. I looked in his tent and there was the thickest air mattress I had ever seen, with a gigantic ghetto blaster pointed directly toward its head. Fortunately the fool had spared us the loud music that tape player was capable of producing. Outside on the cooking grill were the melted remains of a plastic cup in which he had tried to heat water over a flame.

He was a bigger fool than I had originally thought, but he was also a human being who had gotten into trouble. We heard him yell that he was bleeding. We learned later that he had fallen and punctured his arm on a piece of dried cactus. His mistake was to remove the desert wood, because then the blood had gushed from the wound. As he struggled to the pinnacle of rock to signal us, he discarded his gun, his greatest danger having been himself, not the snakes that he was prepared to slay with the weapon.

The fool bled a lot that cold January night and passed out a few times. He was quite weak early the next morning when we reached him. We thought we might have to carry him laboriously down, but the highway patrol was called by radio. An hour later a helicopter hovered a few feet over the top of the pinnacle as we loaded him aboard, and he was whisked off to a Tucson hospital, where he recovered. He was identified as a young man from Ann Arbor, Michigan, who had never been camping before in the desert.

My cautious nature led me away from the contemplated cross-country jaunt and over Porcupine Pass to lunch at North Star Lake. The sun was warm and the wind cold, so I ate behind a clump of subalpine fir and then took a fitful catnap.

The upper Yellowstone drainage, where I nooned, was a study of rock and grass and small lakes: the duplicate of the entrances to the other basins along the Highline Trail. Past Tungsten Lake at 11,344 feet was the pass of the same name. I decided at 2:30 to call it a day at a lake marked 11,268 on the map. My guess was that this lake might be the last good camping spot before Smiths Fork Pass, which I planned to cross tomorrow on my way to the Red Castle area.

I read, then began cooking an early dinner. The sound of horseshoes striking rock alerted me and I looked up to see a string of horses pass by carrying two adults and eight or ten children, heading for Tungsten Pass. I heard the leader shout out loud enough for the whole amphitheater to hear, "All those who want snow cones raise their hands!" On cue all hands popped up, and the entourage obediently halted at a snowbank. It was treat time for all of us as I contemplated my dehydrated stew.

* * *

The land between Browns Park and Fort Bridger was fitfully occupied by settlers after 1870. It was too isolated to attract the large cattle companies, so homesteaders predominated. There were two constants. The groupings tended to be Mormon or non-Mormon, and they were randomly scattered along the creeks that dropped from the mountains. The non-Mormon communities took their names from the landscape. Mountain View was at the foot of the Uintas, in Lonetree there was a single pine, at Burntfork there had been a fire, and Linwood was the common name for a cottonwood tree. McKinnon and Lyman were named for Mormon officials, and Manila was the result of an outburst of patriotism following Admiral Dewey's naval victory in the Philippines. That the settlement was named for a battle fought on water was ironic, because a drier place could not be imagined. Its original name was Sandtown.

The settlement patterns at Mountain View and Manila differed from those of the other communities strung along the military road. At Mountain View settlement was delayed until 1890 when the former military reservation was opened for homesteading. Manila was the result of a land-promotion scheme that capitalized on the passage of the Cary Act in 1894. Congress gave the states desert lands in hopes that they would be irrigated and settled. Salt Lake promoters got hold of most of the land in what they called the Lucerne Valley (previously it had been named Dry Valley), installed a water system, and circulated brochures claiming all sorts of lucrative agricultural possibilities on land that was mainly vegetated with sagebrush, prickly pear, and greasewood. A few Mormon families arrived and began to eke out a living in that far northeast corner of the state.

Midway between Browns Park and Fort Bridger was Burntfork, where the lack of a pattern was more typical of what was occurring all over the West at the time. There was no plan or logic other than the incessant search for grass, water, and free land by people arriving singly, as couples, or as families and scattering about the countryside to build log cabins wherever they wished, unless the land had already been spoken for. Along with these squatters came some cattle and eventually sheep, which were supplemented with strays from Judge Carter's extensive holdings and cattle from Texas and Oregon. By the mid-1870s there were twenty thousand head of cattle on the open range in that region, and the elk and antelope were being pushed out. At the same time a government surveyor found squatters everywhere, including on the military reservation. Following the disastrous winter of 1887–88, there was less cattle. Little changed over the years. It would not be until the 1950s that the road was paved and electricity brought to Burntfork. But by then the hamlet's most famous resident would have come and gone.

Elinore Rupert (later Stewart) sought land and in the process found a husband and made a new life. Congress passed the Enlarged Homestead Act of 1909 in response to the semi-arid states, which wanted to accelerate growth by encouraging dry farming on plots that were larger than the standard 160-acre parcel. Three-hundred-and-twenty-acre parcels became the standard for nine western states, a number of states choosing not to participate in the program because they did not want to be stuck with the arid label. Wyoming, Utah, and Colorado were among those states that were included in the legislation. Wyoming, in particular, aggressively sought new settlers, boasting: "There is absolutely no question as to the fertility of the soil in Wyoming. It is rich, and will produce enormous yields as compared with farms of the Middle West." Settlers grabbed the bait. The number of Wyoming farms and ranches nearly doubled between 1900 and 1910, but the rewards were spotty. Drought years followed. It was a hard life.

In 1909, at the age of thirty-three, Rupert was a widow with a young daughter. While working as a maid in Denver, she read about the new law and caught a good case of the homestead fever, a not uncommon affliction at the time. Her plan was to find a competent rancher who could advise her, while at the same earn a living until she could find and then build a separate place. In response to her newspaper advertisement for a housekeeping position on a ranch, Clyde Stewart, a dour Scotsman and widower, replied. Rupert and her daughter, Jerrine, arrived in Burntfork on a cold April day after twenty-four hours on the train and two days on the stage.

One month later she filed for land adjoining Stewart's sagebrush-dotted homestead, which was bracketed by two streams at the foot of the Uinta Mountains. Like other romantics and outsiders, Rupert first coveted a place "amid the whispering pines" on the peaks, but she soon learned the realities of the harsh Wyoming climate.

Elinore and Clyde were married shortly thereafter. She wrote her former employer: "The engagement was powerfully short because both agreed that the trend of events and ranch work seemed to require that we be married first and do our 'sparking' afterward."

The letters piled up and her Denver employer, whom Stewart described as being a "Bostony" woman, took them back to that eastern city, where they were published in 1914 under the title *Letters of a Woman Homesteader*. They were the basis in the seventies for the movie *Heartland*. Another book, *Letters on an Elk Hunt*, followed the next year and Stewart was well on her way toward becoming Wyoming's most celebrated woman author. The books reveal a warm, compassionate woman who always managed to see the good side of things in the face of the adversities of homesteading on an unforgiving land.

Elinore Stewart rolled with life as it was presented to her at the base of the mountains rather than flail back as Queen Ann did. The couple lost their first baby, a son, and it was a number of years before she could bring herself to write her confidant about the death. Stewart said, "The old sorrow is not so keen now. I can bear to tell you about it, but I never could before. When you think of me, you must think of me as one who is truly happy." She then, literally, counted her blessings: "I have my home among the blue mountains, my healthy, well-formed children, my clean, honest husband, my kind, gentle milk cows, my garden which I make myself." There was more, ending with, "Do you wonder I am so happy?"

When there were a few extra hours or a day or two—a very rare occurrence—Stewart would saddle a horse and ride up into "the great, somber, pine-clad Uintah Mountains." There was a feeling of being released, like a bird, from the cage of a never-ending round of chores into a fresh, pristine world. One such outing occurred after she had completed all the hay cutting, milked seven cows every day, put up thirty pints of jelly, and done the next day's cooking every night during the summer so that she could work outside the entire day. Then the woman homesteader took a day off and, along with her daughter, rode up into the Uintas.

She wrote: "There was a tang of sage and of pine in the air, and our horse was midside deep in rabbit-brush, a shrub just covered with flowers that look and smell like goldenrod. The blue distance promised many alluring adventures, so we went along singing and simply gulping in summer." They caught all the trout they needed with grasshoppers for bait at the end of a string attached to a freshly-cut birch pole. They fried the fish in lard, added a little salt, and ate them with bread and serviceberries for lunch. Mother and daughter returned in the early evening hours, and "a mighty tired, sleepy little girl was powerfully glad to get home."

Within the vast spaces surrounding the Stewart homestead the few neighbors looked after each other. Stewart visited an old German woman on the day of the birthday of the woman's dead son. The woman's husband and small daughter also were buried outside. She had prepared a feast, although she was expecting no one. The two women, who shared the deaths of sons, ate and talked until two o'clock in the morning and then planned to spend Christmas together. Having received training as a nurse, Stewart served as the community's midwife; and when a small child "joined the angels" she helped build the casket and performed the service, there being no minister close by.

Despite the hardships, Elinore Stewart was an unabashed promoter of the homesteader's life for women. "I am very enthusiastic about women homesteading," she wrote. There was less work raising a large family in the country than was involved in having to go out every day in the city and do someone else's wash; what was raised was one's own, and there was no rent to pay. She recognized that it took a certain temperament "and persons afraid of coyotes and work and loneliness had better let ranching alone. At the same time, any woman who can stand her own company, can see the beauty of the sunset, loves growing things, and is willing to put in as much time at careful labor as she does over the washtub, will certainly succeed; will have independence, plenty to eat all the time, and a home of her own in the end."

Longing for a like mind crept into her unpublished correspondence with Grace Raymond Hebard. Hebard was Wyoming's most eminent woman at the time. She was the first woman admitted to the bar in that state, chairman of the University of Wyoming's history department, and an ardent supporter of woman suffrage in other states, Wyoming having granted women the right to vote in 1869. Stewart sought another good mind in her letters, once writing, "Many times I envy your living as you do among things and people of interest." Her letters were warm supplications. In return she received stiff replies from Hebard, who set about collecting historical material on "our noted literary woman of the State."

During World War I, Stewart threw herself into war work, enthusiastically and tirelessly selling war bonds and conducting Red Cross drives. During the twenties, her daughter and the couple's three children were sent to school to Boulder, Colorado, where Clyde Stewart had relatives. She would visit Boulder only to return to Burntfork and joyfully plunge back into ranch work. She never fully recovered from a ranch accident in 1926, and died eight years later in Rock Springs. Elinore Stewart had lived the homesteader's life that she so evocatively had portrayed.

Chapter 7

SCIENTISTS

Bernard DeVoto remarked that the history of the West could be written along radii that emanated from Fort Bridger for fifteen years after its establishment in 1842. That was accurate as far as it went, but he should have extended the length of time. For an intense period centering around the early 1870s men of science and letters, who were regarded as the best and brightest of their gifted generation, passed through and circled around the crude settlement and the Uinta Mountains.

This was the Gilded Age—a time when scientific studies in the deserts of the West were carried out with Victorian aplomb; the hope being that fame, fortune, and honors would accrue in the East. The men who participated in the scientific plundering of the West celebrated themselves by naming peaks in the Uintas after their kind. There was (Clarence) Kings Peak, the highest mountain in Utah, and just south along the same ridgeline, South Kings Peak, and below that, Kings Lake. Nearby were Mount (Samuel F.) Emmons and (Grove Karl) Gilbert Peak and Gilbert Meadow. To the east was (Joseph) Leidy Peak and (O. C.) Marsh Peak. West of the central Kings massif was (F. V.) Hayden Peak, Hayden Pass, and Hayden Lake. In the same general area, between Hayden Peak and Naturalist Basin, was Mount (Louis) Agassiz.

Why this orgy of mutual backscratching and why were the Uintas so honored by the presence of these great men? The repayment of professional debts and the camaraderie of a narrow social and professional class based in the East accounted for the inbred characteristic of the naming process. And, quite simply, the Uintas were the most accessible mountain range for travelers from the East after the railroad was completed. The railroad carried them there and back with unprecedented speed and ease and issued the scientists and their entourages free passes for their trips. In return, the work of the scientists benefited the railroad in either direct or indirect ways.

Fort Bridger was at the center of this scientific activity. The scientists hopped off the train and headed for the supply depot. Heavy bills were run up at Judge Carter's store by Marsh, Cope, Leidy, King, Powell, and Hayden. There they got their supplies and transportation and within a few hours were in the mountains or the desert hunting for rocks or fossils. They did their work in the pleasant summer months and returned to their universities, laboratories, and public agencies with a rich haul of bones, drawings, rocks, and field notes. They published or exhibited their findings, and their careers rocketed upward. The scientists came to think of the West as their own particular province, when actually they were only one shallow presence in a long line of transient occupants.

The Victorian manners of the scientists were ludicrous to the natives, and they seem boyish now when viewed in posed photographs of the time. Seven men from an 1872 Yale University expedition to the Fort Bridger area held guns at the ready in a studio photograph. Rifles, pistols, knives, geologists' hammers, and binoculars dangled from their necks, were strapped to cartridge-laden belts, or were tightly gripped in hands better suited for the classroom or laboratory than handling the harsh realities of the West (which, in any case, were actually dealt with by local packers and detachments of troops sent to escort the gentlemen). In the center of this group was Othniel Charles Marsh, professor of paleontology, head of the Peabody Museum, and an extremely forceful personality.

An assumed nonchalance was also the dominant theme of a photograph taken on the summer grass at Fort Bridger. Strewn casually about were the implements for a game of croquet, with Army officers, civilians, Judge Carter and his family, and, in the center in a dark suit, Professor Joseph Leidy of the University of Pennsylvania. Leidy, an anatomist, was the first to confirm that dinosaurs once resided in North America.

Marsh and Leidy were two of the three leading paleontologists of the day, this being a period when the search for fossils and dinosaur bones was as glamorous and competitive a scientific undertaking as space flight was in the 1960s. Also passing through Fort Bridger was Edward Drinker Cope of Philadelphia, the third in the triumvirate of star scientists. Like Marsh, Cope was an educated man of independent means. These two distinguished men were fierce rivals for dinosaur bones. Each employed spies, double agents, coded telegrams, false names, stealth, verbal vindictiveness, and an unseemly amount of scientific haste in an effort to outdo the other at a time when the outside world was clamoring to get a sight of the giant beasts.

The competition between the three vertebrate paleontologists, who worked separately in the same general area in the summer of 1872, was intense. Arriving at Fort Bridger in early July, Cope took three weeks to scrape together the needed transportation, since mules and wagons were in short supply because of the various scientific expeditions that were already in the field. Cope hired one of Marsh's men to guide him to his rival's sites. Leidy, who had been supplied with free bones over the years from a doctor stationed at Fort Bridger, complained that the other two "offer money for what used to come to me for nothing, and in that respect I cannot compete with them." He soon dropped out of the competition.

There was a rush to publish not unlike the rush to stake mining claims. Within a period of two months, seven genera were named independently by Leidy, Cope, and Marsh for fossils that are now recognized as a single species—*Uintatherium,* meaning Uinta beast. A garbled telegraph message sent from the field by Cope resulted in the wrong name being attached to his find. Leidy's name stuck, since it was in print two weeks before the descriptions of Marsh and Cope. This was not science's finest hour.

* * *

On this cloudless night in the mountains the crisp sky was full of shooting stars and winking satellites, the only hint of a scientific presence. The Milky Way was a broad, iridescent swath laid down over an ink-black pit. In the early-morning hours the scythe-shaped moon rose above the black mass of Kings Peak.

In order to see the light show and with faith in continuing excellent weather, I did not put up the tent that night. The thermometer registered twenty-five degrees when I awakened at seven, and there was a thin layer of frost on my sleeping bag.

On my way to the Red Castle area, I climbed Smiths Fork Pass. The early sun glanced off the flanks of Mount Powell. There was a pecking order among the scientists. Although John Wesley Powell was the first of the scientists into the Uintas, he was the last to get a peak named in his honor. A fellow geologist, Wallace Hansen, noticed the omission and rectified it a century after Powell had passed through the Uintas. Marsh was given a peak while his rival in the search for dinosaur bones, Cope, who was not as well connected, received no such honor.

I wondered what those famous naturalists, vertebrate paleontologists, and geologists would have thought about all the sheep I found grazing on the north slope of the pass. Were all their reports written, the bones collected, and their maps drawn just to bring about the eating of the West?

The overwhelming presence of the animals in the upper basin of the East Fork of Smiths Fork was oppressive. A balance had been lost in the process of finding some grass for domestic animals to eat in the summer months. Their hooves had worn terraces in the clipped grass and bare earth of the mountain meadow and their accordion-shaped droppings were all about.

Then there was their stupid behavior. The sheep simply retreated en masse down the valley as I walked toward them. They did not have the common sense to circle around my benign advance and resume grazing where they had left off, and there was no herder to head off this blind retreat.

Who deserved to be in this mountain meadow, the sheep or I?

Or should the question be phrased in mutually exclusive terms? What basis did I have for complaint? Lamb was my favorite meat, and I clothed myself in wool during the winter months. Was there another place for them and/or me in the West?

The West is crowded with livestock. Cut back on such use of public lands and the effect on the market would be minimal, since the Interior West supplies but a small proportion of the nation's total meat requirements. But ranching is a historic use of this country—at least for the last one hundred years—and there are people and communities who depend upon it. A healthy ranch is visually a lot more pleasing than, say, an open-pit uranium mine.

Leaving the trail and circling around the toe of Red Castle, I came upon the well-trod path from China Meadows. Tents, both singly and in clusters, were pitched along the trail to the west of the castle-shaped rock, which is tinted red, as is most of the rock in the Uintas. Red Castle is one of the major attractions in the backcountry of the Uintas. I have noticed that overly dramatic names with no basis in fact tend to draw people, for example, Devil's Postpile, Hells Canyon, and Old Faithful—the latter being neither old nor faithful.

I was a bit nauseated. The water, some other bug, or my imagination? I could only wait and see what developed. Besides feeling ill, I was also lonely and tired. I was aware, from previous experiences, that a breaking point occurs a few days into such solitary journeys. It is best just to proceed through this barrier because on the other side there is some measure of increased tranquility.

The first clouds of the trip gathered over the peaks in the late afternoon. There were thunder, lightning, and some light snow that evening. I heard rocks falling from the ramparts of Red Castle, as if the resident mountain gods were issuing a warning.

While the paleontologists fought over the bones on public lands, the geologists used the terrain to establish their reputations and thereby obtain federal funding for their competing surveys of the West. Of the three surveys conducted in and around the Uintas, only Powell's served the interests of pure science. The chief beneficiaries of the Hayden and King surveys were the railroads, since their work paralleled existing tracks or delved into areas ripe for development. Such practical applications of science attract congressional appropriations. It is difficult to determine what the average westerner gained from them except, in the case of Hayden's efforts, some poor advice.

Ferdinand Vandeveer Hayden entered the scene as head of the United States Geological Survey of the Territories, which was under the jurisdiction of the Department of Interior. With him as he set out to catalogue southern Wyoming in 1870 were four heavy wagons, two army ambulances, and twenty men, including the noted western photographer William Henry Jackson. Leidy and Cope worked independently and later submitted monographs that were published with Hayden's report that year.

Hayden's survey was the biggest, longest-lasting, and best-known of the three surveys. It was his particular forte to gobble up as much information on an area as was possible and then spew it back in a disorganized manner, emphasizing the practical applications of his observations in the process. Hayden, a medical doctor turned rock and bone collector, said it was his goal "to place before the world in a proper light the magnificent resources, scientific and practical, of our vast [public] domain in the West." In other words, he was a government boomer; and for this he was appreciated by business interests in the West.

This general survey lacked specific goals; and, as a consequence, Hayden and his men hopped around the West wherever money and interest took them. In 1870 it happened to be southern Wyoming. Hayden got a late start, setting out on August 6 for a two-month tour of the countryside. By September 12, when the aspen trees were beginning to turn and it could snow on any given day, the party pulled into Fort Bridger, the most western point of that year's work. Four days later they set off for the Uinta Mountains guided by Carter. His "long residence at Fort Bridger and intimate knowledge of the surrounding country proved of great value to us in our explorations," said Hayden in the report that covered his activities for that year.

Hayden wrote an excellent physical description of the north

slope, capturing it with all the finely etched detail of a lithograph; but then he spoiled it when he departed from reality. Increasingly, he saw the landscape and what could be done with it through rose-tinted glasses and described it in an overly rhapsodic manner.

As Hayden rode toward the Uintas, he gazed about. Wheat, oats, barley, and hay could be raised here in abundance and with ease. The grazing possibilities were unsurpassed. There were excellent roads into the mountains reaching to the 11,000-foot level. The language he used indicated luxuriance, and roads that did not exist. As they gained altitude, the party passed from a "broad grassy valley" to a plateau that "has the appearance of an elegantly pre-pared lawn." The manner was Victorian and the scene could have been England.

Finally they broke out upon the heights somewhere between Blacks Fork and Smiths Fork and Hayden rhapsodized, "The view that meets the eye toward the sources of these streams can hardly be surpassed for ruggedness and picturesque beauty." The peaks resembled "Egyptian pyramids on a grand scale." Then, quickly switching to a culture that also appealed to the Victorian mentality, the physician described another mountain in terms of a Gothic church. His party gave it the name of Hayden's Cathedral, a designa-tion that did not stick.

Hayden continued in this vein of overly lavish praise for a rather ordinary mountain range and emphasized the abundance of agricul-tural riches that could be extracted from the earth. The rich, black soil supported a heavy growth of native vegetation; ergo, it could sup-port extensive cultivation. Of one valley he wrote, "Every foot of bottom land could be cultivated with ease," while of another, "The grass is excellent, and the water pure from mountain springs. The sage shrub grows very rank, which also indicates the fertility of the soil."

Who was Hayden kidding? Outsiders could be fooled, but those few people who lived there knew about the early frosts, the crushing winters, the one cutting of hay, and the struggle to raise other crops. The Mormons at abandoned Fort Supply knew of the hardships, and Carter had suffered agricultural reverses. Surely while traveling in the High Uintas in early fall there was some hint of winter in the air. Yet the government geologist never mentioned climate.

Hayden rode through an imagined paradise with blinders on. He described a grove of aspen trees as being distributed on the rounded hills with a "delicate artistic taste" and praised the "esthetic feeling" of their autumn foliage. It was the "simplicity of structure" and "contrasts so pleasing to the eye" that made the Uintas the most beautiful of all mountain ranges, at least "in an artistic sense," he wrote.

As he returned to the fort, Hayden became more unrestrained in his commercial visions. Judge Carter should be allowed to build a railroad into the mountains, as proposed in a bill before Congress, and land grants to support such construction would not be excessive. Such a project would bring onto the market some 100,000 acres of timber, farm, and grazing lands. Millions of acre feet of timber would be available for the railroads. Farms would be sprinkled everywhere, both in valleys and on plateaus. There could be an "unsurpassed summer resort" for invalids. For those who could get about, the forests would be stocked with game and the streams filled with trout. There would be a new world of beauty available for the artist. This European recreational dream and model of American extractive enterprise would take place amidst the most beautiful and accessible scenery in America.

There was a letdown in the narrative after this point. Indeed, it would have been difficult to sustain such soaring visions as they departed from the fort on October 1 and journeyed eastward across the badlands toward Henrys Fork. But the message was not discontinued, just lessened in intensity. In the valley of Henrys Fork, where the soil was rich and the grass plentiful, Hayden predicted it would soon be "occupied from its mouth to its source." There was no time to slip over to the south slope, but a glance from the crest told Hayden (incorrectly) that it was no different from the north slope. He detected an indication of oil—actually black bat excrement— but found no signs of oil where it would later be produced.

When they got to Browns Park, the party found that 2,200 head of Texas cattle had been deposited there for the winter and would remain until they were driven to California in the spring. Noting the predominance of sagebrush, Hayden remarked, "A small number of cattle or horses could find abundant food for winter, but so large a number as were in it at the time we visited it must consume all the grass in a few weeks." Of the bare, convoluted rocks at the eastern end of the Uintas, Hayden acknowledged that the geology was "very complicated and interesting"; but it would take a week or two to work out all the complexities, and he really had to catch a train.

That the possibilities Hayden foresaw were not grounded in any reality indicated some fault in his vision. The government scientist applied the artificial sensibilities of the Victorian age to the West, and in the process manufactured a different landscape, one that did not fit the facts. Hayden's crime was to mislead people, especially those settlers who read his popular reports or actually carried one in hand as they debarked from the train and rode south to discover for themselves the hard realities of living along the north slope.

Hayden rode back East on the train, churned out a 511-page report, in which he thanked Judge Carter and the railroads for their generosity. The next season, with an appropriation from Congress almost double what he had received the previous year, he headed toward the Grand Tetons and the Yellowstone region, where he described even greater glories.

In contrast to Hayden, Clarence King knew exactly where he was going—a west-to-east path along the 40th parallel that was wide enough to encompass the Central and Union Pacific railroad lines from the crest of the Sierra Nevada to the Front Range of the Rocky Mountains. The route of King's Geological Exploration of the Fortieth Parallel bisected the heart of Sagebrush Country. The purpose of the survey was "to examine and describe the geological structure, geographical condition and natural resources" of this hundred-mile-wide belt. Such a report would be of great help to the railroads and the federal government, since they owned (actually, in the case of the former, would come to own or control) adjoining sections of land along this route, yet knew little about what was upon and underneath those lands.

The survey was an ambitious task for a twenty-five-year-old Yale graduate; but King, called the "best and brightest man of his generation" by his friend Henry Adams, thought big and had the presence to pull it off. King was *the* man of his time, although in later life he would sink into failure and relative obscurity. Well-read, well-connected, charming, literate, aristocratic in bearing, and always on the go, he gathered around him a coterie of privileged young scientists. King tended to select look-alikes. Of the four geologists in the first party, all were New Englanders, all graduates of either Harvard or Yale, and all but one had done further study in Europe. Some, like the geologist Samuel Franklin Emmons, a friend and neighbor of Adams, would rise to prominence in their fields.

So it was a jolly group that took to the field in 1867, only to be felled by the realities of heat and malaria in western Nevada. King was struck by lightning while using a metallic instrument atop a mountain in a storm, but refused to give up. He recovered in one week and proceeded with the survey. Persistence in the face of adversity was the code.

Two years later King's survey party had worked its way east to a summer encampment in the cool meadows of Parleys Park above Salt Lake City. During the summer of 1869 they worked their way through the Wasatch Mountains to the Uintas and the basin to the north of these mountains, finding coal deposits and following the Bear River to its headwaters near the crest of the Uintas. For King, the range was "unlike any other in America, being in fact a great lofty plateau of nearly horizontal strata" capped by a plateau-like summit. He likened the Uintas to the Caucasus Mountains in Russia. Where Hayden saw the mountains through unrelated details, King saw them as a distinct unit. He was drawn to the nearby badlands, whose architectural forms fascinated him. Turrets, towers and "citadel-like masses" rose from the soft marls and sands of Eocene time. King wrote:

There is rarely in one region a more marked physical contrast than may be observed between the stretches of clay desert and Bad Land—in which all the topographical features are subdued by the low vertical scale, where vegetation is wanting, and the whole tone of the landscape is ashen—and the vast, rolling, wave-like ridges of the Uinta foothills sweeping up with their deep green covering of coniferous woods, surmounted by the lofty pyramidal summits whose dark-red strata are traced in level lines across all the surfaces that are lifted above the plane of vegetation.

King perceived it was the grinding action of glaciers that had carved the vast amphitheaters. "The resultant topography is that of an intricate series of narrow ridges and a great procession of angular peaks, all carved out of horizontal beds," he wrote in his analytical work *Systematic Geology*. The difference that he was able to perceive between the two slopes was that the southern slope dropped more gradually and had less faulting. The geologist noted the unusual east-west orientation of the Uintas, the large number of lakes and meadows, and "superb forest growth." King thought that the Uintas and the Alps, although half a world apart, had risen at about the same time.

Two years later the survey was back in the region and split into two parties, one of which worked out of Fort Bridger. Emmons was in charge of this group; and he sent an invitation to Henry Adams to join him. Adams, the intellectual and wealthy descendant of presidents, met King briefly for the first time, had poor luck hunting, and saw plenty of rattlesnakes south of Laramie, where he first stopped. He spurned sleeping in a tent, preferring the great outdoors. Southern Wyoming and northern Colorado were too civilized (there being "no end of farms and cattle in it") for someone who was seeking the real West.

Fort Bridger fit Adams's preconception. As he sat outside his tent, a Shoshoni watched this small, unsure man of letters. And the easterner eyed the Indian in return and wrote: "You ought to see the long-haired cuss and his get-up which is dirty enough and far from poetical." (There is no record of what the Indian thought.) Adams found the fort to be "in an awful wilderness of alkali desert covered with low sage brushes." But he came alive in the mountains. "My last trip in the Uintah mountains was a stunner. I never felt so lively and so much in the humor for enjoyment, and how I did eat!" Particularly toothsome was a fat buck that Adams said was better meat than anything he had eaten in London, Paris, Rome, or Florence.

Duty called, however, and Adams returned to teach history at Harvard with "many longing, lingering looks back." (Also teaching at Harvard was another King supporter, the great naturalist Louis Agassiz.) Perhaps Adams had forgotten this youthful frolic when he later wrote in *The Education of Henry Adams:* "Neither to a politician nor to a business-man nor to any of the learned professions did the West promise any certain advantages, while it offered uncertainties in plenty."

For King it was a busy summer. He was in and out of Fort Bridger and touched bases on both coasts and later with the two parties in the field. They worked into the fall months until the snows threatened to cut off their retreat to the fort. On their way there, King tracked a grizzly bear to a cave in the badlands and crawled in after the beast. It was a foolish act, but at that time King lived a charmed life. He killed the bear with a single shot aimed between two luminous eyes. The survey party boarded the train and headed to San Francisco, where they established winter quarters.

It was from that coastal city that King and a few members of his survey party, including Emmons, returned to Fort Bridger in 1872 to search for the location of a fabulous source of gems that had supposedly been found somewhere in the Interior West—the perpetual location for such mirages. Earlier that year two grizzled prospectors had showed up early one foggy morning at a San Francisco bank with a bag of diamonds that they wanted to deposit for safekeeping. They did not say where they had obtained them, thus immediately piquing great interest.

In this cunning manner, the prospectors unleashed all the dormant dreams of easy, abundant riches in a meager land that had periodically plagued the West since Spanish times. Even knowledgeable persons wanted to believe. Charles Tiffany, the New York jeweler, who had little experience in assessing uncut gems, and a noted mining engineer, Henry Janin, who was more familiar with passing judgment on the location of precious metals than gems, gave very favorable reports—the latter after a visit to the scene. All of this occurred at a time when truly rich deposits of diamonds were being found in India and South Africa. So why not diamonds in the American West, the thinking went?

Rumor fed upon rumor, and a few knowledgeable crooks took advantage of the gullible. Crafty men showed up in Denver and Salt Lake with a few crumbs and some tall tales. The newspapers printed the unverified accounts, and other publications further away copied and amplified those misleading stories. The rumors spread like tumbleweed, bouncing wherever the wind took them. It was said that an Apache Indian had found an inch-long diamond. Garnets were passed off as rubies, and so on.

Caution should have been the password, but delirium, which infected some of the shrewdest business minds on both coasts and in Europe, was the order of the day. Twenty-five persons were invited to invest $80,000 apiece in a mining venture by the directors, who included such luminaries as William C. Ralston, chairman of the Bank of California; General George B. McClellan, who ran for President against Lincoln in 1864; and Senator Ben Butler, an active supporter of the 1872 mining law.

Salting a mining claim, which meant dumping some fragments of riches upon a piece of worthless land, was not an unknown practice in the West at the time (or, for that matter, at the present time). It was, in fact, one way the locals could skim off some of that city money from both coasts that otherwise came to them in minor amounts as salaries for rather menial tasks. Mining and the great amount of chance and speculation that revolved around it were in a separate category from other business activities. Bret Harte wrote, "The ways of a man with a maid be strange, yet simple and tame / To the ways of a man with a mine when buying and selling the same."

While not legal, salting a claim was one of those peculiar western practices that were tolerated. Otis E. Young, Jr., wrote in *Western Mining:* "The very mention of the word salting in mining country will to this day provoke cries of indignation from prospectors or descendants of prospectors, who like the modest lady to her swain will state firmly that they had nothing of that sort in mind, and besides they do not know what you are talking about."

More recently, as the value of precious metals has declined, most salting incidents have revolved around uranium, particularly as that market peaked in the early 1950s and 1970s. The first salting incidents coincided with atmospheric testing of nuclear weapons in southern Nevada during the fifties. The resulting radioactive fallout increased the value of many a mining claim that otherwise indicated no radioactivity underneath the surface dirt.

From a few hints, firsthand knowledge of the region, and careful deduction, which was much in vogue at the time, King and his men placed the diamond find on the bare, wind-swept slopes of what subsequently was named Diamond Peak, just northeast of Browns Park. The party of geologists turned fortune hunters left Fort Bridger at the end of October and made their way in bitterly cold weather along the north slope of the Uintas until they reached the Green River four days later. After fording that river and other streams, wrote Emmons, their horses' legs were encased in ice and sounded like clicking castanets.

As they approached the peak they found increasing signs of recent activity: a fresh blaze on a cottonwood tree, a written claim for the water that would supply the nonexistent Golconda City, and freshly staked mining claims. Tracks led up to a rock-strewn plateau. "Throwing down our bridle reins we began examining the rock on our hands and knees, and in another instant I had found a small ruby. This was indeed the spot. The diamond fever had now attacked us with vigor, and while daylight lasted we continued in this position picking up precious stones," wrote Emmons.

The next day, after the fever had abated somewhat, patterns were noticed in the distribution of the gems that did not conform to nature's more random ways. For every dozen rubies, there was one diamond, and the gems were found only in areas that had already been disturbed. Rubies were buried in anthills where footsteps were discerned close by, but were absent from places where no footsteps were evident. The number of gems decreased, then they disappeared entirely as the geologists sifted further away from the plateau. Some accounts credited a packer with finding a cut stone; but, in any case, it was clear from all the evidence that a tremendous hoax had been played on the financiers.

King wrote his report, and the survey was praised for making a practical contribution to the knowledge of the West. It was the geologist's finest hour. Then King passed on from the Uintas. The two prospectors, whose claims were purchased by the mining company, made off with their money. A grand jury in San Francisco investigated, but no one was indicted.

John Wesley Powell was a different man. He thought in regional, not worldly terms. In 1876 Powell wrote in *Report on the Geology of the Eastern Portion of the Uinta Mountains and a Region of Country Adjacent Thereto,* that the Rocky Mountain region had four things in common. These similar attributes were high altitudes, precious metals, no navigable streams, and aridity. Powell would expand on the theme of aridity and the West in a subsequent work. In his Uinta Mountains report he sketched a region and the geological forces that shaped a particular set of mountains. Powell had this to say of the Interior West: "Above all it is the rocky region; rocks are strewn along the valleys, over the plains and plateaus; the cañon walls are of naked rock; long escarpments or cliffs of rock stand athwart the country, and everywhere are mountains of rock. It is the Rocky Mountain region."

A self-taught, practical man, who nevertheless had the ability to crank out the purple prose when needed, Powell eschewed Victorian overstatement in his scientific writings. He wrote: "The Uinta Mountains are composed of elevated valleys, tables, and peaks, the latter having a very irregular distribution, due to geological structure." To him the Uintas, with their east-west orientation, were a geological oddity.

Since 1868 Powell had traveled in and around the Uinta Mountains. They were the barrier through which his famous voyages down the Green and Colorado rivers first passed. Altogether Powell made two boat trips and four pack trips through the eastern portion of the mountains. The Uintas were his launching point into the arid lands to the southwest, where he made his mark as an explorer, geologist, anthropologist, and conservationist. Powell, who was less grandiose than either Hayden or King, would nevertheless outlast his contemporaries as a government scientist and have a more profound effect on how land was used in the West.

His constant message was that there was very little arable land, and a lot of water was needed to make that land bloom. Along with land commissioner Sparks, Powell was among the first to suggest limits; and, of course, he suffered the same political consequences. The West tended to run roughshod over those who attempted to rein it in.

Born in densely vegetated upstate New York and raised in the fertile Middle West, Powell lost his right arm in the Civil War, in which he served as a major, the rank he became known by in later civilian life. Following the war he taught natural science in an Illinois college. In 1867 when Hayden and King were successful supplicants for federal funding for their surveys, Powell, as an unknown, was unable to obtain any federal help for his proposed adventures. This did not deter him. Instead he gathered funds from various Illinois colleges and set off for a modest exploration of the Front Range that summer.

Each succeeding year he penetrated more deeply into the heart of the West with a propensity toward haste tempered by precise planning. In 1868 Powell and his small party, which included his wife, Emma, were back. That fall they made a reconnaissance of the eastern edge of the Uinta Mountains; and instead of retreating from the field for the winter, as was customary for such groups, they spent it in three small log cabins near the Green and Yampa rivers. In March of 1869 the group proceeded toward Fort Bridger via Browns Park and the customary trail up Henrys Fork. At the fort they were welcomed by Carter, and the major and the judge sat down in the latter's comfortable library to discuss Powell's projected voyage down the river.

Not a man to hesitate or miss an opportunity for adventure and the acquisition of scientific knowledge, within six weeks of his return to the East Powell was on his way back with the boats and supplies for a six-month voyage. Four narrow boats, more suited for rowing on lakes than shooting the turbulent rapids of the Green and Colorado rivers, and ten men departed on May 24 from Green River City for a journey down the "River Styx," as one of the men put it.

On the first day, as related later by Powell in his florid account, *The Exploration of the Colorado River and Its Canyons,* they ran aground on a sandbar, broke one oar, and lost two others to the river current. As was his habit, Powell took to the high ground for a view. He wrote, "Away to the south the Uinta Mountains stretch in a long line—high peaks thrust into the sky, and snow fields glittering like lakes of molten silver, and pine forests in somber green, and rosy clouds playing around the borders of huge, black masses; and heights and clouds and mountains and snow fields and forests and rocklands are blended in one grand view." It was clear that Powell could write for different audiences.

From the badlands "interrupted here and there by patches of *Artemisia,* or sage brush" they entered the mountains and the fast water. Ashley's incised name was noted, but the date was partially obliterated after the passage of forty-four years. (The name and place were entirely obliterated nearly one hundred years later by the rising waters of Flaming Gorge Reservoir.) Powell honored an earlier presence, whose exact identity he did not know, by naming the place Ashley Falls.

Of the first part of the voyage through the Uinta Mountains, boating historian and river runner Otis Marston wrote:

> Heavily overloaded and with inexperienced boatmen, the Powell party reaped a harvest of unnecessary mishaps and adventures, and after a succession of collisions, linings, portages, spinning whirlpools, soakings of dunnage and supplies, fire in camp, and the loss of one boat in the rapid they named Disaster Falls, they got out into the Uinta Valley on June 26, a little more than a month after they had left Green River, Wyoming. A significant part of the mileage had been overland, and one of the basic scientific facts established had been that most of the rapids had shores adequate for lining and portaging.

Two months later, with two remaining boats and five men, the others having deserted along the way, the major emerged from the depths of the Grand Canyon and the arduous journey ended. Powell and those of his party who remained with him for the entire trip most probably were the first to make it all the way from the canyons of the Uintas through the Grand Canyon; and he was the first to have an account of such a voyage published.

The ambitious geologist wrote the popular account to draw attention to himself. Powell succeeded admirably. Its publication in

1874 catapulted him into the ranks of Hayden and King. He obtained his own survey, for whom the noted geologist Grove Karl Gilbert worked, and later replaced King as head of the United States Geological Survey. The major had made his reputation off the West.

The scientists did not remain in Sagebrush Country for long. The scientific novelty of the region wore off quickly, there being only a half-dozen years of intense activity in and around the Uinta Mountains. The various hunters after fame, fortune, and recognition in their respective fields either sought other opportunities elsewhere in the West or, as was the case for most of them, drifted back to permanent residence in various eastern institutions after a few seasons "out West."

Scientists did not reappear in the shadow of the mountains until the first decade of the present century, when there was a renewed interest in dinosaur bones on the south slope. "Fossil hunting," wrote Edwin H. Colbert, a curator of vertebrate paleontology at the American Museum of Natural History and a bone collector himself, "is something of a fever, like the search for gold [or diamonds], and every individual in the field soon becomes infected with the desire to make the best and most spectacular discoveries." Those discoveries—"probably never equalled in the history of dinosaur collecting," to use Colbert's words—were made in 1909 in the desolate foothills of the Uintas a short distance from where Escalante had crossed the Green River and where Powell noticed "reptilian remains" during his second voyage down the river in 1871. A local resident who stumbled onto the bones in what was to become Dinosaur National Monument thought they were the remains of sea serpents.

The driving force behind this discovery was Andrew Carnegie, the steel tycoon, who wanted a choice dinosaur skeleton to present to the King of England and something "as big as a barn" to fill up the new wing of his museum in Pittsburgh. To realize these ends, Earl Douglass, a paleontologist recently hired by the museum, combed the bare hills west of Split Mountain. Hayden's survey indicated these sculptured mounds were formed during the Jurassic Period, within which era the bone-rich Morrison Formation came into being. The report first brought Douglass to this treeless, summer inferno in 1908.

Douglass was a slight, bespectacled man from the Middle West who had come to the museum after studying at state schools in South Dakota and Montana and at Princeton University in New Jersey. He was dispatched back to the West to find Carnegie some dinosaurs. The pressure mounted. Nothing, except a weathered thigh bone, had been unearthed the first summer; and now it was August 19, 1909, and another season was about to end. Finally, there *it* was in the gray sandstone incised by gullies—eight dinosaur tail vertebrae joined together as if in life. Two shots were fired to summon his companion. Douglass exclaimed, "What a beautiful sight." The local folks trooped out and discussed how the Uintah Basin would become famous for the discovery.

Actually, the fame would accrue to the Carnegie Museum of Natural History, not Vernal, Utah. Like minerals, livestock, and timber the bones were shipped out of the region and the locals were given wages and a few leftover bones in exchange.

The word was flashed back East. Douglass wrote William J. Holland, the museum director: "Carnegie wanted a Dinosaur for the king of England. If he wants one now there is a fair show that we have it." Actually, the King did not get this dinosaur, but another one. This dinosaur was named *Apatosaurus louisae* in honor of Carnegie's wife, Louise, and it was mounted for display in the Carnegie Museum of Natural History.

Douglass set about extracting the remains in a methodical manner, using the techniques of a miner. He constructed a frame tent and then a log cabin, the residential evolution of many a western mining camp. The overburden was "mucked out" with picks, shovels, and occasional shots of dynamite, loaded into mining carts mounted on small rails, and dumped on a tailings pile. A road was built to the diggings, and from the quarry horse-drawn freight wagons hauled the crated fossils fifty miles to the mining camp at Dragon, Utah, where they were loaded on board a narrow-gauge railroad for the trip to the transcontinental line in Colorado. This was how gold, silver, and lead were mined and transported out of the region.

The work proceeded that first winter in the freezing cold in order to satisfy Carnegie's hunger for bones. Douglass complained privately that he was poorly paid and had received no recognition from Carnegie for his amazing find. But he was a loyal employee, and plodded on with the help of some local laborers. During the thirteen years Douglass worked the quarry for the museum, he shipped 446 crates of fossils weighing 700,000 pounds back to Pittsburgh. It was an abundance of material and overwhelmed the museum staff. Some crates remained unopened as late as the 1980s. Dinosaur remains from Utah eventually found their way, much like Carnegie libraries or American steel, throughout the nation and the world. A beautifully articulated skeleton of *Diplodocus* was found and named *Diplodocus carnegiei*. A cast was made of the skeleton and the resulting plaster-of-paris model was presented to museums in Europe (King Edward VII was a trustee of the British Museum), Central and South America, and this country. A fiber-glass replica wound up on the main street of Vernal.

All of this activity was fine, except there was one slight problem. The Carnegie Museum was a squatter and a trespasser on the public domain. When the land was thrown open for homesteading, the museum, through Douglass, moved fast and applied for a mining claim. No, said the government, fossils are not minerals, at least not within the intent of the mining law. Douglass despaired: "So we, after expending thousands of dollars here, have no more legal right to it than anyone." That was a correct interpretation of the situation.

The dignified Carnegie Museum approached the problem like any common western land grabber and lobbied for the site to be set aside for its exclusive use. The difference between, say, a western livestock association and the eastern museum was that the latter was exceptionally well-connected. The director of the museum talked with the secretary of the Smithsonian Institution, who discussed with President Woodrow Wilson the idea of declaring the quarry site a national monument. The chief clerk of the General Land Office noted that the proposed monument would have no public interest once all the objects for which it had been created were removed. The Secretary of Interior pointed out that Carnegie had already "partially exploited" the site; and it should be reserved so that the Smithsonian—the national museum—got its share of the bones.

In October of 1915 President Wilson set aside eighty acres as Dinosaur National Monument. The Vernal newspaper trumpeted in its usual overheated manner: "Our Notoriety Becoming National."

The Carnegie Museum obtained the yearly permit to excavate dinosaur bones in the monument. It would be renewed, Douglass was assured by Holland, "until we may finally adjudge that it is no longer expedient for us to carry on our work in that spot." By 1922, following the death of Carnegie and decreasing funds, it was judged to be no longer expedient; so the museum surrendered its rights, first to the Smithsonian, and then to the University of Utah, which wound up its activities at the site with Douglass as supervisor in 1924. The bones were transported to Salt Lake with all the hoopla of a winning team returning home.

One of Douglass's last observations, before moving to Salt Lake, where he eventually became a consulting geologist and died in comparative poverty, was that he was "more convinced than ever that there is oil in the basin and where I supposed it and that it will be found when one goes at it right." Oil and other energy minerals would be discovered in the basin by others, and the search for and extraction of those minerals would be similar in outline to the plundering of dinosaur bones. There was profit, albeit of a different type, for both science and industry in such minerals.

Chapter 8

SETTLERS
(SOUTH SLOPE)

Compared to the northern slope of the Uinta Mountains, the south slope was a historical backwater: a stagnant, desert slough versus the fast-moving river of history that crossed the Wyoming plains. The basin was a desolate place; and the dominant white culture to the west, the Mormons, hesitated to enter it. The ferocity of the Utes discouraged settlement from the Colorado side. But, when previously conquered lands became crowded, the Indians were tamed, and mineral riches were suspected of lying underneath the surface of the desert, the whites, in a move duplicated elsewhere in the West, invaded the basin and began to eke out a living from the inhospitable terrain.

The result of this movement was a classic example of resource domination by the most powerful culture and a constriction of the Indians' land base. The whites, both those who entered the basin from the west and those from the east, became remnant outposts of their separate cultures outside the basin. They were on the fringe. Prosperity was their perpetual illusion. A difficult, spare land was the reality. There were recurrent hopes, but those periodic booms—much like the brief flood surges of a desert river—repeatedly dashed, and still splash, against an unyielding terrain.

The basin is a 23,000-square-mile trough in northeastern Utah and northwestern Colorado that slowly subsided as the Uinta Mountains rose. Bounded on the north by those mountains, the Wasatch Range to the west, the Tavaputs Plateau to the south, and a low incline to the east, the basin lies within the rain shadow of the two mountain ranges. The average rainfall along the contour line of the highway connecting the small towns that cling to the south slope is seven inches. Temperature extremes range from 105 degrees to minus 30, making the basin one of the coldest regions in Utah and insufferably hot during the summer months.

The Uintah Basin is neither fertile nor beautiful. Less than 3 percent of the land area within the counties of Duchesne and Uintah, which encompass most of the trough, is arable; and the crop yields on these lands are historically low owing to drainage problems in the soil. There has been a historic fantasy concerning the sustained, large-scale extraction of energy minerals from the basin, but nothing of consequence has ever materialized over the years.

The basin lacks the spectacular aesthetics of the canyonlands to the south, being undulating instead of incised, and colorless instead of vibrant. Thus, tourists do not flock there. Dinosaur National Monument is a minor attraction that the locals have attempted to make the most of over the years. ("Pull for Dina," "Push for Dina," urge the chamber of commerce signs, which are adorned with dinosaur symbols and placed above the handles on the glass doors of Vernal's commercial establishments.)

Highway 40, which parallels Escalante's line of march, is a secondary route. Transcontinental traffic prefers the interstates to the north and south. No road of consequence runs vertically through the depression.

In short, the Uintah Basin has suffered from stagnancy. What existed here were pale imitations of greater expressions of cultures headquartered outside the basin, the Fremont being a segment of the greater Anasazi Indian culture, the Uintah Utes being the poorer cousins of the Colorado Utes, and the Uintah Basin Mormons striving to keep up with their Salt Lake brethren. Determination and hope, of which the Mormons have more than their share, have been the only visible currents within this Sargasso Sea of the West.

Fourteen years after the advance party of Mormons arrived in the Salt Lake Valley and following colonizing missions that were dispatched northeast to the Fort Bridger area, north into Idaho, south to the Virgin and Colorado rivers, and beyond into the periphery of the Los Angeles Basin, the Mormon leadership decided it was time to secure their eastern flank. At the direction of the Mormon leader Brigham Young, a list of names was read off in the Salt Lake Tabernacle on August 25, 1861, and two advance parties set off for the basin within two weeks of being called to serve.

As at Fort Bridger, the purpose was to establish a buffer against the encroaching gentiles. Young said he had handpicked the experienced company because "The Gentiles will take possession of that valley if we do not, and I do not wish them to have it." Like their well-organized mass migration from the Middle West to the Salt Lake Valley, the colonization of the further reaches of the territory was a cooperative venture directed from above.

The Mormons moved out in a mass, and retreated in a mass.

As they departed from Salt Lake, it was decided that should any Indians be encountered "they will be dealt with in a summary manner." By September 19 most of the potential colonizers had returned to Salt Lake. Their report was printed in the newspaper under the headline "Uinta Not What Was Represented." The basin, stated the story, "was one vast 'contiguity of waste' and measurably valueless, excepting for nomadic purposes, hunting grounds for Indians and to hold the world together." The land of the "walnut and vine" was not to be found there, even if it had been so represented by "hunters, trappers and other wanderers." The account went on to state:

> Why men who have lived for years in this country, have roamed over its mountains and sterile plains, and have witnessed the experiments that have been made in tilling the soil, where any exists, have not by observation learned that portions of the desolate wastes can, and cannot, be cultivated, we are unable to say, but such is the case as had been demonstrated more than

once. The men who were sent out, in the instance, to view Uinta, and select a location for a settlement if one could be found, were persons of experience in such matters and in their report the most implicit confidence is placed, consequently all arrangements for establishing a settlement there have ceased.

The exploratory effort was called off rather quickly in view of Young's seeming determination to settle the region and considering similar but more prolonged efforts attempted elsewhere in even less hospitable terrain. It was not the Mormons' nature to admit defeat so easily.

Other factors were circling about in the background. Young knew the federal government was interested in the basin as a possible reservation for the Utes, and such a move—if, indeed, the basin was not worthy of immediate settlement—would accomplish two objectives at one time, with great benefits and little cost to the Mormons. The Indians could serve as a buffer against the encroaching gentiles, and the Utes would be removed from the arable lands around Lake Utah that the Mormons coveted and would be placed in the inhospitable basin. The Mormons, by demonstrating their interest in the Uintah Basin, might goad the federal government into the desired action.

At the time the Mormons were locked in a battle with Washington. Each wanted to dominate the territory. The Utes became the tennis ball that was bounced back and forth, and finally out of the court and into the basin. Forty-five years later the state and federal governments, who by then had made an uneasy peace, cooperated to reduce greatly the Ute land base. Their separate goals meshed so perfectly by the turn of the century that their purposes were achieved in a smooth and peaceful, if not quite civilized, manner.

The clouds and my stomach ailment had mysteriously departed when I awoke on the morning of the seventh day. I faced a long day hiking out of the Red Castle area, crossing two passes, and coming to rest somewhere in the Painter Basin late that afternoon. The first pass I was familiar with, it being the simple retracing of my steps back through the sheep. On gaining Smiths Fork Pass the clouds swooped back in and the wind picked up. The season changed, just like that.

I was reminded of the treeless Alaskan tundra and the southern Andes rising from the Patagonian desert, where the feeling was one of being encompassed by the global sweep of weather. The sky at the ends of the earth pressed close to the ground and the violent alterations in weather felt like ancient, timeless forces coming out of the vastness of Siberia or the Pacific Ocean.

The blasts of wind played with my frame pack like a red sail about to jibe and caused me to take an unplanned step or two. I donned my parka after swallowing some raisins and chocolate for quick energy and warmth.

My route was a shortcut from the south slope of the Smiths Fork Pass to the base of Anderson Pass, where I would again pick up the Highline Trail. The level walk along the 11,600-foot contour line was intermittently through tundra, across rock flows, and through grassy fields of boulders that resembled ancient monuments. My parka hood protected me from the wind, and I concentrated on the immediate steps ahead and the wanderings of my mind. As I made my way through a maze of standing boulders, I heard voices.

What I heard was a large number of human voices babbling just below the threshold of being individually decipherable. I know I heard them. I had heard them before, two or three times already on this trip and once a few years before in the Sierra Nevada when I was descending from the heights after a few days alone in the mountains of California. The only constants that I have been able to establish are that the voices occurred when I'd been alone for a few days and they became audible near standing rocks that were approximately of human height. They can be men or woman, or both sexes combined, as has most often been the case.

The voices sounded as though they were in a large, resonant hall through which I was circulating as a silent observer. It was a social setting, which was interesting because what I was doing—hiking alone through a mountain wilderness for a number of days—was an asocial experience.

The voices, when I first heard them, startled me. They arrived without warning. I was not frightened, just momentarily puzzled as I looked up and saw only rocks and tundra and felt the cold wind passing by. The voices continued to circulate within my head as I walked. They had a decisive beginning but an indecisive end. I could not recall when they faded out.

I have met one other person who has heard voices in the wilderness.

I once rode into the Superstition Wilderness Area of the Tonto National Forest with a forest ranger who was going to check on the prospectors searching the Arizona mountains for the Lost Dutchman Mine, one more western legend of instant wealth.

The Superstition Mountains east of Phoenix crackled with heat, the rattles of diamondback rattlesnakes, and occasional gunshots in the late spring. They were, and had been for some years, an armed camp inhabited by searchers after a fantasy. People had been warned, assaulted, and shot, not necessarily in that order, over the years. Some prospectors later swore in court that they feared the mountains were being invaded by Russian soldiers. The miners wore fur-lined caps with ear flaps in the heat, saw unidentified flying objects, or called themselves by such names as Crazy Jake and told grandiose stories of multiple killings, while sporting enough hardware to, at the very least, intimidate the questioner.

Those men and at least one woman did everything besides find gold and buried Spanish treasure. The search was the end, and the end of the lives of some fifty persons along the way.

Anyway, after facing the black hole at the end of a pistol held by a young miner, who put the weapon down when the ranger identified himself and then picked up a small puppy and cuddled it, we visited the camp of Al Morrow in Needle Canyon. Al was the oldest resident, having camped in the mountains twenty-one years. During that time he had dug numerous tunnels in the hillsides and twice copied the Old Testament onto lined notebook paper, in the process translating the stilted English of the Gideon Bible into the vernacular.

Al had been shot at by fellow miners and had watched them shoot each other up, yet he refused to carry a weapon. "If you bring fear and greed into the mountains, you will not take any gold out," said this gentle, thin man.

There was a certain fault line in those dark, volcanic mountains, said the old miner, which if followed would yield some startling telephone conversations and comforting music.

I took a picture of Al, sitting with a cigarette dangling out of the side of his mouth while transcribing the Bible for the third time. On the adjacent table was a box of Quick Quaker Oats. The picture accompanied a newspaper story I wrote, and the Quaker Oats people called me to ask where they could send Al a carton of the cereal. I told them care of general delivery, Apache Junction, Arizona.

I hope he got that box.

A short time later I heard that Al was killed when one of his tunnels collapsed on him.

By the middle of the nineteenth century the Ute Indians had not passed far beyond the hunter-gatherer stage of existence. True, some had horses and guns that widened their hunting range and killing radius, but those technical advances were mainly confined to the Utes who lived around Utah Lake and along the White River in northwestern Colorado. The Uintah Utes—known also as Uintats, Uinta-ats or Unitah-ats—who lived a primitive existence in the basin, were less fortunate in a material sense but better off geographically because the lands they roamed were not immediately sought by the whites.

As the emigrants kept pouring into the Salt Lake Valley and more land was needed for the expanding population, the Mormons moved south from Salt Lake to the Provo area. As they neared the fertile shores of Utah Lake, the contacts with Indians increased.

The Indian policy of the Mormons differed from that of other whites in the West in that they did not shoot first, most of the time. The Mormons tried patience and food, and when they ran out of both, or felt sufficiently provoked, the shooting followed. The Indians discharged their weapons, and there were deaths on both sides. The policies shifted from patience to killing to control. The federal Indian agent for Utah established three farm reserves for the Indians during the 1850s on the west side of the Wasatch Range;

but they failed because of resistance by Indians, disorganization, funding problems, and entanglement in the federal-Mormon power struggle. A Ute publication later noted: "Most Utes remained reluctant to settle in one place, where their enemies could attack them. Others regarded farming as demeaning. Many refused to accept the arbitrary boundaries established by the treaties. In addition, farming was impractical, if not impossible, in many of the areas assigned to the Utes."

The Utes suffered. They were described as being in a "state of nakedness and starvation, destitute and dying of want."

Within a day or two of Young's tabernacle announcement, the federal Indian agent wrote the Commissioner of Indian Affairs in Washington informing him of the Mormons' intent to move into the basin and suggested that it be made a reservation, a move that would foil the attempted colonization. On October 3, which was exceedingly fast considering the length of time it took to get a message back East and through the bureaucracy at a time when the country was engaged in civil war, the Secretary of Interior forwarded the request to President Abraham Lincoln, who immediately signed the executive order that set aside the reservation. Because of haste and lack of firsthand knowledge of the country, the reservation boundaries that Lincoln approved were quite vague. The reservation was to include "the entire valley of the Uintah [Duchesne] River within Utah Territory, extending on both sides of said river to the crest of the first range of contiguous mountains on each side."

The federal machinery ground away, eventually producing a report in 1862 stating that the land "is understood to be ample in extent, containing two million acres, abounding in valleys of great fertility, with all the necessary water-power for mills, and having an abundance of timber; indeed, as being admirably adapted for the purposes of a large Indian reservation. Many of the Indians exhibit a desire to be placed upon it, and undertake in earnest the pursuit of agriculture." The report proved that the condition of the basin was in the eye of the beholder. The supposed desire of the Indians was wishful thinking: the threat of removal led to the Black Hawk War—the bloodiest conflict ever fought on Utah soil.

Following the uprising, the defeated Utah Lake Utes were broken at last. They wandered off in a number of directions, one of which was toward the Uintah Basin and a reservation that had been provided for them in an 1865 treaty in which they had surrendered their lands west of the Wasatch Range in exchange for the reservation to the east. At the treaty ceremony, Young bluntly told the Indians: "Do you see that the Mormons here are increasing? We have been and calculate to be friends all the time. If you do not sell your land to the government, they will take it, whether you are willing to sell it or not." He asked if they understood. The Indians said they did and made their marks upon the document, which was never ratified by Congress.

The treaty provided annual payments to the Indians for their loss of land; but because the treaty was never ratified, the Indians did not receive the payments. Yet the whites maintained they had lost their land. A tribal history noted: "The history of negotiations with the Ute People is a history of intimidation and bribery. It is a history of broken promises. The Ute People usually complied with their part of the treaties and agreements. Often they had no other choice. However, the government seemed to forget its part of the bargains."

When the Indian agents finally set foot in the northwestern end of the basin, where the new reservation was located, they were confronted with the reality of the place. The new agent, there being a rapid turnover among these federal employees, reported to his superior in Washington: "The broken character of the land, by streams, slough, rocky and alkaline patches, makes it discouraging, even to skilled laborers; much more is it so to those unaccustomed to habits of industry." Nevertheless, the Indians were encouraged to farm, with little success. They were uneasy. Rumors kept circulating that the reservation was about to be thrown open to white settlement.

During this same period the Utes in Colorado and northern New Mexico were being squeezed west of the Continental Divide by the encroaching whites; and following the killing in 1879 of Nathan Meeker, an Indian agent, they finally lost their reservation in western Colorado, whose governor advocated their extermination, and were banished to the Uintah Basin.

By this time the basin was becoming an object of desire to the whites, who gradually impinged upon Indian lands. In the 1870s Mormon settlers homesteaded the Ashley Valley, a fertile piece of ground adjacent to the Green River that had been left out of the Indian reservation. In this manner they leapfrogged and surrounded the Indian lands and established a bastion closer to the Colorado border.

Browns Park, a favorite wintering ground for the Utes, was settled at this time by the Bassetts and others. Cattle and sheep grazed over large portions of western Colorado and eastern Utah. On the other side of the basin some six thousand livestock from the Wasatch Front illegally grazed on the reservation's western fringe. Roads were built across Indian land, military forts were established, and finally gilsonite miners excised a seven-thousand-acre strip from the eastern flank of the reservation.

The Utah inspector of mines, criticizing "certain sentimentalists," reflected the dominant mentality that Indian land should be put to productive use. "Tell me," he asked, "how a man who has located a gilsonite claim has robbed an Indian. Why the loafer never was known to dig for anything, and can never be taught to." The Mormons came to regret the enclave because it became a strip of sin, no governmental entity having legal jurisdiction over "men and women without means of existing except gambling, selling whiskey to Indians and prostitution."

The predicament of the Utes was not unusual. They fit within the pattern of Indian policy as it was practiced nationwide. From the East Coast to the Middle West the policy up to 1887 was to remove Indians from their traditional lands and relocate them elsewhere. From Georgia, sixteen thousand Cherokees walked along the "Trail of Tears" to Oklahoma, where they would lose reservation lands in a land rush more celebrated but similar to the coming Ute experience. Going in the opposite direction were the Navajo, whose three-hundred-mile "long walk" took them from northern Arizona to southern New Mexico. The Utes actually had much shorter distances to travel.

The policy changed from encouraging separateness to assimilation, and would continue to evolve through these two basic cycles, which later became known by different terms. (For "removal and relocation" read "separateness." "Allotment" meant assimilation into the white agricultural economy and loss of their land base.) The new policy of assimilation became official with the passage of the Dawes General Allotment Act of 1887. That act allotted an Indian who was the head of a family a 160-acre tract (single persons and children were to receive, respectively, 80- and 40-acre parcels). The Indian then needed to farm his allotment, and, after a period of twenty-five years of proper management, could own it outright and become a citizen of the state in which he resided. Private property and a farmer's mentality make a civilized person, the thinking went.

The remaining lands within the former reservations were then opened to white settlement, thus precipitating a number of land rushes in the West, including one on the Ute reservation. From 1887 to 1934, when the policy reverted again to one of separateness, Indian landholdings shrank from 138 to 48 million acres. Two scholars of Indian policy wrote of that period: "Everyone could agree that the Indians owned too much land and that holding land in tracts of millions of acres unnecessarily impeded the orderly settlement of the western states."

Hanging on to the policy of allotment and assimilation was the thread of consent, a tradition not only of Indian law but also of a democratic society. Herein lay the problem with the Utes. They did not want to lose any further land, and were adamant on that subject. The solution, for the whites, was to sever the thread. Westerners were getting quite adept at legislative legerdemain when it came to acquiring land and water, and now they went to work on the Utes, to whom the whole process was alien. History and their intuition taught the Indians to be distrustful of white intentions, against which, in the end, they had little recourse. Besides the white settlers, who were predominantly Mormon, two agencies of the federal government emerged as the biggest winners in that land grab.

As I climbed Anderson Pass, it began to spit snow. Wet flakes descended on a slant from the west but did not stick to the ground. The trail zigged and zagged up some switchbacks, then held steady for a low point in the north-south-running Kings Peak Ridge, thus putting the snow at my back. My hands were cold. Below my shorts my bare legs kept pumping away.

I had considered shucking my pack at the 12,600-foot pass and making a dash to the highest point in the range, but the visibility was nonexistent. Also, the climb looked like a dull traverse over broken slabs of rock, so I gave up the idea—better to leave something for a return visit.

I ate a quick lunch at the first combination of sheltering rock and flowing water on the descent. From my niche I had a fine view of the upper end of the Uinta River watershed. There were nearby rock, further swatches of green forest, and a hazy blue veil over distant objects. The haze resembled a river of warm air ascending from the Uintah Basin on a hot day.

Halfway through the Painter Basin the Highline Trail veered off to the left to parallel the divide while the more frequented path continued down toward the distant trailhead at the U–Bar Ranch. I was thrown off a bit because I was accustomed to walking along the main route. My guess was that the majority of foot traffic was from the trailhead to the peak or from the trailhead to the lakes stocked with fish at the eastern end of the amphitheater. My way lay along the less-traveled portion of the triangle between the peak and the lakes.

The Highline Trail sputtered here, sometimes visible, sometimes not. I had to look sharply and consider where the trail was most likely to go and proceed in that direction until I either picked up the path or realized that I had gone astray. If it was the latter case, I would then return to the last discernible mark and begin over again.

The trail, when I found it, was marked by weathered pine poles that resembled gigantic pencils stuck in the ground, eraser first. Their tops were sharpened to points. One visible set of horse tracks was my only guide for portions of the way.

I plodded on, sweating now although I had shed my outer clothing. The landscape changed, becoming rounder and drier. The Kings Peak massif, reaching its apogee at 13,528 feet, then dipping no more than 100 feet to take in Gilbert Peak to the north and Mount Emmons to the south, was a climatological curtain across this mountain range. Streams that were marked perennial on the map did not run in the late summer, the vegetation was much further advanced into the dry season, the forest undergrowth sparser, and patches of raw earth were interspersed among the dry grasses of the meadows. The dust rose, powderlike, from the trail.

Although I had lost no altitude, I felt as if I had entered some intermediate zone between the mountains and the desert—a place where one presages the other.

Finding water suddenly became a problem. I was thirsty and for the first time regretted that I had not brought a plastic water bottle, having relied on dipping my cup into almost instantly available streams and lakes and thinking I did not need, like the desert civilization below me, to store any water. Up a rise, which dehydrated me further, then down a long drop through a lodgepole pine forest and I saw water and a green meadow ahead.

It was a great relief. I dropped to my knees and drank, then lay against my pack to smoke a pipe and lazily enjoy the last slanting rays of sunshine. Four horses grazed peacefully in the meadow, but I never did see any humans about.

I camped there beside Gilbert Creek, which joined the Center Fork of the Uinta River a few feet downstream. The Center Fork gathered in the North Fork and Shale Creek and then became the Uinta River, which eventually passed through what remained of the Ute reservation. My Forest Service map declared: "The Uinta Mountains were named after the 'Uintats' (Ute Indians) who were mountain dwellers." Well, perhaps for a small portion of the year. The map also shows the "Old Indian Treaty Boundary" in a series of straight, unnatural lines that connect the major landmarks along the crest.

To whom did this land really belong? Proceeding backward, it was mine for this one night at least. Perhaps the horses, and almost certainly their owners, felt some proprietorship, at least in terms of grazing rights. Technically the land belonged to the United States Government; that means you and me and the person or persons who own those horses. The Forest Service, an agency within the Department of Agriculture, administers the High Uintas according to all the laws and regulations that cover wilderness areas and national forests. Such administrators have a proprietary feeling about "their" lands, as do the congressmen whose districts lie within them.

The state of Utah—more than a state, more a state of belief—and its white citizens regard the Uintas as "their" mountains. The state's fish and game laws are applicable there. If a crime is committed, the sheriff from the appropriate county will investigate and take action. However, the Utes, who live on a shrunken reservation at the foot of these mountains, have gone to court to dispute these outside jurisdictions. They believe the land is theirs, both in terms of what their ancestors once roamed and what was once officially ceded to them by the government.

The Utes, who were pushed out by persons of European descent, in their time had displaced another Indian culture. The Spanish and the Mexican governments, which briefly laid claim to these mountains and the surrounding territory, renounced their claims— under pressure, to be sure. For all I know, there might be unresolved Spanish or Mexican land-grant claims here, as there are elsewhere in the West.

Such claims are a live issue in the Carson National Forest of New Mexico, where Forest Service officials that year were trying to temper their anglicized laws to the Pueblo Indian and Spanish cultures, which predated the concept of federal lands on this continent. The locals, angered because so much of the highly desired piñon wood was being exported to California and Texas, were going into the mountains without permits and cutting their yearly supply.

Of course, there was nothing new about this practice. Antonio Luhan, the Taos Pueblo Indian who was the husband of copper heiress Mabel Dodge, had gone into the same forest in 1928 with other Indians and cut down a dozen Douglas fir trees. Luhan's wife, who was D. H. Lawrence's hostess in the West, paid the fine of $343.79. Forest Service officials thought the settlement would have "a wonderful effect on the Indians and other petty forest violators," but the wood was still being illegally cut.

Needless to say, there was no such salutary effect because both the Indians and the Spanish, for different reasons, thought the forest on the slopes of the Sangre de Cristo Mountains belonged to them. The Indians had been there for thousands of years, and the Spanish for hundreds. The Forest Service had arrived within the current century. In the late sixties violence erupted in the mountains when Hispanics challenged Forest Service restrictions on what they regarded as lands stolen from their ancestors. There are still isolated acts of defiance, vandalism, and sabotage on federal lands in the region.

Wisdom, or the lack of it, was not restricted to any one culture when it came to using land in the West. Both cultures regretted that the piñon trees had been cut down to make room for more livestock. The Forest Service had found that it was costly to maintain these open spaces, which tended to be invaded by sagebrush. A few years ago Manjo Trujillo stated at a Taos meeting that twenty years before his father had driven a tractor that crushed the piñon trees. "If he could see now what he did, he would turn over in his grave," said the son.

There was no ultimate legitimacy to claims for these lands. History showed that the mountains and deserts belonged to whoever possessed them and was most powerful at a given time. The passing cultures shared the blame for what had gone wrong or right during their times of occupancy.

Tonight this place belonged to me. Tomorrow I will be gone. What's for dinner? Freeze-dried rice and beef. Let's eat.

In 1903, when William Henry Smart, who was president of the Mormon stake (a local organizational unit) that claimed religious jurisdiction over the Ute reservation, rode into the Uintah Basin on a tour of inspection, he halted and walked into the woods to pray. "I was filled with peculiar feelings as I knelt down here on the divide between the known and the unknown country. I felt a strong sense of responsibility ahead of me and prayed for light and wisdom," he recalled. Apparently Smart received the guidance he sought because the spare, stern man dedicated the remainder of his life to bringing the basin, and the Indian lands within it, under Mormon control.

In a sense, although there are essential differences between them, Smart was the William Carter of the south slope. Carter exercised power through commercial monopolization, while Smart was the personal representative of a socio-religious-economic conglomerate. Both came to hold a brief monopoly on their respective lands. Carter died from pneumonia, caught while trying to enlarge his empire by building a road into the Uintah Basin, while Smart, once a prosperous merchant, lost his money during his twenty-year colonization effort but gained salvation. On both slopes the Indians, who were in disarray, had no chance against the monolithic forces these two men represented.

Smart was a zealot for the cause of his church. His great-granddaughter later wrote that "he was a severe man. It was a severity, however, born of a quality that characterized the building of Utah and made it unique among western states: an absolute, single-minded, selfless devotion to a cause." Kristen Smart Rogers added, "Because of that devotion, there's a difference in the way Utah was built."

The boundary between Utah and the remainder of the West was as clearly distinguishable as order is from disorder. The Mormons knew what they wanted, and acted as a cohesive group to gain and maintain it. The others fumbled their separate ways through history.

To acquire Ute lands, the Mormons depended upon a small but unified delegation in Congress. The main problem was to achieve the appearance of consent. The Indians were represented at congressional hearings by their trustee, the federal government in the persona of the commissioner of the Bureau of Indian Affairs, who sided with the state. Commissioner William A. Jones testified: "There is a sort of feeling among the ignorant Indians that they do not want to lose any of their land. That is all there is to it, and I think before you can get them to agree to open the reservation you have got to use some arbitrary means to open the land."

And that is just what transpired in Congress with the full knowledge that a clear precedent was being established, not only for the Utes but also for other tribes on some fifty million acres. The chairman of the Senate Committee on Indian Affairs, William Stewart of Nevada, said, "This is a grave question. It involves the prosperity of almost the entire West." An unabashed spokesman for mining and railroad interests, Stewart believed that leasing of mineral lands from the Indians would result in confusion; therefore, he pushed for allotment of some lands to Indians and opening the bulk of the reservations to white settlement.

Should this policy not be followed, Stewart warned gravely, "I want every senator to think of the responsibility to be assumed in throwing away half of the mineral lands of the United States." Of course, he was vastly overstating the case; but few senators outside the West were knowledgeable enough to catch him on it.

Utah Congressman George Sutherland, later to become a senator and an associate justice of the United States Supreme Court, argued that consent was not needed because the Indians were not the rightful owners of the land. Before 1865, the lawmaker said the Utes did not "occupy" the basin, but rather "were wandering Indians, had no fixed abode." Since the treaty had not been ratified, the congressional act that earlier had set aside the reservation could be easily undone. No Indian consent was needed to return the land to the public domain since none had been given for some smaller reservations that had disappeared elsewhere in Utah. Allotments would be provided simply "out of a desire to do justice to them," Sutherland told a Connecticut senator.

Eastern humanitarians, who saw the policy of assimilation as a means of rescuing the Indians from poverty, were allied with westerners who wanted the additional land. Thus, the Indians' most effective "protectors" were lost to them on this issue. A recent report on Indian problems by the United States Commission on Civil Rights stated, "Allotment and other assimilationist practices received strong support from 'friends' of the Indians. Many believed that these policies represented the only alternative to Indian extinction." With the help of a favorable Supreme Court ruling stating that Congress could allot and open an Indian reservation without tribal consent (*Lone Wolf v. Hitchcock,*, referred to as the Indians' Dred Scott decision), Congress passed a bill in March of 1903 that provided for the opening of the reservation and allotment of Ute lands without their consent, if such was not obtained by June 1. President Theodore Roosevelt signed the bill, and grateful settlers later named a town in the Uintah Basin after him.

Thirteen days before this deadline, with the Utes having heard nothing about this change in policy—indeed, believing that they had been assured on a recent trip to Washington that their land was irrevocably theirs—an inspector from the Indian bureau showed up on the reservation to seek their consent to sever that relationship. The stenographic record of the six continuous days of afternoon council meetings at the Indian agency in Whiterocks is a classic record of how two cultures misunderstood each other on matters of land. Their words and thoughts passed each other by like separate arrows loosed at shadows.

James McLaughlin, the inspector, was the very picture of Victorian rectitude. A distinguished mane of gray hair was complemented by a handlebar mustache set in the middle of a stern visage. McLaughlin, who had dealt with Indians for more than thirty years, saw his role as mainly diplomatic. He believed in a diplomacy that was "administered without weakness on the one hand or a show of ill-temper on the other." To the inspector, the Utes were an "irresponsible, shiftless and defiant people" who "had not gone far enough on the road to civilization to have an adequate knowledge of the fact that the government was proceeding in their ultimate interest in giving them lands in severalty." These thoughts were laid out in a 1910 book that McLaughlin wrote. It was entitled *My Friend the Indian*.

At the marathon council sessions "friend" was a word McLaughlin used repeatedly, as did the Indians. In fact, the word was used so often that its employment seemed to have shaded into mockery. The inspector was straightforward as he proceeded through the charade of seeking consent. Again and again, to the point of exasperation, but not anger, McLaughlin attempted to hammer home the point that the opening of the reservation was not the issue. Whether they would accept the allotments was the issue. But the Indians saw it differently.

On the fifth day, with 120 Indians in attendance, McLaughlin said:

My friends, you seem not to have grasped the thought that what you have been discussing is already past, and all your talk on that line amounts to nothing. You are on record as being opposed to it. The reservation, my friends, will be opened not withstanding your protests. I will repeat what I have said before: that it is unnecessary to discuss that line any further. The question that you should give your attention to is whether you want to accept allotments or not.

An unmoved John Star replied:

My flesh is black. You have good flesh. You are white like this paper here. My flesh looks like the ground. That's the reason I am going to keep it. Why should I give it away? I like it. I was raised here. That's the reason I have got it right in my heart. I am pretty well acquainted with the white man. I know him. The white man wants something all the time. They want everything. They are after this land and are troubling me all the time.

Charley Mack spoke:

Before they passed such a law, someone ought to have come here and spoken to the Indians first. That is the reason the Indians are so scared. It has come so sudden. They were not expecting anything like this. What are the Indians going to do? It is like sand. You throw water upon the sand and it will cave in and wash away. So with the Indians. After a while there will be none left. If they take this land away from us, we can find no more land to go to.

Fear, sadness, anger: there was even some humor in the form of bitter allegory. An Indian named Quinn asked:

Where did you find the key to this reservation to open it? That's the reason I don't understand even if you do say it is provided for. I don't believe it. You say you are here, that you have this paper as your authority. If they find the key to this reservation to open it, we will give it to you. You come and throw it on the table and say, "Here, I have the key to this reservation." Throw it down here so I can see it. When you throw your key to the reservation out here, I will believe you.

Tim Johnson said the white men were already stealing the water and dynamiting the fish in the streams. He continued:

> You talked to me before in this house. You told me to put my children in school. You said then, "The white men will not bother you about your land at all." Now it is changed. You said, "If any white man comes here about your land don't listen to him." Where have you thrown that talk now? You were there when this law was passed in Congress, and you ought to have told Congress that you had promised us to hold it. It seems that you had thrown Washington's mouth away. I am not telling you this because I am mad. I am telling you this because you are my friend. Now I want you not to say anything more. You can't gain anything by talking here any longer.

But the firm McLaughlin did continue to talk. He said he felt called upon to correct some of the statements of his friend Tim Johnson, and then embarked on a lengthy civics lesson. He concluded, "I feel, my friends, that I have done my duty in the matter. I have explained it so clearly that you cannot fail to understand it fully, but it is very difficult to convince persons who do not want to be convinced."

The next day, which was the last of the council sessions and eight days before the deadline, McLaughlin presented a paper for the assembled Indians to sign that gave their assent "to the provisions of said acts," referring not only to the 1903 bill but one passed the previous year that also dealt with allotment. The oral opposition had been unanimous. During the next week, while the inspector prepared his report, 82 out of 280 male adults signed the consent form. This number was far from a majority, and, according to the Ute history book, "several of these may have been bribed or were school-aged children."

Now other segments of the federal government stepped in and carved sizable chunks from the Indians' domain. The Reclamation Service and the Bureau of Forestry, which were later renamed the Bureau of Reclamation and the Forest Service, were formed at this time and aggressively sought to survive, sometimes at the expense of the Indians.

In addition to illegally grazing cattle on the reservation, farmers in the neighboring Heber Valley had for years unlawfully diverted water from tributaries in the upper Strawberry River watershed, as Tim Johnson had pointed out. In the waning years of the nineteenth century, Utah Senator Joseph Rawlins unsuccessfully sought to have the practice legalized for his constituents. The U.S. Geological Survey made a hydrological survey of the area and reported the illegal diversions, which it judged were not injurious to the interests of the Indians at that time, since they were not using the water.

The farmers in the Spanish Fork Valley near Provo also wanted more water, and the Strawberry Valley on the reservation was a prime reservoir site from which a tunnel could be run under the Wasatch Range to the western slope, a plan that was vigorously opposed by settlers around Vernal. A Bureau of Indian Affairs official commented, "The people of Vernal, Utah, and elsewhere in this vicinity are quite wrought up over the possibility of any of the water which now reaches the Green River being diverted to another watershed as contemplated in the Strawberry Reservoir project. It is reasonable to presume in this connection, however, that their anxiety does not wholly arise from an apprehension that the Indians will lose water by the process."

The Reclamation Service, located within the Department of Interior as was the Bureau of Indian Affairs, wanted to build that dam and reservoir. The Bureau of Forestry, within the Department of Agriculture, desired to add to its burgeoning domain. So a natural alliance, which did not have the Indians' interests in mind, was formed. George L. Swendsen, the service's Utah engineer, and Gifford Pinchot, the chief forester, arranged with the Utah congressional delegation to obtain most of the reservation lands.

Pinchot and Swendsen reinforced each other's interests. Swendsen feared the local farmers would undertake the project if the service did not move quickly, and he asked for Pinchot's help in securing legislation setting the site aside as a reservoir and thereby thwarting ranchers who would claim it for grazing purposes once the reservation was opened for settlement. In turn, Pinchot asked Swendsen to certify that a greatly expanded forest reserve (the equivalent of a national forest) was needed to protect the reservoir. Pinchot wrote the engineer: "It would help matters greatly if you could send me a brief statement about the Utah Lake project, especially in regard to the importance of protecting the forested watersheds now included within the lands temporarily withdrawn."

The chief forester worked through Utah Senator Reed Smoot to obtain the March, 1905, legislation and resulting presidential proclamation, which added slightly more than one million acres to the Uinta Forest Reserve and set aside sixty thousand acres for reclamation and reservoir purposes. Smoot's and Utah's interests were best served by working with the two administrators, since a forest reserve would be open to white mining and grazing interests and Smoot's constituents were pushing for the reservoir site.

The senator wrote Pinchot, who was close to Roosevelt, in early 1905: "I believe that if you show the President that it is this session or never for the Uintah Bill, because the opening takes place on October [September] 1 next, and how desirable the bill is for the allotted Indians, he will be willing to ask Mr. Knox to carry the bill along as adroitly and rapidly as possible." In such a manner did the state and federal government overpower the Indians, who were speechless in that particular forum.

The acquisition of land, as John Star pointed out, became the desired end in itself. There was little or no discussion of its suitability for white settlement or any demonstration of actual need. Greed, or perceived need, obscured reality. The chief engineer for the Indian agency took a tour of the reservation in May, 1905, and reported to the Secretary of Interior that he found "the situation somewhat disappointing, as will many prospective settlers who regard this as a land of milk and honey." The best lands were high and thus difficult to irrigate, the rocky soil "would discourage any New England farmer," most of the benchlands were "a huge bed of boulders mixed with a small percentage of sand and clay and covered with a few inches of loam," and in the valleys bisected by streams there were patches of alkali that would be harmful to crops.

But the boomers were vigorously beating the drums. On the back of the stationery of the treasurer of Uintah County was a glowing description of the basin and this statement: "The Uintah Reservation soon to be opened and which is tributary to Vernal has some of the finest streams of water in the State, and many thousands of acres of as fertile land as can be found anywhere. With its million and a half acres of farming lands thrown open to settlement, thousands of settlers will locate in this section who will remain permanently."

Expectations were not only high for the new white settlers, but also for the fortunes of the Indians. A Browns Park rancher wrote in an agricultural publication, "Verily, the Indian is a greater states-man than his white brother, and I acknowledge a liking for him. He is a winner every time. He pays no taxes, no rents, no salaries, no interest. Now, we will see the Uintahs rent their lands to white men and they will continue to live by the labor of whites who till their ground, while the bonds received for the sale of their surplus land at interest will in time make their daughters a good catch for foreign lords."

Fear and divisiveness were abroad in the land as the opening approached. The whites thought the Indians were purchasing more than their usual amount of guns and ammunition and engaging in war dances. Not so, said the Indian agent, who termed the fears "exaggerated" rumors. Nevertheless, he took no chances and imported additional Army troops.

William Smart was busy marshaling Mormon manpower for the opening. Smart, who was close to the Mormon leadership, wrote a form letter to stake presidents and bishops throughout Utah that stated: "We are acquainting ourselves with tracts of land which we feel are most desirable for settlement, and which, through land office connections being formed by us, can be chosen by those who may be in touch with us."

The virulent anti-Mormon press exploded when that letter was obtained. The gentile-owned Salt Lake *Tribune* stacked up the following headlines on a front-page story:

Hierarchy Wants the Earth
"Counsel" Given To the Faithful
"Connections" Formed With the Land Office At Vernal
How Senator Smoot Could Have Helped
Along the Conspiracy of His Brethren

That story and subsequent ones accused the Mormons of a land and water grab. The Mormon-owned Deseret *Evening News* replied that the orderly registration process and "facts" proved that it was not a Mormon land grab, "as some insinuated it would be."

What happened, once again, was that the Mormons organized while others dallied. Hotels were filled to overflowing and a tent city sprang up in Provo as more than 30,000 registered for the drawing during twelve days in August. There was a traveling-circus aspect to acquiring Indian lands. A newspaper noted that the next opening was on the Flathead reservation in Montana, although no date had yet been set. "Nine bright boys" from local schools drew the numbers, and the first went to a young Provo rancher who "is said to have in him the right kind of material that will make a good homesteader."

The boys drew a total of 5,772 names, and these persons were allowed to homestead on the reservation. By foot, horse, and wagon they passed hastily constructed shops that sold liquor and supplies on the way to the borders of the reservation, where soldiers checked credentials before they were allowed onto the land. All went smoothly, said the report, and the *Evening News* editorialized: "On the whole, we believe that a large portion of the reservation will in a few years be converted from sterility and barrenness to beauty and abundance."

Approximately 300 dispirited Utes fled the reservation and wandered about the West for two years, during which time the Sioux, who were having their own problems, turned down their bid for an alliance. The nomadic Utes returned from South Dakota and, along with those who had remained on the reservation, were allotted a maximum of 80 acres per person, for a total of slightly more than 100,000 acres. (In contrast, public land laws at the time limited a single white person to 320 acres.) They were also given a 250,000-acre grazing reserve and some miscellaneous lands.

Six years after the opening Inspector McLaughlin, in company with a chief supervisor, revisited the reservation. They reported that the white superintendent of irrigation had been speculating on Indian lands, and the white settlers were infringing on Indian water rights. Their conclusions, as stated in another report that was not published, were:

They [the Utes] feel that against their wishes one million acres of land was taken from them and opened to settlement, and that another million was placed in a forest reserve with the understanding they were to receive the revenue until 1920. They have witnessed the settler on the ceded lands improve his claim with timber cut from the forest reserve under a free use permit. They have been helpless to prevent the cattle and sheep of the white men from crossing their exclusive range of 250,000 acres to reach the forest ranges for which the white man pays but no part of which goes to reimburse the Indians, and they realize that greater returns are being derived from the reserved lands than they can ultimately receive from the vestige of the reservation that was allotted them. They know that every dollar received from the sale of the ceded lands has been expended to conserve the water of the former reservation, which will in all probability be appropriated by their white neighbors. Jurisdiction of their rights has been transferred from Federal to State control and they live in a community where they must witness the inexorable march of progress and pay for it the inevitable price of the weaker people.

The white settlers discovered that they had landed on some pretty tough ground. Shortly after their arrival they asked the Indian agent if they could share the government irrigation ditches, and in 1909 the Utah Legislature appropriated $7,500 for the "needy settlers" to buy seed. They were supposed to pay the money back by working on public roads. In 1912 they successfully petitioned Congress to place a moratorium on their token land payments. This money was supposed to go to the Indians. Only a few of the homesteaders remained permanently in the basin. A 1910 photograph of Roosevelt, headquarters of the Dry Gulch Irrigation Company, showed a bleak, treeless desert town. Telephone poles were more numerous than people on Main Street. Trash blew about the false-fronted buildings.

William Smart formed development companies, bought banks and newspapers, and visited his charges in his familiar white-topped buggy drawn by two white mules, all in service to his church. In the end the basin broke him, too, as it did Earl Douglass and others. After a Duchesne bank failure, he ended his days in Salt Lake in "respectable poverty," as a descendant put it.

So ended the era of settlement on the north and south slopes of the Uinta Mountains. It was an era that was pivotal to the West. Like the Oregon Buttes, it was midway through the journey. All that came before was new. All that came after were variations on already established themes. As with music, however, it is best to follow the score all the way through to the conclusion for the sake of continuity and the possibility of a surprise or two along the way.

Chapter 9

REGULATORS

In an account of the origins of their town written by the grade-school students of Maybell at the eastern end of the Uintas, the eras of prehistory and history were bridged by hoofed creatures. The children wrote:

> The last buffalo left in Moffat County stayed near Black Mountain. This buffalo stayed with the cattle. One spring he did not go with them. He was too old and sick to go up on the mountain. Some Indians came through in 1885. They saw the old buffalo and killed him. They put the head on a post and danced around it for eight days. It was the first buffalo the Indians had seen for a long time.

At the turn of the century history in this part of the country meant cows, the cowboys who herded them, the rustlers who stole them, the ranch owners, the merchants who serviced the livestock economy, and the federal government, which interceded for the first time with some regulations for the use of public grazing lands.

To put it mildly, the intercession was not taken to in a kindly manner by the locals; and those reverberations have continued to this day in Sagebrush Country. Defiance of the federal government was greatest when forest reserves were established in northwestern Colorado. G. Michael McCarthy wrote in *Hour of Trial: The Conservation Conflict in Colorado and the West* (1891–1907):

> In a day when most other areas of the Colorado range had been pacified by the federal government, the Park Range still stood out as one of the wildest, most lawless regions left in the West. From Steamboat to Yampa, from Meeker and Hayden north to Wyoming and west to Utah, the area was a lingering remnant of the old frontier where, literally, the strongest survived. The only law on the Park Range was determined by the cattlemen—generally the handful of barons who dominated the region. Disputes were settled as they always had been, not in courts of law but on the range itself.

Into such a volatile situation rode Harry Ratliff one day in January of 1901, looking for a horse that had strayed toward Browns Park. Instead the young rancher found Vice-President-elect Theodore Roosevelt and his party avidly hunting cougars. Roosevelt spent five weeks "scampering" about northwestern Colorado in search of mountain lions. His party managed to bag fourteen, Roosevelt having killed the largest lion. While Ratliff waited in the camp that day, Roosevelt sent lunch over to him; and then the cowboy took the party's mail to Maybell.

That night he slept at the Two Bar Ranch, where his bunkmate was the hired killer Tom Horn. Horn had served as a Rough Rider under Colonel Roosevelt in the Spanish-American War, but there was no record of the two ex-soldiers meeting in Colorado.

Seven years later Ratliff, by then supervisor of the Park Range Forest Reserve, came across an echo of his former bunkmate, who had been hanged. Ratliff accidentally stumbled across the section of the minutes of the Snake River Stockgrowers Association that stated an executive committee would "contact and employ a range rider [Horn] to rid the country of thieves" and assess its membership for the service. Hi Bernard, foreman of the Two Bar and later Ann Bassett's first husband, was one member of the three-man committee. Ratliff burned the minutes so that the issue—already partially settled by Horn's 1903 execution—would not interfere with obtaining the cattlemen's cooperation with the Forest Service.

On that winter day in 1901 Ratliff rode back to his ranch just north of Steamboat Springs. Roosevelt soon returned by train to New York, then departed for Washington, where he fretted as a powerless Vice President. The following September President William McKinley was assassinated and Roosevelt became President. Within a few days the former Dakota Territory rancher began making plans that would drastically alter the history of the West by setting aside large blocks of lands as forest reserves and tightening the controls over their use.

President Roosevelt did not initiate the first large-scale conservation movement in the country—one that would be channeled through government agencies specifically created to achieve those ends—but he brought it to its apex. Throughout the last twenty-five years of the nineteenth century there was growing concern over the exhaustion of the nation's timber supplies because large swaths of forest were being cut down by lumbermen from the northeast to the northwest coasts. A rash of newspaper stories, magazine articles, books, and reports condemned the destruction of the forests on public lands.

The popular upswelling, like the environmental movement of the early 1970s, led to legislation, in this case passage by Congress of the General Revision Act of 1891, whose Section 24 provided for the setting aside of appropriate public lands as forest reserves. There was little discussion of Section 24, which was proposed by professional forestry and scientific organizations, and it slipped easily through Congress and was signed by the President, just as the precedent-setting National Environmental Policy Act was enacted some eighty years later.

Prior to passage of the 1891 act there had been a few scattered withdrawals of public lands for conservation purposes, such as the grant of the nucleus of what would become Yosemite National Park to the state of California in 1864 and the creation of a two-million-acre Yellowstone Park in 1872. By 1900, four million acres had been set aside for national-park purposes.

In comparison, during the administrations of Presidents Benjamin

Harrison and Grover Cleveland, thirty-three million acres were designated as forest reserves. The 1891 act was the "first step in the conservation of the natural resources of the country," wrote Paul Gates. Together with the Forest Management Act of 1897, which set up the regulations and administrative apparatus for the forest reserves, the free and unrestricted use of a large portion of the public domain was slowed for the first time in the country's history. "For a country whose policy from the outset had been to pass the public lands into private ownership as speedily as possible, this series of acts to preserve areas of considerable size in public ownership was a remarkable change in attitude," Gates concluded.

It was a change the West resisted when it caught onto the significance of the legislation, because with little warning and less explanation the rules on which people's livelihoods depended were suddenly altered by outsiders. This first contact with the realities of colonialism—meaning that power was wielded in a unilateral manner from outside the region—led to the forging of the modern West. No longer was it a matter only of bursting outward, then settling in, and beginning to harvest the resources; now survival meant a collectivization or marshaling of forces for legislative and legal battles with outsiders. It became apparent that while one eye looked forward toward growth, meaning the consumption of natural resources, the other eye had to be cast backward to the East, and later the West Coast, not only to determine what the markets were but also to resist interference with filling orders. This bifurcation of vision led to a type of walleyedness, even schizophrenia; and the symptoms increased as the century waned.

With the creation of reserve after reserve, the West was in a state of upheaval by the end of the nineteenth century, a condition that would be duplicated some eighty years later during the Sagebrush Rebellion. The anger climaxed when President Cleveland on George Washington's birthday in 1897, without any warning, created thirteen new forest reserves totaling twenty-one million acres, the irony involving Washington and the famous cherry tree being intentional.

Those lands became known as the Midnight Reserves because the President was due to go out of office in ten days. Public-lands historian Roy M. Robbins wrote: "Needless to say, this executive order unleashed a storm of protest from the West on the subject of public lands, the like of which had not been witnessed since the mid-nineteenth century, when sectionalism held its greatest sway." Cleveland's action "set the West aflame," wrote another historian, and similar hyperbole was used to describe the Sagebrush Rebellion in its time. The objections to the creation of the reserves were that the President took this unilateral action at the behest of eastern conservationists who had never even seen the country, and that the local economies would be devastated.

There was heated talk, by western representatives, of impeaching Cleveland. The outgoing President angrily vetoed an amendment to a bill that would have restored the forest reserves to plain public-domain status. President McKinley calmed the West's fears by some adroit compromises, thus setting the scene for the boisterous entrance of Roosevelt into the fray some months after returning to Washington from his hunting trip.

Even before Roosevelt took office, he and the equally patrician Gifford Pinchot were a team. While Roosevelt was governor of New York, the Yale- and European-educated Pinchot was TR's advisor on conservation matters. Like Roosevelt, Pinchot enjoyed being out in the field; but he was most at home building an empire back in Washington. There, as chief forester of the bureau that was to become the Forest Service, he could insert into public policy his conservation philosophy of wise use of natural resources based on scientific principles. In terms of forests, trees were considered a commodity and were to be harvested on a sustained-use basis; a rather malleable concept, meaning there should always be some trees left to be harvested. Such a policy, which later came to be known as management of resources, was considered an obstruction by the timbermen and overly permissive by the other conservationist faction.

Pinchot and his followers preempted the term "conservationist" for themselves during the early years of the new century, thus splitting the movement into those who advocated regulated use and the others, from the "let it be" school, whose most forceful advocate was John Muir. Muir and others like him fought for nonuse or preservation of forests and such park lands as Yosemite, where they were unsuccessful in stopping Pinchot from getting the Hetch Hetchy reservoir site detached from the national park. Both factions tended to be from the same social groupings, centered around Boston, New York, and San Francisco. Stephen Fox, a biographer of Muir and historian of the conservation movement, wrote, "Conservation was never more an elitist conspiracy than at its birth." There was, and is, a social and class enmity between the majority of conservationists and most westerners based on manners and attitudes.

Roosevelt, the former rancher and enthusiastic hunter, leaned toward Pinchot's reasonable, practical, and politically reliable advice. A natural partnership evolved between the two men, and the newly formed Forest Service was the chief beneficiary of that liaison, its annual budgets blossoming under their combined paternity and nurturing of the new agency.

The chief forester, known with respect as "the chief" to his men, was out front as the most visible implementer of natural-resource policy, and thus absorbed most of the vitriolic criticism from the West and the distrust of the other conservationists. Pinchot was depicted as "Czar Pinchot" in a cartoon in a Denver newspaper. He sat on a throne with a crown and a scepter. Behind him were "His Cossack Rangers," for some reason wearing fezzes. They advanced menacingly with raised whips about to fall on the kneeling, bowed-head subjects, whose wide-brimmed hats, held meekly in hand, were labeled "stockman," "irrigationist," "miner," "new settler," and "pioneer."

Actually, who was flogging whom was a little difficult to tell shortly after the Park Range Forest Reserve was created in Colorado by Roosevelt on June 12, 1905. Originally 757,116 acres, it was subsequently enlarged to 1.1 million acres in 1907 and its name changed to Routt National Forest. By the end of his second term in 1909, Roosevelt, with Pinchot's help, had managed to set aside 132 million acres of forest and park lands and enforce a semblance of control over their use. And Harry Ratliff, who was now in the Forest Service and venerated his chief and the hunter who had fed him lunch, was right at the center of the action at the eastern end of the Uinta Mountains.

Ratliff was a man who did not hesitate; indeed, he sometimes acted too precipitately. It was a characteristic in demand at the time, but it is missing from today's more timorous and circumscribed federal land managers. He is remembered as effective and knowledgeable, but somewhat lacking in tact. Pictures of Ratliff when he was with the Forest Service show a short, feisty man who appears to be uncomfortable in suits. His wide-brimmed hat is pushed back, revealing a lock of dark hair hanging over one side of his forehead. With eyes narrowed, Ratliff calmly took the measure of the camera.

Ratliff had been the first white child born in a small settlement of pioneers in Ute country in southwestern Colorado. His father died at an early age, and the son and mother moved first to Idaho, then to California. Ratliff had little or no formal education, but he had plenty of the other type of learning. At the age of fifteen, he left for Alaska on board a ship that was hauling horses to the far North and learned navigation from a friendly captain. The young man worked in the woods of the Northwest as a lumberman and then went south to Sonora, Mexico, where he was a horse packer for a mining operation. Ratliff returned to his native Colorado not long after his twentieth year, arriving in Meeker the day four youths from Browns Park, who were emulating the Wild Bunch, held up the bank. Three were killed in the resulting melee.

He worked as a cowboy for various ranches in northwestern Colorado; and then filed a homestead claim on a 160-acre tract on Mad Creek, north of Steamboat Springs, and began to make the necessary improvements in order to own the land. (Recently this tract and the "improvements," including an old barn, were purchased by the Forest Service as an addition to Routt National Forest. Found inside the barn was a false wall behind which was a two-foot-wide room. Forest officials speculated that Ratliff used this room to hang poached elk meat. This illegal activity presumably occurred before he joined the service, where one of his duties was to act as game warden. As game warden, Ratliff said, "We had to be tolerant. I myself had to pass grouse feathers for rabbit a time or two, but the lecture I gave left a lasting impression, I know.")

The locals were angered by the formation of the forest reserve in 1905. Inferring that "Lord Pinchot" had the power of life or death over the newspaper, the *Steamboat Pilot* editorialized: "As long as the Pilot has permission to live and circulate it will denounce the formation of the timber reserve, and the new regulations as an iniquity and a shame upon the people who have made Routt County a habitable place."

A forestry inspector from Washington later characterized the paper as being "very radical against the service," and the same could be said of the region's citizens. Proclamations were passed by local business organizations, one of which noted: "The present regulations governing timber reserves are calculated to retard the growth of the country, are unjust to settlers, to stock growers, miners and others."

The settlers, large cattlemen, and their suppliers—which was just about the entire countryside at the time—thought they were engaged with a paper tiger. Then a forest supervisor appeared on the scene looking for a local person to serve as forest guard on the western slope of the range. Jack Ellis, a rancher, took the job. The forest guard went to visit his former partner, neighbor, and friend, Harry Ratliff, and brought his family with him.

While the womenfolk visited inside, the two men went outdoors to talk where the newly cut logs that Ratliff had hauled to his homesite to serve as the timbers for the new barn and poles for the corrals were quite noticeable. Their conversation, as preserved by Ratliff in a later report to Gifford Pinchot, was a classic western confrontation that took place (and still does) throughout the region. It went like this:

> We sat down on the logs and Jack said, "Where'd you get the logs and poles?"
> I pointed to the east and said, "Up on the hill."
> And he said, "Well, you can't do that Harry."
> I answered, "The hell I can't. I've done it."
> He said, "It's against the law."
> I said, "What law."
> "The new law of the Reservation. I can't allow you to do that."
> I said, "Why?"

"Because," he said, "it is unlawful to cut timber without a permit."

I asked him how to get a permit and he replied, "Come to me. All you have to do is ask, and I will give it to you free."

I answered, nearly as I can recall, "You mean to say that I have to hunt you up every time I want to cut a stick of timber?"

"No, take a permit out for enough to do you for several months at one time."

I said, "But what if you are not around?"

He said, "Well, you can wait until you find me."

I did not feel very good about this.

From timber cutting to grazing, the two men covered the main concerns of what was happening on the denuded forest lands of the Park Range. The elk had almost disappeared by this time, decimated by hunting and the inexorable push of cattle onto a range rated "scarcely equalled in the world" in the 1870s to one that had become greatly depleted, even by the admission of the cattlemen, at the turn of the century. Their conversation resumed:

My cattle were grazing on the bare meadow and Jack said, "How many cattle have you, Harry?"

I replied that I had about seventy-five or a hundred head of cattle and some horses.

"You'd better take out a permit for them."

I said, "Do you mean to tell me I have to have a permit for my cattle and horses and my corral poles, house logs and fire wood and I have to hunt you up, too?"

Jack said, "Dammit, I didn't make this law, but that is what it is and you have to do it."

And I said, "Jack, you take your little old permit for sticks, stumps and steers and get the hell off my ranch!"

Well, Mr. Pinchot, Jack went and we were both mad.

For a number of reasons, including the fact that he did not want to give up his five thousand head of cattle, Ellis did not relish the job; and the forest guard, the forest supervisor, and the local cattlemen soon went looking for someone else. They settled on Ratliff at a meeting that he did not attend.

Ellis and the supervisor went out to his ranch, and Ellis shouted as they approached, "Don't shoot, Harry. We're peaceable."

The cattle business was not going too well for Ratliff, so he consented to take the $720-a-year job and sold his livestock. He passed the required examination, which consisted mainly of cowboy arts, and assumed a post as replacement for a forestry guard who had died under mysterious circumstances near the Wyoming border. The guard was buried before it could be determined whether he had expired of poisoning from bad water, bad whiskey, or bad cattlemen.

His constituents, Ratliff said, pictured a forest ranger as "a person, supposed to be a man, with a white collar, narrow shoulders, side seated pants, like a woman's bloomers, with spindle shins wrapped in a sort of bandage, that didn't know which end of a horse the collar went on or whether the horn of a saddle faced to the horse's head or to his tail." In 1909, when the question of a uniform arose, Ratliff, who was then forest supervisor, suggested that the "standard" outfit should consist of two well-broken saddle horses, one pair of winged chaps, a good riding saddle, a Frazer pack saddle, a Stetson hat, a bed roll, and a revolver of not less than .32 caliber. These were pioneering times for federal land regulators.

With this outfit in hand, and the ability to use its separate parts effectively, Ratliff, at the age of twenty-seven, set off to do his job. There were some problems, since the local cattlemen were in the habit of setting forest fires just to entice rangers into gunshot range. Then there were the timbermen, a no less intransigent breed.

Ratliff followed up on the investigation by two Forest Service employees into a timber trespass case against a company owned by the Union Pacific Railroad. He found that one of the government workers had gone to work for the company, and the other was being guided by it in the investigation. The latter refused to hand over government property, so Ratliff used "fisticuffs" with the man, who subsequently turned informer to Ratliff's enemies. Ratliff took over the investigation that eventually led to a settlement.

Another timber cutter, George Suttle, an influential citizen of the

Steamboat Springs area, chased inquiring forestry officers at gun-point off land that he claimed was his property. Since there was no accurate survey of the area, his contention was difficult to disprove; and the officers accordingly retired from the scene. Ratliff investi-gated the charges of illegal cutting and hauled Suttle into federal court, where he was convicted. Suttle vowed to shoot Ratliff on sight if he should ever set foot on his property and conspired with the cattlemen to put the forester in jail.

Neither the loggers nor the stockmen in northwestern Colorado were pleased with Ratliff's administration of the federal lands, so they set out to get him through the courts. First came warnings from their minions. Ratliff was told by the president of the local bank not to fool with the big cattle outfits. Then in February of 1908 his old friend Jack Ellis "came to see me and virtually told me that I would have to 'play [ball] with the big outfits.'"

Ratliff, who was forest supervisor by this time, failed to mend his ways; and a charge was trumped up against him. It was alleged that he had sold a mortgaged horse. After two trials Ratliff was acquitted, although the legal weight of the whole county, which extended at that time to the Utah-Colorado line, was brought against him. Ratliff said, "Their first purpose seemed to be to convict me of being a forest officer." When the records of the trials were returned from being reviewed in Washington, they bore the initials of "G. P." and "T. R."

Next, the cattlemen turned to fouler means to eradicate this government pest from the range. About this time Bob Meldrum, whose wooden pistol grip bore fourteen notches, arrived in the small Wyoming cow town of Baggs, just over the state line, and took up residence as a lawman and paid gunman for the northwestern Colorado cattle interests. When Ratliff showed up in Baggs, Meldrum challenged him to a gunfight on the street but was beaten to the draw by the forest supervisor, who disarmed the gunman and walked away with Meldrum's pistol stuck in his belt.

After this embarrassing incident, Meldrum lost his badge and extra pay. When he killed a popular local cowboy, he was jailed for a few years. Recorded history last mentioned Meldrum working as a harness maker not far from Baggs, where he came to an untimely end. A number of people had cause to heartily dislike the gunman, who, like Tom Horn, tended to shoot when he thought the advantage was greatly in his favor. In 1948 when Ratliff furnished the current supervisor with some notes for the forest history, he posed a number of questions that could not be resolved by the old files, such as, "Was it true that Bob Meldrum fell on a pitch fork or was it a bullet that punctured him?"

Gradually through attrition, the law, and Ratliff's unconventional methods of enforcement, the Forest Service began to take control of the federal lands under its jurisdiction and win acceptance in northwestern Colorado. When "three ladies from the underworld" toured the sheep camps in a wagon on payday, thus resulting in the scattering of the animals all over the range while their herders were otherwise occupied, Ratliff arrived on the scene and tied the madam to a tree, vowing to keep her immobile until she agreed to leave the forest. She agreed. For good measure he cut her hair off, tied it together with a ribbon, and nailed it to the wall of the Whiskey Park Ranger Station as a warning.

With the arrival of sheep in the forest, the cattlemen prepared to fight for the diminishing range. Ratliff defused the confrontation by appointing the son of the president of the cattle association to keep the sheep above the grazing demarcation line. Along the way there were more mundane chores, like building the road over Rabbit Ears Pass and fighting forest fires.

When Pinchot overtly challenged the Secretary of the Interior and was fired in 1910 by President William Howard Taft, Ratliff and other first-generation foresters like him became cynical about the Forest Service. "This set the Service back, I firmly believe, many years; and it seems to me there followed a period of stagnation, a time when we staggered like men beaten down by some power not understandable," he wrote.

The power was the political club, which the western users of federal lands used to bludgeon obstreperous land managers like Ratliff into submission. Far easier and less messier to call a congressman and have him complain to the relevant superior, or threaten an agency's program, than to hire a gunman. With increasing regulations and poor pay in the offing, Ratliff resigned from the Forest Service in 1914, and in his mid-thirties became a different type of western man: one who made his living by extracting resources from the public lands.

I had been pounding the trail fairly steadily for three days, and it was time to take a break. The plan was to get an early start, push hard for two hours, then collapse somewhere in the vicinity of the Kidney Lakes.

It was an uneventful plod to the two lakes, which, naturally enough, were kidney-shaped, the western mind being fairly literal. The ground around the lakes was shorn clean of vegetative growth from extensive human and animal traffic over the years, so I headed toward the crest to find more virgin territory.

The place I finally settled upon was the southeast shore of an unnamed lake hard by Rainbow and Wilderness lakes. I found a windless niche for my tent behind some bowed subalpine fir and a few sheltering rocks, where I nestled the stove. There was a view toward the crest of the range. Below, the Uintah Basin was a pale blue sea lapping against the foothills. In relatively short order I had once again erected the perfect home for a one-night stand.

There was no shortage of things to do. The sun was hot enough for me to bathe in the frigid water and dry myself on the solar warmth of a rock. After doing the laundry, I resumed reading with a certain reluctance since I was nearing the end of the novel.

In order to prolong the pleasure, I took up the other book I had brought with me. The field guide, *Western Forests,* was an intimidating presence on this trip. First of all, it was quite thick, and second, it was heavy. I had packed the guide because I felt some responsibility for describing the natural surroundings with some specificity. But I neglected to do so because I rediscovered that I had no inclination just to label things. I preferred placing things within their context and examining their connections.

Besides, I am continually frustrated by field guides. There is usually doubt about identifications—whether because of season, sex, age, or another shifting factor. Only infrequently could I make a picture or word description mesh perfectly with an observation. Also, a comprehensive field guide that takes in a whole landscape type lacks depth in specific areas; but I was not about to pack a whole nature library into these mountains.

I took a brief turn around the lake and identified leafy-bract asters, yarrow, Scouler willow, and Rydberg's penstemon, plus other assorted wildflowers and plants that I was less sure about. Such names meant little to me.

They meant even less thirty-five years ago when I was fifteen years old. My father, who frequently vacationed on horseback in the West without his family, took me on a grand tour of the region in the summer of 1950. We traveled in Pullman cars, limousines, and tour buses and stayed in first-class hotels, none of which really interested me. As an adolescent I was more obsessed by the mysteries of females, smoking, and liquor than by western landscapes.

It was during that trip that I got my first sighting of a regulator. This particular person was a Park Service ranger, whose face was topped by the broad-brimmed campaign hat that was part of his uniform. I saw him, and even see him now, in partial silhouette to my right as he explained the workings of Old Faithful in Yellowstone National Park. I thought that with such a uniform and profile I, too, could attract girls.

Earlier this year I revisited Yellowstone for the first time since my father and I had been there. My first stop was West Yellowstone, a honky-tonk tourist town that lives off the visitors, who number close to three million a year to the national park. I had no memory of the town, but the stone Union Pacific station was familiar. That was where we alighted after a long train ride from Chicago, during which I had multiple nosebleeds and a few surreptitious cigarettes on the platform between cars as the train gained altitude and entered the West.

Parked outside the station, now a museum, was one of the canvas-topped tour buses that had driven us to Old Faithful Inn. The bus was now an exhibit.

The drive to the inn, an improbable architectural mixture of Swiss chalet and the trapper-settler periods of the American West, was past a bewildering variety of license plates and over a road full of chuck holes. It ended as I took a turn onto the freeway-like overpass and halted in the mammoth parking area. There was no park ranger to personalize the story this time, so I went to the visitor center to determine what had changed since my last visit.

Old Faithful, neither old in terms of geologic time nor really very faithful, was erupting at an average of every seventy-two minutes. In 1950 the average had been sixty-three minutes. "Average" is a tricky word, and should not be depended upon. The eruption that I waited for occurred twenty-five minutes past the average interval.

We got a bit dazed waiting. Cameras from the large crowd jerked up at each sign of incipient activity, then were lowered. We sat on benches while a light rain fell. A few people departed. The eruption, when it came, was anticlimactic; and the crowd quickly dispersed as a few newcomers drifted in for the next show. The park had a frayed feeling, as if its appearance could not be maintained with so many people coming and going during the continuous performances.

I drove to the park headquarters at Mammoth Hot Springs, where I searched in the basement archives to find out what had happened in the park that long-ago summer. The postwar travel boom was beginning to taper off; but, nevertheless, the park had logged in one million visitors. Nearly seventeen thousand came, as we did, by train. The superintendent's report complained of "insufficient personnel and limited appropriations" to keep the park in good shape. During that unusually cool, wet summer, Governor Adlai Stevenson of Illinois visited the park and, perhaps not by coincidence, the Illinois entry in the American Legion parade passed through on its way to Los Angeles. It was a model of the U.S.S. *Illinois,* which surely must have made an interesting sight in that setting. In July eleven persons had received minor injuries from grizzly bears.

There were still problems with the grizzlies. A "Dear Friends of Yellowstone" letter sent out by the superintendent the same year that I returned stated: "Management of Yellowstone's bears is frequently the source of controversy, but scientists agree that the population has declined and needs immediate attention to effect recovery."

The bison within the park had been infected with brucellosis and were not welcome outside the park, where ranchers worried about their livestock's catching the disease. The large elk herd tended not to pay attention to the park boundary and damaged adjacent pastures.

Some new visitor facilities, such as restaurants, gift shops, and the like, had been built at Grant Village, while others were being removed at West Thumb. What to do about the development at the Fishing Bridge area was an issue of great controversy.

Mining and oil and gas leasing had increased just outside the park, while there was a continuing worry that development of geothermal resources on public lands outside the park would lower the geysers within it. (All these problems would be obviated, and new ones incurred, by the great fire of 1988.)

I crossed the street to hear what the new director of the National Park Service, William Penn Mott, Jr., had to say. He was meeting with various members of his constituency. They included representatives of the tourist industry, conservationists, recreationalists, campers, park rangers, fishermen, concessionaires, researchers, and representatives of state parks, youth hostels, and wildlife interests. Most of the people were from either the west or east coast. There were no representatives of the common, everyday type of westerner who might use the parks for grazing or mining or horseback riding.

Mott presented a twelve-point program for his tenure as director, and stated that crowds and traffic jams were what people had come to accept as normal in their lives, whether in a wilderness setting or a city. The parks could not be everything to everybody, so they must begin to restrict the number of visitors, in fact had already begun to do so at Yosemite.

I had known Mott in California when he was director of the State Department of Parks and Recreation under Governor Ronald Reagan. He was straightforward, competent, and highly opinionated. In a year or two his twelve points would have been forgotten and not too far down the line someone else would take over his job with, perhaps, a nine-point program. Federal land managers come and go.

The Uinta Forest Reserve was one of President Cleveland's Washington's Birthday presents to the West, but the cries from Utah were muted in comparison to what was heard from the remainder of the West. The Mormon concept of stewardship, meaning that natural resources were to be wisely managed for the good of God's children, found a parallel in the conservation movement. And Utah, in its own particular way, was part of that movement. Newly formed commercial clubs and chambers of commerce, along with the Union Pacific Railroad, extolled the beauties of the surrounding mountains. Professors at the University of Utah and Brigham Young University led natural-history classes into the wilderness. Artists took to the hills, as did the inevitable Utah picnickers and campers. When it came time to create forest reserves, small groups of users—such as stockmen, farmers, and city water users—petitioned for their establishment.

Utahans had their champion in Washington. The senior senator, Reed Smoot, a high official in the Mormon Church, was a powerful force in such matters during the thirty years that he held office. Following Pinchot's departure from the Forest Service, the acting forester wrote: "In Utah a special condition exists with reference to additions which amounts in substance to this office refraining from making additions that are objected to by the senior senator." (Other powerful western representatives and senators, such as Wayne Aspinall and Carl Hayden, came to possess similar veto powers over land use within their states and, to some extent, elsewhere. They replaced the gunmen, and, on occasion, represented a broader range of interests.) A history of the Wasatch National Forest stated that Smoot "gave local influences a most effective voice."

The Uinta Forest Reserve, which one would have thought would be the mother of them all, rapidly began to lose large chunks of its territory to its more aggressive neighbors, the Wasatch and the Ashley national forests, in a process of bureaucratic infighting that went on after the forest lands were first carved from the public domain and Indian reservations. The Uinta lost nearly one million of its two million acres in 1908 to the newly created Ashley, a jurisdictional gift to the white settlers in the Roosevelt and Vernal areas. Then 355,000 acres went to the Wasatch, whose core had been created along the populous Wasatch Front in 1908, this newest addition nearly doubling its size in one stroke. The three ranger districts along the western and northern slopes of the Uintas came to represent about one-half of the total acreage of the Wasatch-Cache National Forest.

A number of factors went into who got what slice of the forest pie as the century progressed. Local users, through such men as Senator Smoot, had a lot to say. They wanted the forest headquarters or ranger district to be conveniently located, meaning that they would not have to travel far to obtain permits and make their needs known. Convenience was a large factor in the creation of the Ashley National Forest, whose headquarters was in Vernal.

Additionally, federal regulators continually sought to tidy up their units for bureaucratic purposes and increase their turf. When the supervisors for the Ashley and Wasatch forests fought to a draw over the sizable Blacks Fork and Fort Bridger additions, and eventually asked the regional forester in Ogden to make the final decision, one of them wrote to their superior, "Am glad you are taking it upon yourself to settle this inter-forest boundary. It is apparent that Mr. Nord and I couldn't settle it. Both too selfish, I suppose." Whatever forest A. G. Nord served as supervisor tended to increase its boundaries; and, except for Senator Smoot, he was credited with being responsible for acquiring the most forest lands in Utah.

Along the north slope of the Uintas the forests had been cut down during the 1870s and 1880s for railroad ties, mining timbers, and charcoal for the smelters in Salt Lake. Then they went through a period of rest and recuperation until around World War I, when more grazers and timbermen took to the woods, streamsides, and mountain meadows. In the twenties and thirties the proposed additions to the forests were down from the one-million-acre category to 100,000 acres, just about the size of the proposed Summit County addition to the Wasatch that filled in the space between the northern boundary of the forest and the Wyoming border.

There was a new attitude abroad in the West. Although relatively small, the Summit County addition was vital since it took in the headwaters of the Weber and Bear rivers. Local opposition had effectively blocked its inclusion in the forest reserve in 1906, but thirty years later almost everyone was for it. In 1931 seven forest fires had blackened 5,400 acres in the proposed addition. A pine-beetle infestation was ruining timber. Burned timberlands and those that were heavily grazed increased downstream siltation, thus reducing reservoir capacity. More runoff caused flood damage to such towns as Evanston. Washington thought the addition was too small; but the local and regional offices prevailed and the land was folded into the forest in 1933, thus completing its basic external boundaries.

The locals had come to accept and even to call for the creation of such jurisdictions. Now the battles would center on what to do within the forests and parks.

I decided to go to Yosemite to see what Mott was talking about. In that national park there had been close to three million visitors in 1985. During the Memorial Day weekend, when a national television network was televising a climb of Lost Arrow Spire, the park service had planned to seal off Yosemite Valley to further automobile traffic should it become overcrowded. That unprecedented action was not necessary, as the expected crowds did not materialize. Perhaps there were fewer visitors because of the well-publicized Teamsters strike in the park, or perhaps the plan to limit cars was enough to discourage the average Californian from visiting Yosemite.

That was the summer when a woman camping alone in the park was stabbed by a man, but managed to make it out of the wilderness, where she said, "I wasn't going to die because of that turkey."

Hang gliders, parachutists, a gory murder-suicide, lightning strikes that killed two, 472 traffic accidents, drugs, charges of park rangers making an improper drug investigation, a follow-up congressional investigation, a budget cutback, acid rain, a pending multi-million-dollar commercial development just outside the western park boundary, and bears were also on the agenda that season. During the summer, there was the usual newspaper story about Yosemite and national parks in general being in trouble. Over this particular article was the headline "Trouble in Paradise." Such an imagined paradise—really, just another western fantasy—no longer existed, nor had it been a reality for some time.

I remembered standing outside the Ahwanee Hotel with my father many years ago and watching the firefall from Glacier Point.

When I went West some years after that, I spent my first night in
California camped in Yosemite Valley during a July 4th weekend. It
was crowded then, but bearable.

The firefall was eliminated in 1969 because of the crowds it had
attracted. When I camped in Yosemite this last time the only fires
that I saw were in the campgrounds. A thick layer of wood smoke
hung over the valley, choking lungs, stinging eyes, and reducing
visibility—one reason why I never go anymore to Yosemite.

Such an ordinary place as the Uinta Mountains just suited me
fine. For dinner beside the unnamed lake I had spinach pasta,
sour-cream gravy, and mushrooms. At twilight a coyote loosed a
single cry. Then there was silence, and I was alone again.

Stabilization and sorting out were the dominant features of the
first half of the twentieth century. Sagebrush Country needed to
recover from the turbulence of the preceding century and the first
few years of the current one. The pattern of unrestricted use of
public lands that climaxed in the decisive period of settlement, and
the reaction to that surge westward—the traumatic arrival on the
scene of the regulators—were eventually adjusted to and life on the
range resumed its regularity.

Energy development waxed and waned along relatively shallow
graph lines while agriculture, meaning livestock mainly, began a
slow decline. Mining has always been a minor matter in the West,
except for scattered flurries of activity and the wide-ranging peregrinations of prospectors. Although tourists began arriving on the
scene in trains and increasingly in automobiles, they tended to
congregate at the "crown jewels" of the national park system, leaving
the vast remainder of the West to itself.

The two world wars came and went, and more than the usual
amount of natural resources was extracted from the West. There
was a marked increase in the military presence on public lands
during World War II, be it proving grounds, training centers, or air
bases.

There is a noticeable lack of materials for documentation of this
period. It was as if the people just lived and did not consider the

passage of their lives worthy of recording. Settling in was much less dramatic than breaking new ground. The people who lived there, those outside the region who saw it as a quaint, romantic place, and the scholars who occupied themselves with its past began to look increasingly, and longingly, to the Indians, trappers, military, lawmen, and outlaws of the previous century, all of whom gained in mythic glory because of the unspectacular present.

As a result of this misplaced sentimentality, the everyday life of the present was neglected. The historical hiatus resembled a gap in a geologic record of the earth's crust. The record was resumed in the second half of the century when the extraction of natural resources became the dominant issue. Meanwhile, a few scraps of history were preserved from the intervening years.

Evanston's oil boom in the early years of the century did not last long, and the town reverted to pinning its hopes on employment from the railroad and serving the surrounding ranching community. The population of the town between 1920 and 1930 declined from 3,500 to 3,000. Halfway through that decade the best indication that things were not going well was the appearance of promotional literature stating that Uinta County was "The Land of Opportunity." It was a place "where Mother Nature, in one of her rare moods of unrestrained generosity, has wantonly showered her choicest boun- ties," stated the pamphlet put out by various civic organizations, which seemed as concerned about shoring up their own confi- dence as about attracting outsiders.

After prohibition ended, things began to look up. Becker Uinta Club Beer opened a brewery in town that employed fifty to sixty persons; an underpass was constructed under the Union Pacific tracks (an overpass being part of the loot from the energy boom of the last decade); and by 1940 the population had rebounded to 3,600.

The Works Project Administration guide for Wyoming noted that Evanston was at the center of a farming and dairy area and added, "It has comfortable houses, well-kept lawns, parks, and gardens, and many shade trees." Most of the activity was along Front Street, which faced the gothic railroad depot. The Lincoln Highway, U.S. 30, snaked through town, and at Christmas motorists could see the

Three Wise Men, their camels, and the Star of Bethlehem outlined in electric lights on the hill below the insane asylum.

The trains roared through Evanston during World War II, hauling troops and supplies both ways. In the late fifties the last steam engine was retired from the Evanston run. By 1960 the population had jumped to nearly 5,000 following what was labeled as a building boom in mid-decade that consisted of five new homes, a drive-in featuring soft ice cream, three service stations, and a funeral home. The local newspaper, which looked for the bright side of every happening, reported that the county "did not have its best year in 1961, nor did it have its worst." The railroad and tourists were pluses, but the farmers had to seek federal aid following a drought.

Ten years later there were fewer inhabitants, but more promotional literature. The town was desperate for growth. It described itself thus: "Key city of south-western Wyoming, Evanston is a thriving, aggressive community with a rich heritage of pioneer development from the days of the western migration." The Chamber of Commerce pamphlet neglected to mention that more people passed by Evanston in one month during the height of the western movement than lived there now. Retail trade was the biggest industry in town, and Uinta County had the highest percentage of persons employed by the government of any county in the state.

These were not exciting times, but they were comfortable times that were about to end.

For the smaller communities strung along the foothills to the east of Evanston, changes, with one exception, were even slower in coming. There was no electricity out as far as Lonetree, Burntfork or McKinnon until 1951, and even then it took another half dozen years before everyone was hooked up to the line. A planning document written in the 1970s for Mountain View had to go as far back as 1919 to list the last happening of historical significance, that being the opening of a branch bank in town.

What conflict there was centered around the question of whose children would go to what school, since Mountain View was dominated by gentiles and neighboring Lyman was heavily populated by Mormons. In 1959, a student writing a thesis on the Mormon presence in the Bridger Valley, which had rebounded in the present century after the disasters of the previous one, predicted, "The future of the valley seems very stable with little growth or decline in population expected."

Following the vast amount of words and paper that constituted the debate over the controversial Colorado River Storage Project Act of 1956, a concrete arch rose in Flaming Gorge and blocked the Green River to those who would duplicate the journeys made by Ashley and Powell. The river became a shimmering blue lake encased by red cliffs at the eastern end of the Uinta Mountains.

There were ripple effects. The road that linked the small ranching communities along the north slope was paved; and once the reservoir filled, cars from Salt Lake hauling boats on trailers flashed past the clusters of ranches and rotting log cabins that marked the homesteads of such previous inhabitants as Elinore Stewart.

Keith Smith, a sheep rancher, had to move as the reservoir waters inched upward. A graduate of Andover Academy and Yale University who remembered his meals at Mory's restaurant with pleasure, Smith had lived for sixty years in the small community of Linwood. Incorporated into the structure of his home was the log cabin that was built by the first white settler on the north slope. The history of the region was like the wind passing through the nearby cottonwoods that were about to be inundated by the rising waters of the reservoir.

But Harry Ratliff was a survivor in the different Wests. When Ratliff left the Forest Service, his aim was to make money; and he eventually succeeded, not to any great extent but certainly enough so that he could live a comfortable life on the south slope. His salary as forest supervisor had been $1,800 a year. "Therefore, I resigned and entered the employment of the Denver & Salt Lake Railroad as an exploration engineer, and I am glad to say that I have improved my financial condition," he wrote in 1944. Ratliff centered his efforts on moneymaking in the Uintah Basin and made Vernal his home.

He went to Vernal in 1914 to negotiate rights-of-way for the railroad across the basin, a planned extension that never materialized, much to the disappointment of the local residents, and to make a general survey of the basin's natural resources. Previously he had been in Idaho on railroad business and had inspected some phosphate deposits in that state, so he was familiar with this mineral that was being avidly sought at the time. The president of the railroad went down with the *Lusitania*, so plans changed and Ratliff no longer worked on acquiring land and inventorying natural resources. Instead the railroad sent him on some more immediate assignments. He set off on horseback to see some Utah ranchers who wanted to ship their cattle from Craig, Colorado, which was the end of the line.

Along the way toward Diamond Mountain Ratliff decided to do some prospecting for himself. He stopped in Big Brush and Little Brush creeks for a few days, and chipped off rock samples and carefully inspected them for signs of phosphate. A local rancher and a geologist with the federal government were also in the area, searching for the same mineral. These three men had set out to locate phosphate deposits because of growing demand for it in the rapidly expanding fertilizer market.

Sensing competition, Ratliff acted quickly. He took the samples to Denver, where they were confirmed to be phosphate, then returned to Vernal, hired some unemployed men, and had them stake about one hundred claims on the southern flank of the Uintas, just to the north of Vernal. The names given to the various claims spoke of love and quick riches: Lillie, Gold Coin, Monarch, Jack Pot, Mabel, Golden Eagle, Lucky Gus, Ida May, Hercules, and so on.

It took Ratliff thirteen years to gain title to the land he had claimed. During that time he was aided by A. F. Humphreys, a successful Denver mining engineer who financed Ratliff's efforts. In return Ratliff was given one-quarter interest in Humphreys's Phosphate Company. The claims were eventually sold to the San Francisco Chemical Company, passed on to the Stauffer Chemical Company, and finally to the Chevron Resources Company in 1980.

Chevron was not interested in history but in numbers; and the numbers told the San Francisco–based company that it would be profitable to build a phosphate-slurry pipeline from the mine to a processing plant near Rock Springs, Wyoming, to which sulfur would be shipped from the firm's Carter Creek natural-gas-processing plant. At Rock Springs the two products would be mixed to make fertilizer, the combined legacy of Harry Ratliff and William Carter.

While phosphate was a winner, the mining of the more glamorous hard-rock minerals in the Uintas, such as gold or silver, was never of any great consequence. Although there were Tungsten Lake and Tungsten Pass in the High Uintas, those landmarks were probably named for minerals that only resembled scheelite, the tungsten mineral. At the end of the nineteenth century some copper, gold, silver, and lead were taken out of the Dyer Mine, north of Vernal. The easterners who ran the mine retained the name, although Lewis R. Dyer had bowed out early in the game when he made off with the money that was loaned him to start the mine. It was soon played out, leaving the rotting timbers of the mining camp, known as Camp Misery, to remind later visitors of the ephemeral dreams that flitted back and forth across this landscape.

Throughout the last decade of the nineteenth century, prospectors combed the eastern end of the Uintas, always just on the verge of a great discovery that never occurred. (Some of their colleagues in Park City, across the narrow valley that separated the foothills of the Uintas from the Wasatch Range, had much better luck.) Eventually they disappeared, but some interest was revived by Ratliff's phosphate claims; and hope has not been completely abandoned to this day, even though there has been little evidence of mineralization. The U.S. Geological Survey made a thorough search of the mountains for minerals whose presence might hinder the creation of a proposed wilderness area in the High Uintas, and reported in 1967: "The area that was studied contains no known mines or mineral deposits."

Growth flowed sparingly into the Uintah Basin during the great hiatus, despite the constant references to the basin's being the promised land. A newspaper of the time gushed, "Assuredly the land is one of 'milk and honey.'" The wilderness had been penetrated, the desert subdued, barrenness and sterility were banished "and in their stead stand the pleasant homes and the fruitful fields of a contented people." The predominantly Mormon residents were proud that Vernal had the distinction of being the only city in the nation that did not levy a municipal tax, having managed to finance its activities by license fees.

There were hard times, and hundreds of people drifted away.

Crops failed year after year "and the majority of the people were in abject poverty," stated a county history. The local newspaper, with the clarity and courage of ten years' removal from worse times, looked back from the late thirties to the prior decade and stated, "Many had left the country and more were ready to leave. This land of promise had failed to be what advance publicity had represented, this through no fault of the land itself." But still there was hope. The town of Moffat, named for the railroad builder who had failed to deliver, was rechristened Gusher for the oil well that never gushed.

At the other end of the basin the town of Myton, named for a dishonest Indian agent, sprang up quickly after the opening of the reservation. In the first year a white man killed an Indian, after which he left town quickly. The promising town boasted two banks and a flour mill, all three of which went out of business in the twenties. This was a time when fires were set for insurance purposes, a stigma that became attached to the town, along with its reputation of being a center for alfalfa seed. Myton's residents hoped for a railroad, a phosphate plant, and a sugar-beet industry, but were disappointed on all counts. In 1930 there were 469 people in Myton. That number was down by some thirty persons ten years later.

The residents of the basin pinned their hopes on a railroad that never arrived. They beseeched the federal government, via the state legislature, for such a miraculous deliverance from economic stagnation. "The Federal Government is the only source to which we can now look for assistance in constructing a railroad . . . to develop the vast resources of this rich section of our state," said the petition forwarded by the two counties. But no manna came from that direction for the purposes of railroad construction. The basin residents would eventually share in the largesse of federal water development, but always believing that the Wasatch Front was robbing them of their rightful share. "Fellow citizens of Uinta Basin it is time for us to assert ourselves and protect our rights," exclaimed the local newspaper when it addressed the water issue in 1931.

Through the thirties the basin stabilized somewhat, although agriculture, which was the mainstay of the economy, began to decline. The value of farm holdings in Uintah County had increased

on the whole since 1910, but a "noticeable decrease" occurred
around 1935. The assessed value of farms was down, there were
fewer cattle, and the farm mortgage debt had increased during the
Depression decade. To counterbalance the decline in the agricultural sector, automobile and tourist traffic was up, with the completed paving of U.S. 40. In 1930 there were 9,035 whites and 783
Indians in Uintah County, and by 1940 the white population had
increased by some 850 persons.

But still growth did not match expectations. So the locals went on
the offensive with a promotional campaign that even exceeded the
imaginative quality of Evanston's fantasies. The Uintah Basin, stated
the Salt Lake *Tribune,* was "a land of milk and honey, blessed with
nature and man-made opportunities" and "enriched with almost
unlimited resources." It but remained for man to make the most of
these opportunities in the basin, whose "fame and fortune in the
making are attracting widespread attention in investment and development circles."

The Uintah Basin was actually a wasted province. Although
livestock grazing had been placed under controls in the forest lands
of the high country, grazing was not regulated on the flatter, drier
public-domain lands surrounding the mountains until the creation
of the federal Division of Grazing in 1935. Herders rushed onto
these lands in every season to beat their neighbors to the diminishing
grasses. It was a free-for-all that was not helped by less rainfall and
plummeting beef prices. The result was predictable. A range survey
of the basin undertaken in mid-decade by all the relevant federal
agencies stated:

Early misuse of the range lands coupled with a period of
abnormally low precipitation have brought about on the lower
ranges marked reductions in palatable forage and serious increases
in erosion. Observations over large areas of the low lands showed
that none of the ranges outside national forests were making
permanent improvement, and that more than 85 percent of the
lower ranges were deteriorating still further. On more than 60
percent of this land area, erosion was dangerously accelerated.
Tremendous losses of both water and topsoil occurred, which

conditions are serious because the area is already limited in both
of these vital resources.

The report noted that similar conditions could be found throughout the West. The demoralized livestock industry, no lover of
federal controls, reluctantly agreed that, since transfer of the public
domain to the states was not feasible, although the Hoover Administration had pushed for such a solution, some form of federal
regulation was needed to rescue the situation from chaos. However,
the stockmen also agreed that the Forest Service, which was charging grazing fees close to their true market value and actually, in
some cases, reducing the number of cattle on the range, was not the
agency for them.

They went shopping in the Department of Interior, where, through
their congressmen and Secretary Harold Ickes, who was constantly
trying to enlarge his domain, they set up an agency in their own
image. The Taylor Grazing Act, named for a powerful Colorado
congressman who was known for protecting western interests, was
passed in 1934. It set up grazing districts and enabled the Secretary
of Interior to issue permits for use of the range, to improve those
lands so more livestock could be put upon them, and to set fees. Of
the fees that were collected, one-quarter went to the federal treasury,
one-quarter went to financing range improvements, and half went
to local governments. Along with imposing a modicum of regulations,
the bill was a western relief measure. Only in such a hermaphroditic
state could such legislation be passed.

The Taylor Grazing Act was ranked in importance with the 1891
bill that made it possible to form forest reserves and the 1916 act
creating the National Park Service. Ickes, who had a vested interest
in the act, called it the Magna Carta of the conservation movement.
With two scratchings of President Franklin D. Roosevelt's pen
on paper, one to sign the act and the other to bar the former
public-domain lands from further private entry, the previous national
policy of giving away such lands was changed to one of holding on
to and conserving them. "For over forty years historians had been
heralding the passing of the frontier; without a doubt the old
frontier had now passed," wrote public-lands historian Robbins.

One hundred and forty million acres of the public domain, fifty million acres of Indian lands, and almost the entire state of Alaska could now be regulated to some extent. With the divided nature of the enabling legislation in mind, the Interior Department set up the Division of Grazing in such a way as not, it was hoped, to ruffle too many westerners. Leasing fees were to be less than the market value of comparable private range, administration was decentralized, advisory boards consisting of local users were to have a role in decision making, and westerners were given preference in jobs in order to avoid the eastern stigma of the past Forest Service days. These early employees, and later ones who thought and acted like them, came to be known within the agency as "cowboys." To make a slight stab at covering that vast amount of territory, the number of employees in the Grazing Service rose from 36 in 1936 to nearly 150 in 1942; and the appropriations increased from $250,000 to $800,000 within the same time frame.

Even with this minimal oversight, westerners were upset, and they struck back through their congressmen. They were successful at lowering appropriations and reducing the nationwide staff to one hundred employees after World War II. Grazing regulation, trespass control, and construction of improvements were virtually impossible under these conditions; and stockmen once again grazed livestock when, where, and in what numbers they liked. By the early seventies the Bureau of Land Management, as it had come to be called, had recouped some control; but it was still essentially a captive agency.

If the BLM was the agency for the livestock and mining interests, then the Park Service belonged to the John Muir–type conservationists, and the Forest Service was the province of the Gifford Pinchots of the nation. That seemed like a fair division of the spoils. The problems arose when one grouping or philosophy of land use was, or appeared to be, in ascendancy over the others. By mid-century the three principal federal land-management agencies and their separate constituencies were in place, and an imbalance ruptured the uneasy peace.

The West had come a long way since Harry Ratliff's early days. In his later years Ratliff prospered. He looked like a local banker in his three-piece suit, gray hair, steel-rimmed spectacles, and hearing aid set in his left ear. He bore little resemblance to the rough-and-tumble forest ranger who had to aggressively carve a niche for the regulators in the western scene of that earlier era. The country had changed in like manner. Before, there was uncertainty and turmoil. The regulators brought safety and dependability to the use of land. That was why they were eventually accepted and folded into the dominant society.

Ratliff purchased three ranches, one being the Escalante ranch next to the Green River, where the Spanish priest and his party had camped 175 years earlier. He sought what he needed to extract the natural resources from the land that he owned or controlled. "Power from Echo Park will permit large tonnage production of phosphorus and make possible the reclamation of many thousands of acres of fertile lands along the Green River," said Ratliff, who died in 1956—the year that Congress deleted the controversial Echo Park Dam from the legislation and finally managed to pass the Colorado River Storage Project Act.

Before Harry Ratliff died, he wrote a poem that summed up his life in the West. It began and ended with the following refrain:

> *I had to go. I had to know*
> *Why deserts starve, while the rivers carve*
> *And tear out a mountain's heart.*

Chapter 10

PRESERVERS

The emotional unsettling of the West began slowly after World War II and reached a discordant crescendo in the early 1980s. This disquietude corresponded to a rapid spurt in growth. It was growth of a size, type, and intensity that would have disrupted any pubescent culture, particularly one that had not yet defined its place in the scheme of things.

In the absence of internal cohesion, outside forces shook the region; and during the resulting upheaval Sagebrush Country passed through episodes of helplessness, euphoria, anger, and despair. At the end there was the customary period of decline and retrenchment. Outside the region, in the centers of influence, conflicting forces manipulated the strings that controlled the gyrating dance of the West. There were those on both coasts during the modern era who wanted to preserve the Interior West as a pickled specimen in the time warp of a glass jar or, alternatively, to rip its innards out to feed the needs of others.

The first symptoms of disturbance arose just before the war when Nevada cattlemen, a particularly independent lot, refused to pay grazing fees to the federal government. They not only objected to paying for what they had previously enjoyed free of charge but also wanted long-term leases on public lands. Their case was lost at the

Supreme Court level and their complaints put in abeyance until
after the war.

The two national livestock associations, the American National
Livestock Association and the National Wool Growers Association,
met in Salt Lake City in August of 1946 and passed a resolution
asking for the sale of the vast bulk of public-domain lands administered by the Bureau of Land Management. Deeper hostility was
expressed at the meeting toward the more restrictive Forest Service.

A war of words ensued. Nevada Senator Pat McCarran thought
the natives knew best and should be left alone. "We of the West feel
that we know our country and the responsibility it has toward the
rest of the nation. Here we have hardy pioneers in every walk of life
having to do with the plains, the forests, and the mines," said the
senator. Wyoming Representative Frank A. Barrett, who conducted a
series of subcommittee hearings on Forest Service practices throughout the West, said of the criticisms being leveled at his constituents,
"These poor people of the West can't be charged as being robbers
and thieves."

The cry of the westerners was for some type of recognition of
independence. "Do we have statehood in the West? We do not. The
public land states are more correctly referred to as 'our western
provinces,'" said a representative of a livestock association. As a
result of their request for the sale of public lands, the livestock
interests said they expected "the baying of the pack of pool hall
conservationists who will be needled into action by the threatened
[federal] bureaus. Few of them have anything at stake, or any
constructive ideas. They are full of misguided information and a lot
of enthusiasm and don't know what to do with it except howl."

And howl they did, to a pitch of shrillness and effectiveness
unexpected by the westerners. It was a harbinger of things to come.
E. Louise Peffer, a historian of the public lands, wrote: "The most
articulate of the conservationists, chiefly the recent converts, resorted
to the muckraking tactics of that period." Each side, she said, was
"guilty of stretching some facts, ignoring others." The stockmen
were badly led and misadvised. Peffer wrote: "Shut off in isolated
ranches as they are, hearing little but the general righteousness of
their cause as fed to them by their own officials and propagandists,

they have been genuinely hurt and surprised by the vigor of the opposition." Similar reactions by the principal antagonists would be repeated in years to come.

By the end of 1947 the takeover attempt had been routed, primarily because of the repeated thrusts of a writer who was born and raised just west of the Uinta Mountains. Bernard DeVoto demonstrated that the printed word was an effective political weapon in the arsenal of the conservationists: one that could "save" mountains, rivers, deserts, and national parks and forests. It was a weapon that westerners could not match because they had few writers who had access to national magazines or book publishers in the East.

DeVoto had enough of the West in him to exude some local flavor, when needed, and he possessed the right literary credentials to allow him access to the eastern publishing establishment. The son of an Italian Catholic father and a Utah Mormon mother, DeVoto was brought up in Ogden, Utah, which he later recalled as being that "scurvy Mormon-Catholic dump that created all my neurosis." As a lonely boy he roamed the foothills of the Wasatch Mountains, plinking at objects with his gun and visiting his grandfather's farm in the small settlement of Uinta up against the mountains.

The Forest Service was a benefactor to DeVoto's kind, having reforested the mountain slopes which had been picked clean by the railroad, settlers, and livestock in their times and which, in the form of mud, had periodically cascaded down with devastating effect upon the communities below. When McCarran, Barrett, and the livestock associations launched their postwar attacks on the Forest Service, the Ogden Chamber of Commerce came to the beleaguered agency's defense with a statement that ended: "In recent years we were required in self-protection to purchase privately owned grazing lands in the mountains east of our city and to give these lands to the federal government so the Forest Service could control and correct erosion caused by overgrazing, a condition threatening the security of our water supply. Our community will perish if our watersheds are destroyed." DeVoto would remain loyal to that particular federal agency and its personnel when he became a writer of influence.

In 1914 he left the duplex on Monroe Avenue and a family that was sliding into genteel poverty for the University of Utah, where, as a result of the continuing conflict between Mormons and gentiles, one of DeVoto's English teachers was fired from the church-dominated institution and fifteen faculty members quit in protest. As one of the few campus radicals, DeVoto fled the next fall to Harvard University and the East, to which he would be intellectually wed for the remainder of his life.

DeVoto graduated with honors from Harvard in 1920 and five years later struck back at his roots in *The Taming of the Frontier,* a bitter polemic that castigated Mormons and Ogden alike. Needless to say, this book and subsequent works failed to win for DeVoto the hearts and minds of Utahans or, for that matter, westerners of a more general stripe. Years later an Ogden librarian who wrote mystery novels for teenagers occupied far more space in the city authors' file in the county library than the single mention of DeVoto, which was a Boston newspaper clipping of a favorable review for his first novel.

There followed some false starts, tribulations, and hard work that finally gained DeVoto a secure niche. He taught at Harvard, was editor of the *Saturday Review of Literature,* turned out novels and award-winning western histories, and from 1935 to his death in 1955 wrote the Easy Chair column for *Harper's.* However, DeVoto's emotional attachment was to the West; and most of his nonfiction writing centered on aspects of that region.

Short, somewhat pudgy, long in the face, and bespectacled, DeVoto had a gift for indignation that was best exercised in the name of a cause. But it was not until he returned to the West in 1946 for an extended trip, and in the process discovered the religion of conservation, that he found the crusade that fit him best. DeVoto's biographer and fellow Utahan Wallace Stegner wrote: "In the years before conservation and environmental concern became a mass movement and a shibboleth, the Easy Chair was its stoutest champion. Without it, the effort to preserve in the public interest the grass, timber, and scenery of the West would have been very much weaker and less effective."

The pugnacious DeVoto sounded the bugle call for the charge that set the conservation troops off to engage in battle with the

Philistines of the interior West. However, his greatest contribution was in establishing a written identity for the region itself. Unfortunately, few in the West were familiar with his writings.

The battle, actually more of a skirmish, was a mismatch from the start. The amount of verbiage expended by DeVoto and the conservationists was excessive. They somewhat vindictively blew the livestock associations out of the water with a broadside when all they needed was a pinprick. The associations were, in effect, talking among themselves when their conversations were discovered by DeVoto. The stockmen did not manage during that round to get to Congress with their proposal for selling public lands.

Using information gleaned from his 1946 trip and fed to him by his Forest Service friends, DeVoto wrote a series of columns in *Harper's* on what he called the "biggest" land grab in American history. The columnist wrote in the opening salvo, entitled "The West Against Itself," that the future of the region depended on whether it could defend itself against its own rapaciousness. He saw the dilemma thus: "It is the recurrent lust to liquidate the West that is so large a part of Western history."

Then, not content to wage the battle alone, he contacted other eastern journalists; and other publications followed up on his stories. Soon an avalanche of articles were published on the cowmen's plans. A young Katharine Graham wrote in a Washington *Post* column on magazines that "honors for the finest piece, though, go to the chunk of honest, explosive prose by Bernard DeVoto." DeVoto loved the controversy and attention and was not loath to boast. He wrote, "Inasmuch as my first article was the first public announcement and the others rallied around it, we can reasonably say that a considerable amount of the credit for the victory can be charged to *Harper's.*"

The match was grossly uneven. The stockmen returned the fire with scattered potshots in obscure journals, such as the *American Cattle Producer,* saying that "There is a bevy of writers with nothing at stake but their pens whose oily ability to arouse an uninformed public might be put to better use than to promote that which is neither good government nor good Americanism." In addition, the stockmen said that they did not want to be bossed around by "a bunch of communist-minded bureaucrats." The Tonopah, Nevada, *Times* headlined a story about DeVoto's columns "Cow Dung."

The other tactic of the stockmen was complaint, and that fell upon deaf ears. The Wyoming Stockgrowers Association wrote Frederick Lewis Allen, the editor of *Harper's*, that "Western ranchers, engaged in the business of producing livestock on the ranges of western states, are unable to understand why a man or the publisher of such a high class magazine as *Harper's* could be led into publishing such unfair, discriminatory articles as have appeared in your magazine under the authorship of this man DeVoto." Allen supported his writer.

The torrent of columns continued, and perhaps the editors felt the subject was a fly on the wall that had been sufficiently swatted to death. DeVoto wrote a Park Service informant, "The only trouble is they have made me a muckraker in the minds of the *Harper's* editors and I am being assigned a number of subjects I care for a good deal less."

DeVoto was somewhat fawning in his dealings with these bureaucrats. To Newton B. Drury, the Park Service director, he wrote: "Please understand that I want to conduct myself absolutely in accord with your wishes and am writing only to find out how I can most effectively serve them." He subsequently was named to the Park Service's advisory board of prominent citizens and served on it with another eastern literary lion, the book publisher Alfred A. Knopf. Both would participate in an upcoming conservation battle.

The greatest service that DeVoto performed was accurately defining the West in broad, historical terms. The plundered-province and self-abasement themes ran through his work, which totaled some forty conservation polemics on western matters over a period of eight years. The region had been plundered by easterners and abased by its own inhabitants, said DeVoto. He wrote of the West in realistic terms. It was a resource West, not a cowboy, Indian, or outlaw West.

He also spoke of limits. The West's ultimate limit was its aridity. Besides water, its most precious asset was public lands. In matters of water and land the West exhibited its basic schizophrenia. This developing resource society was dependent on the federal government for basic survival and productivity, yet constantly tried to dictate the terms of the largesse. DeVoto put it bluntly and succinctly, as was his manner, by describing the constant refrain as being one of "get out but give us more money."

The solution that DeVoto recommended lacked detail but indicated a general direction. With the conservationists but not of them, he wrote in a 1954 letter to Adlai Stevenson, who was between presidential campaigns: "There is no greater domestic need than a comprehensive program for the West. We need bold and imaginative thinking about resources, thinking on a large scale, and most of all new thinking." He added that the solution did not lie with the conservationists alone. "Conservation thinking suffers from repetitiousness, hidebound tradition, and an inability to realize that the world of 1950 frequently requires different answers from those that were satisfactory in 1900."

DeVoto launched one more crusade in the early fifties. Western land use had traversed the historic path from free, unfettered use, to limited payments and controls for the sake of conserving resources, to what the Echo Park Dam controversy in Dinosaur National Monument came to symbolize—the principle of inviolate preservation of land. From the maelstrom of that controversy, the modern conservation movement was born. It differed from the movement of a half century earlier that focused on setting up the government agencies to conserve land and water. This movement now attacked those very same agencies for being the despoilers. Like the cattlemen, the bureaucrats were stunned, hurt, and angered by the unexpected assaults.

From his seat on the National Parks Advisory Board and from the promptings of his Park Service friends, DeVoto perceived the threat of dammed water to pristine land. In 1950 he wrote of national parks and the proposed dams: "[The parks] were set aside to the sole end that they should be preserved as they are, that there should always be places where Americans could have the inestimable experience of untouched wilderness, unspoiled natural beauty and unmarred natural spectacle. That end is now in danger of being subverted by engineering construction." The article appeared in the *Saturday Evening Post* and was excerpted in the *Reader's Digest*. The resulting backlash from the West and the Washington water establishment was enough to blacklist DeVoto from the *Post* for the few remaining years of his life and, along with his other work, gain him a life membership in the conservationist Sierra Club.

DeVoto stood halfway between the two eras. He most frequently singled out commercial interest groups and the fantasies of the region. Only near the end of his life did the Bureau of Reclamation and the Corps of Engineers, the two dam-building agencies, become objects of his criticism. DeVoto did not live to see his beloved Forest Service and Park Service attacked with the vehemence that was to be exhibited by the environmentalists in the coming years. When he died in 1955 his ashes were scattered in a Montana national forest.

That Dinosaur National Monument received so much attention in the fifties was an anomaly. It was a backwater, an unlikely candidate for a confrontation of such magnitude. After the bone hunters left, the national monument reverted to a period of somnolence, not to reawaken until the dam builders and conservationists rediscovered it.

The Park Service took little notice of the eighty-acre national monument until the 1930s, when local river runners brought the scenic corridors of the Green and Yampa rivers to the agency's attention. A 1933 letter from a Colorado schoolteacher citing the beauty of the river lands found its way to Assistant Secretary of the Interior Oscar L. Chapman, and a Park Service representative was subsequently dispatched from Denver to survey the remote domain. He reported that the rivers made an attractive oasis, but any expansion of the monument would have to take into account prior plans for power development. However, he pointed out that it would be possible to make a trip through the scenic canyons in a motorboat, should there be reservoirs. It was thought that dams and a park could coexist. Through the early thirties local residents, mostly from Vernal, pushed for national-park status.

Portions of the Green River had been reserved, through the influence of power interests, for dam and reservoir sites by the Reclamation Act of 1902. Periodically private interests, the state, the United States Geological Survey, or the Bureau of Reclamation made inspection trips on the Green and Yampa rivers, which led to studies, plans, and reports. Through the thirties plans solidified for a major interbasin diversion of water, what was to become known as the Central Utah Project. Expectations for prosperity reached a fever pitch in Vernal during the late thirties, when it was predicted that "land values will shoot skyward and the Basin will see an era of prosperity never before attained." By then dams had replaced national-park status as the key to wealth in the minds of the local citizens.

In 1938, while yet another Bureau of Reclamation survey party was on the river, President Franklin D. Roosevelt enlarged the monument to 203,885 acres by attaching the Green and Yampa river corridors to the national park system, subject to prior water and power claims. There were plans for six dams along the two rivers at this time.

The hopes of the residents of the Uintah Basin for near-instant prosperity were seemingly dashed forever in October of 1940 when the Bureau of Reclamation announced that the dam projects were not feasible, nor would they become so in the foreseeable future. World War II quickly changed that assessment. The locals once again rejoiced, and the Park Service acquiesced in the face of "a greater national interest," for power from dams. During the summer of 1945 a party of Campfire Girls from Colorado, who had camped in Echo Park, declared that a dam would be "a crime against one of the most natural and scenic spots in the United States." The sides were lining up for what Wallace Stegner, the western historian and novelist, termed "the first great conservation battle of recent times."

In June of 1950, one month before DeVoto's article appeared in the *Saturday Evening Post,* Oscar Chapman, by now Secretary of the Interior, approved plans for Echo Park Dam "in the interest of the greatest public good." The battle was on.

Whether public agencies or private conservation groups best represented the public good has been debated, sometimes with bitterness and acrimony, for the last forty years. The debates began with Dinosaur and included the Wilderness Act, the Grand Canyon, the Santa Barbara oil spill, coal mining on Black Mesa, Alaska lands and offshore oil. What they all had in common was a reference to public lands.

* * *

I had planned to spend a layover day at this unnamed lake, but since I was so close to the end of the trip and my food fantasies were so overwhelming I decided to strike for the roadhead at Spirit Lake, despite the fact that I would arrive one day ahead of my ride back to Salt Lake.

A city. It seemed strange to be making that mental adjustment when I had not even left the lake on this fine, windless morning.

The pack had been decidedly lighter these past few days; and I knew I was stronger as I easily lifted it to my bent right thigh, then hoisted it smoothly with one practiced swing onto my back and automatically adjusted the straps.

I said goodbye to my last refuge and set off on the gentle descent toward the Kidney Lakes, where I found a number of campers who had not been there the day before. They included a large Boy Scout troop camped on the bare ground that I had shunned. I was back in scout territory, which meant I could expect to see a fair number of people today. The boys were just beginning to stir as I passed by early in the morning and rejoined the Highline Trail via the Kidney Lakes' onramp.

I quickly covered the four miles to Fox Lake, a high country reservoir whose level was depleted late in the irrigation season, passing two fathers and their sons on their way to fish. They asked me how the fishing was; and when I replied that I did not know, they looked at me incredulously.

Of Fox Lake the guidebook states, "It fluctuates through the summer but even so is a popular lake for camping and fishing for cutthroat and brook trout." Between the dark green treeline and the sparkling blue water there was a no man's land of notched, sandy shoreline across which were scattered gray stumps and footprints. The waters of the eighty-acre lake were being fished quite avidly by numerous persons. They seemed perfectly content with the unnatural setting.

A rusted horse-drawn earthmover sat near a log cabin by the lake. I had not expected to see a Fresno scraper this high up in the mountains. It was one of the less-publicized implements that had helped win the West. Few areas in the West had been immune from the scratching of such land-leveling tools. Perhaps it had been used here to build and maintain the low dam.

Beyond Fox Lake the trail led up to Divide Pass, where I met two couples on horseback coming over from the north slope for a day of sightseeing and fishing. We passed with only a wave exchanged between us. I had not realized until this moment how inferior the position of a walker is to that of a mounted rider and how prejudiced both are toward their respective means of transportation. The "digger" Indians in the Uintah Basin may have had similar feelings when their mounted cousins from Colorado rode up.

The drop from the pass to Island Lake, another fluctuating reservoir, is fairly abrupt, and I had my noon meal at the north end of the lake, whose shoreline was encased by boulders. For some reason I had felt weak and depleted after my second bowel movement of the day. My notes stated: "Really want to get out of the mountains. I've had enough." But the mountains were not going to surrender me without some resistance.

It was the Hatch brothers of Vernal who drew the Park Service's attention to the Green and Yampa rivers in the thirties and hauled conservationists down the streams in their boats to see the canyons in the fifties. The Hatches were among the original settlers in the Ashley Valley, the first settlement having been named Hatchtown after Jeremiah Hatch, who was known for his ability to get along with the Ute Indians and for fathering thirty children.

Bus Hatch, a grandson of Uncle Jerry, as he was called, caught the river bug in the 1920s. He was a free soul in a society hemmed in by strict rules of behavior. Hatch and his friends drank, hunted, fished, and joked, all in or around the Green River and Dinosaur National Monument. A carpenter by trade, young Hatch began building boats to cross the river to hunt and fish. The expeditions in the twelve-foot boat that held three passengers were the unrestrained rompings of boy-men. Bus wrote his brother, Alton, who was in Brigham Young University at the time, and related a river crossing by an unaccomplished paddler: "There is no retreat in History to equal the way old Jimmy pulled out. He ducked his head, socked the paddle into the water about six feet and the race was on. He paddled too much on one side and, like the cow puncher who had been shot in the heel and was chased by the lion, went in a circle. When he was on the third round he broke the circle and started back."

Hatch's first boat was built in one day of pine planks and held together by nails. Needless to say, it quickly came apart in the river. From Nathaniel Galloway, an old trapper who was an accomplished river runner, Hatch learned how to build boats and manage the river after the trapper was bailed out of jail for a minor offense. It helped that the sheriff was a Hatch relative and wanted to take a river trip. That was how things were done in Vernal.

Hatch and his companions, most of whom were relatives, first took a short run on the Green River through Split Mountain and managed to make a movie of their exploit, complete with the mock capture of a bandit. Then in 1931 they repeated the perilous voyage made by a few others through the entire breadth of the Uinta Mountains.

The four men departed from Linwood, near Manila. On the first day most of their provisions were lost overboard and the men tried unsuccessfully to rope a mountain sheep. For the next four days they subsisted on five pounds of jerked venison, four potatoes, one onion, and a tomato. Oars were broken and holes knocked in the bottom of the boat, repairs were made, the trip resumed, and on the fifth day the exhausted men emerged from the river at the Jensen bridge.

There was no mention in the local newspaper of Ashley or the others who had preceded the locals, although it was noted that a number of unsuccessful attempts had been made to run the Green River in recent years "with the result that the boats have been wrecked and the occupants forced to swim or walk the remainder of the journey." Three years later they ran the Yampa River, and the Vernal paper reported, "They believe themselves to be the first group to ever successfully navigate the stream." The administrative history of Dinosaur National Monument notes the Hatch trips, the movie, and the role of river runners in bringing the "canyons' beauty" to the attention of the Park Service.

Hatch and his friends ran other rivers, being among the first fifty people to traverse the Grand Canyon on the Colorado. Most trips were for fun, but he slowly developed a business from his hobby and it expanded when the first rubber rafts became available shortly before World War II. After the war, Hatch's sons joined him in the family business. Don recalled, "It was like a tree growing; the more boats, the more people. Our philosophy was if someone could not afford the trip we would take them for nothing. We never took the fun out of boating."

In 1952 the Hatches conducted a trial trip for the Sierra Club, and for the next few years, as the dam controversy grew, the business expanded rapidly. In 1954 six-day Sierra Club trips, consisting of fifty persons apiece, departed downriver every week during the early summer. Bernard DeVoto inquired about joining one of these trips, then decided against it. Others went, took pictures and notes, and wrote or spoke about the beauty of the canyons.

A book published by Alfred A. Knopf was the result of one such trip. Containing pictures by Bus Hatch, Martin Litton, and Philip Hyde along with words by Stegner, Knopf, and others, *This Is Dinosaur* served as a prototype for the later Sierra Club coffee-table books that were published in an attempt to influence the outcome of various conservation causes. Stegner wrote in the introduction to a 1985 reprint of the book: "David Brower and the Sierra Club originated the idea. Lovers of the national parks contributed their skill and knowledge as text and pictures. I edited their contributions. Alfred Knopf published the result in an astonishingly short time and with small regard to profit." A copy was given to every member of Congress.

Don Hatch, who had been raised in the isolation of Vernal, suddenly found himself surrounded on the river by quick-thinking, strange-talking people. It was an exhilarating experience for the young man. Brower, the executive director of the club, was particularly charismatic. Don Hatch learned about the viewpoint of preservation and was greatly influenced by it. He joined them, not an easy thing for a Hatch to do, and later remembered the dam fight and his association with the Sierra Club at that time as being the "greatest involvement" in his life. Besides running river trips, Don

Hatch taught school in Salt Lake City, where he distributed anti-dam literature, made speeches, and showed movies for the cause.

The attitude of Hatch's family, friends, and neighbors in the Uintah Basin was strongly pro-dam. To deprive them of a dam was like denying bread to their children. The Sierra Club was evil incarnate. Hatch's alliance with the outsiders was not taken lightly by his family or friends.

The family split on the issue. A cousin said Don was no longer a member of the family. Bus Hatch, by now a realistic businessman, explained his precarious position to a family friend in a letter that differed markedly from his free-wheeling style of earlier days: "I keep hearing that I am against the dam thru the grapevine. I guess most of it is caused by Don. I have been keeping my nose out of it entirely and asked Don to do so, but he has his *own* ideas. As you know, we both put in a lot of time and money working for it and because, for business reasons, I try to keep out and am keeping out, I seem to be getting classed as against it."

The conservationists thought that the elder Hatch was on their side. Brower, who had gone down the river with Hatch on a Sierra Club trip, told a House subcommittee: "Gentlemen, I hope you all meet Bus, and I especially hope you leave him the chance to make the thousands of people happy who have just begun to learn about those wonderful wilderness river trails."

The family friend to whom Bus Hatch wrote was Bill Slough, the owner of the Vernal Cadillac-Pontiac dealership, which was not doing very well at the time. Slough wrote Don Hatch a letter of warning a few weeks later: "I am sure there have been many unkind remarks made about you which were uncalled for but when a group of people want something they need as badly as we need Echo Park Dam they do not like people to oppose them." He continued: "I am certain in my mind that the dam will be built in spite of anything you might do and you are certainly hurting yourself and your dad by taking such an open stand. Surely you have a right to your opinion, but just as surely if you keep on you are running a big risk of ruining the franchise that you and your father have."

Bus Hatch was caught between the proverbial rock and a hard

place. He decided to surrender passively to the prevailing current. For his son, it was a different matter. He became actively involved. The conservationists came, saw, and then returned to both coasts from where they declaimed against the dam. But Don Hatch remained to be harried.

For Uintah Basin residents, their perceived stakes in the Echo Park Dam were nothing short of survival in the desert. At a time when oil was just beginning to be produced in the basin, the foretaste of a boom was in the air. Deeper than usual drilling in 1948 had resulted in the first commercial oil well in the Ashley Valley, and in Utah. Surplus World War II jeeps, loaded with geologists and their gear, were combing the remoter portions of the basin for the liquid mineral. Since Vernal was the town located closest to the proposed dam, it would obviously benefit from the resulting construction activity, and power from the dam just might spur the location of industries in the remote valley. Bigger things were on the way for basin residents, who had been conditioned to expect more than they had ever received.

There was an additional reason for vehemently supporting the dam that came closer to a true survival issue. The Central Utah Project, which would intercept water flowing from the southern slope of the Uinta Mountains and transport it to the urban regions around Salt Lake, had been a gleam in Utah's eye since 1903. Utah, in this instance, meant those populous regions along the Wasatch Front. Uintah Basin residents believed such a project would drain them dry, so the quid pro quo was that they would be reimbursed with additional water from the Green River.

For all these reasons and more the dam was perceived as a basic necessity, and the most intense pressure for authorizing its construction was exerted by Vernal, a town of some four thousand inhabitants, whose strident, unified voice had a disproportionate effect on the debate. Interior Secretary Chapman said he could not find two people in Utah who agreed on the dam. The subsequent reaction from Vernal forced the secretary to revise his opinion. He said that a majority of Utahans favored it. The state-funded 21 Counties Association, with headquarters in Vernal, was a conspicuous lobbying group for the dam. Utah's congressional delegation, followed by Wyoming's, was the most active in pushing for the dam. Again, Utah knew what it wanted and acted in a unified manner to obtain it.

The house of cards that consisted of delicate, interlocking water agreements expanded out from Vernal to include all of the Sagebrush West. There was something in the dam for almost every state. For instance, Echo Park Dam was to have been the physical manifestation of the 1948 compact whereby Utah, Wyoming, Colorado, and New Mexico—known as the upper basin states—apportioned water from the Colorado River system. The dam was also desirable for more immediate reasons. Southwestern Wyoming was in the grip of a drought in 1953 and 1954, and the railroad had closed the coal mines in Rock Springs when it converted to diesel engines. Unemployed Wyomingites cried for help in the form of a dam project from the federal government and felt their well-being threatened, as did Utahans, by the distant preservationists who did not live and work there and who, at the very most, floated the river once with Bus Hatch and became instant experts.

For the conservationists, livelihoods and prosperity were not the issues, but instead the integrity, the sanctity of the national-park system. For these coastal residents national parks and monuments were supposed to be inviolate. One conservation leader went so far as to refuse to fly over Dinosaur on an inspection trip because he considered it a pristine wilderness area. If portions of Dinosaur were flooded, then other parks would fall like dominoes to intrusive human activities, went the argument. The remembrance of the loss of Hetch Hetchy almost fifty years earlier helped rally the conservation troops. Echo Park became the first preservation showdown of major dimensions since Hetch Hetchy.

Given the passionate level of commitment on both sides, and their different perspectives, there was no hope for compromise. "The opposing sides did not mean the same thing when they spoke about the best management of the nation's natural resources for the essence of the reclamationist aim was alteration, while the conservationist was generally thinking in terms of the preservation of primeval conditions in the national parks," wrote Owen Stratton and Phillip Sirotkin in *The Echo Park Controversy*.

It did not bother the conservationists that they had no following in the Interior West. They knew the battle would be won in the East, and it was, with the help of Southern California, which hoped to keep as much water as possible for itself. The reclamationists were bitter. Said Michael Straus, the Commissioner of Reclamation:

> From their air-conditioned caves overlooking the wilderness areas of Central Park in New York, Lincoln Park in Chicago, and Boston Commons in the adopted city of a transplanted western writer [DeVoto] who has a tendency to forget his heritage, these self-appointed guardians have taken it upon themselves to safeguard the canyons of Dinosaur National Monument for the handful of brave souls who dare to explore the area by boat.

The conservationists' silent conspirator was the Park Service, whose personnel surreptitiously fed them information from within the Truman and Eisenhower administrations. Fronting for the western water users, because it had the blessings of two Interior secretaries, was the Bureau of Reclamation, whose budget, personnel, and clout far exceeded those of the Park Service. Each agency assisted its favored clientele and in turn was assisted by them. This reciprocal relationship was typical of how dams got built and national parks established.

The conservationists mounted a tremendously effective campaign. With national sentiment aroused against Echo Park Dam and congressional mail running 89 to 1 against it, all the other water projects on the western wish list included in the bill were threatened. The Echo Park proponents gave way, the dam was deleted from the legislation, and Congress passed the Colorado River Storage Project Act and President Eisenhower signed it in 1956.

With the concurrence of the preservationists, who later came to rue their acquiescence and to oppose what they once had backed, Glen Canyon was selected as the alternative site, and coal-fired power plants were substituted for the cleaner hydroelectricity that would have been generated at Echo Park. Although conservationists hailed the defeat of Echo Park Dam as a victory, there was no winner in terms of the eventual tradeoffs. Preservation was not absolute, just relative.

A few years later dams were being proposed for the Grand Canyon, and the same sides formed again in the same coalitions around the same issues, refined the same techniques, and forgot that a precedent was supposed to have been established by the defeat of Echo Park Dam in the previous decade—a span of time in Sagebrush Country during which memory can be scoured clean by the wind that blows across the unobstructed landscape.

Before, during, and after the Echo Park Dam battle there were scattered calls for designating Dinosaur National Monument a national park. Thirty years after their victory, the coastal conservationists were not present in Vernal when the latest version of this proposal was aired at a public hearing. But Don Hatch—with graying hair, half glasses, and the thick arms of a boatman—was there. He was the only one who spoke in favor of the name change. It was Echo Park revisited, but few knew it.

A strange odyssey began after lunch. I became disoriented and lost.

I set off across the outlet from the lake and headed east down a trail that ended, in its steady state, at a seasonal hunting camp and then became intermittent at best. There was just enough trail to draw me on, and using the large-scale map, I could imagine, without true conviction, that I was on course.

But the fit between the landscape and the rendering of it became tenuous, and finally there was no fit at all, no trail, and a great deal of desperation on my part. I knew that if I just proceeded east I would eventually come to Spirit Lake. All I needed to do was hug the treeline on the north slope, which I did.

I heard an elk bugle to my left as I walked along a remnant of trail that soon petered out. From the soggy meadows below I traveled up a stream to a low divide, then down into another small basin, where I found myself among some small lakes. I had the choice of either circling around the end of a ridge or climbing it and getting a view. I decided on the latter alternative in hopes of locating myself.

Near panic gave me the strength in midafternoon to climb the steep slope with no hesitation. Once I passed above treeline, marvel upon marvels, I found a string of cairns that led me to the ridge-top and a view over Fish Lake and McCoy Park. They fit my map perfectly.

I sat down beside a small stream to calm myself and savor being able to place myself within a known landscape, which is what this book is about.

With a false sense of victory the preservationists, now a part of the western equation, quickly leapt into their next encounter with the indigenous residents of the West. Having secured the integrity of one small, remote portion of the national park system, they sought to preserve large sections of national parks and forests in official wilderness status. "At this juncture the Echo Park victory gave promise that statutory wilderness preservation might be more than a dream," wrote wilderness historian Roderick Nash. Instead of working to defeat a proposal, the conservationists were now advocating a measure. The process of building a consensus in Congress took much longer than destroying one. From 1957 to 1964 nine congressional hearings were held on the subject, six thousand pages of testimony were taken, and the bill went through sixty-six transformations. "Congress lavished more time and effort on the wilderness bill than on any other measure in American conservation history," wrote Nash.

From the two coasts came the preservationist leaders, like priests, chanting Thoreau, Muir, and Aldo Leopold to congressmen. Behind them were the parishioners who flooded congressional offices with mail. From the Interior West came a smaller number of residents and their representatives, who feared for their livelihoods and instinctively distrusted anything that diminished what they perceived as their legacy of use.

The westerners did not write many letters, but they and their trade organizations worked with those western congressmen who held the most important positions on the key Interior committees. Such federal land-management agencies as the Park Service and the Forest Service had no great love for a wilderness bill that would limit their administrative discretion and was aimed at ending what were viewed as capricious land-use decisions by bureaucrats. The nature of the act bred conflict. It was finally passed in 1964 with a number of limiting features, chief among them being that Congress, not the administration, would decide what areas were wilderness. The gathering of minerals and grazing of animals were allowed to continue.

In no other state was the creation of wilderness more painful than in Utah, where the Mormon land ethic rebelled at the thought of locking away what might one day prove useful. The fact that 240,000 acres of the High Uintas had been designated as a primitive area in 1931 by the Forest Service meant little, except that roads and most structures could not be built there. On the other hand continued logging, grazing, and water development were allowed. In 1942 and again in 1958 the Forest Service studied whether it should administratively change the primitive to a wilderness area designation, but gave up on both proposals before proceeding very far since there was little local enthusiasm for such an action.

The Ashley and Wasatch national forests completed another study of the primitive area in 1966 and recommended that it be expanded into a 322,998-acre wilderness area. Despite the act's "untrammeled" provision, the two national forests thought that the area possessed wilderness qualities. There were fourteen lakes, such as Fox and Island lakes, whose levels were artificially maintained by small earthen dams. The high country was inundated by forty thousand persons, whose average stay in the wilderness was three days. Sheep were grazing the area extensively. "Forage production has been reduced considerably below the pristine level by overuse," the report noted. The predominant range condition in the primitive area was listed as "fair to poor."

In October of 1966 a public hearing on the Forest Service proposal was conducted in Salt Lake City. Sixty-six persons spoke, and three hundred more submitted written statements. The Utah hierarchy, from the governor on down, wanted any action on the proposal deferred until after it was determined if any land within the proposed wilderness area was needed for the physical facilities of the Central Utah Project. The Wilderness Society hoped for a 374,000-acre wilderness area. The Mormon *Deseret News* was torn in two directions: "In a state that needs both water and tourists as much as Utah does, it's hard to know which to put first."

In early 1969 the Department of Agriculture recommended to President Lyndon B. Johnson the creation of a 322,998-acre wilderness area; but the Johnson Administration went out of office without acting on the matter and there the proposal languished until 1983. Meanwhile, energy developments impinged upon the mountains.

The times were frenetic for the Sagebrush West. The seventies began with the deep penetration of the environmentalists into the internal matters of the West, progressed through a tidal wave of energy developments, continued with a huge influx of population, escalated to the administrative challenges of the Carter years to western resource concepts, and finally climaxed in the Sagebrush Rebellion. By the early eighties the region was emotionally wrung out. Then came a decline in oil prices and a concomitant drop in exploration and production of energy minerals. It all went bust once again, and people began to drift away.

The times, actually a previous time, were perfectly caught by E. L. Doctorow in his novel *Welcome to Hard Times,* which was set in the West. A territorial official says, "Over this land a thousand times each year towns spring up and it appears I have to charter them all. But to what purpose? The claim pinches out, the grass dies, the well dries up, and everyone will ride off to form up again somewhere else for me to travel. Nothing fixes in this damned country, people blow around at the wiff of the wind."

And the wind did blow in sharp, erratic gusts.

Around the time of the first Earth Day in 1970, which signaled an emotional surge in the conservation movement similar to what had occurred in the late nineteenth century when the forest reserves came into being, the Sagebrush West was rediscovered. As part of the back-to-the-land movement, coastal residents—some in conscious imitation of the mountain men—temporarily took to western trails and byways in record numbers. Others seeking the good life migrated inland for longer stays. The net result was greater interference in the internal affairs of the Sagebrush West by these newcomers. They brought different perspectives and, along with the coastal conservationists, to whom they were related, their most important contribution was the presentation of alternatives.

While these people generally desired less or no development, or development of their sort, the energy people wanted more, sometimes in places treasured by the environmentalists. The natives usually sided with the developers, only to find out later that they had less to say about what happened once they had given their initial support, and frequently the results were unpalatable. It all tended to get out of hand. The traditional, local power bases—those centered on ranching, small energy production, or tourist needs—either adapted, began to crumble, or were entirely subverted. The common denominator was quick change.

The energy companies arrived on the scene when oil prices rose, opposition to power plants developed in urban areas, and the escalating costs of nuclear power facilities and their questionable safety features forced utilities to look elsewhere for alternatives. In the Interior West they found oil, coal, natural gas, synfuels, and uranium. Impossible promises were made, outrageous hopes held out, and once again the West was willingly seduced.

In 1980, *Time* magazine ran a cover story entitled "Rocky Mountain High: Soaring Prospects for the 80s." There was no mention of possible down times that were soon to come.

Then Randall Meyer, president of Exxon, held out the shimmering vision of a startling bonanza. The numbers were simply stupendous. He estimated that the oil-shale and coal reserves in the West were worth $858 billion. To extract them Meyer said that 870,000 persons would be directly employed while a total of 4 million other people, out of a total population of 11 million in 1980 (up 37 percent from 1970 for the eight interior western states), would benefit to some extent from such massive activities. "Now the western states are likely to become centerstage in the United States energy development," said Meyer in an overly optimistic address to students at the Colorado School of Mines who were about to embark on careers that depended on the employment that the executive and others like him could offer.

One year later, on a day that came to be known as Black Sunday, Exxon bailed out of its western Colorado oil-shale operation, thus signaling the start of the region's most recent decline, as worldwide oil prices began to tumble.

Others could see the times in their proper context. Just before the most recent inundation Wallace Stegner wrote:

> The whole history of the West is a series of consecutive raids. The Beaver West gives way to the Gold West, gives way to the Grass West, gives way to the Irrigation West [gives way to the Energy West]. Everything has to be readjusted about once a generation. It's not quite the same as being a cotton farmer in Mississippi, where the same kind of cropping goes on for three or four or five generations.

Looking back after the latest debacle Ed Marsten, the editor of *High Country News,* the only publication that attempted to cover the region as a whole, echoed Stegner's theme. "It is a tragedy," he wrote, "that so many communities in the Rockies are tied to extractive industries, and that those industries lead nowhere but to booms and busts, followed, perhaps in this decade, by the final bust." Marsten was mistaken; the cycle would repeat itself again. That was a given of western history.

The most recent boom for the region in and around the Uinta Mountains began a few miles from where the ninety-degree arrowhead of the southwestern corner of Wyoming pierced Utah. A joint venture of three oil companies drilled four thousand feet deeper than others before them and came up with oil in the crucial year of 1975. For eighty years the region had been known as a driller's graveyard. Now a stampede was set off to what became known as the "dazzling" Overthrust Belt, a sinuous, geologic swath that extended from northern Alaska to southern Mexico. The central section of the belt—a two-hundred-mile-long gentle arc beginning in west-central Idaho, bowing into western Wyoming, and ending just beyond the arrowhead in Utah—was supposed to save the country from dominance by the Arab nations and other oil-producing foreigners. The major oil companies, independents, roustabouts, and assorted flotsam and jetsam flocked to the Evanston area to take part in the bonanza.

By 1981, at the height of the boom, there were forty-five to fifty drilling rigs operating within thirty miles of the congested former railroad town. Two large gas-sweetening and -processing plants were under construction to the north, more such plants were planned, and pipelines spread all over the countryside to collect the riches and ship them out. *Western Oil Reporter* predicted, "The boom very likely will last for some time to come." Forgotten were the migrating Mormons, who used oil from the springs near Fort Bridger and then passed on; Judge Carter, who briefly produced some oil there; and the short spurt of commercial production just after the turn of the century.

From 1977 to 1982 the population of Evanston jumped from 5,077 to 14,400, and along with the energy workers, their paraphernalia, and their transient lifestyles came all the ills and some of the benefits of a hastily imposed urban environment. There were drugs and crime and traffic jams in Evanston: but no longer did a resident have to drive all the way to Salt Lake City to buy a decent bag of groceries, have dinner at a Burger King, or see a newly released movie. It was more likely that a Salt Lake resident would drive to Evanston for some easy access to liquor or fireworks and listen to music at Billy's Country Music Emporium, a cavernous sheet-metal structure on the edge of town that was the latest reincarnation of the hastily-constructed saloons of the railroad building era.

Over on the other side of the mountains there was a touch more restraint in Vernal, where the Mormons were somewhat more successful in keeping a lid on the energy boom and more united in the drive to profit from it. From the discovery of oil in 1948, its production had grown slowly in the Uintah Basin until the mid-sixties, when three hundred horsehead pumps were referred to as a "boomlet."

First with an increase in oil and gas drilling in the early seventies, proceeding with the construction of the Central Utah Project along the south slope of the Uintas and a coal-burning power plant southeast of Vernal, and ending with an influx of people preparing for nine gigantic synfuel projects that never materialized, the population of the basin swelled in that decade—a 62 percent growth rate for Uinta County and a 72 percent increase in Duchesne County. There was a housing crunch, schools were overcrowded, traffic was incessant, juvenile delinquency increased, marriages got shaky, apathy was prevalent, and there were conflicts between Mormons and non-Mormons.

Suddenly the survival of the existing Indian and white cultures within the basin was threatened by the new waves of emigrants. One report noted: "Like the traditional Mormon community, the Uintah Utes have a culture and lifestyle that might not survive." At last there was commonality.

Neither culture was obliterated. The rising tide of energy developments that threatened to swamp them retreated, leaving behind, once again, the familiar residue of hard times in the Uintah Basin. Besides economic uncertainty, there was fear—fear that the Ute Indians might control, or at least influence, the destiny of whites in that God-forsaken place.

The Utes had hung on tenaciously to their remaining lands. Their grip was strengthened with revenues from oil and gas projects, awards for land claims, and a successful legal challenge to the status quo that sent tremors through the white community. The Indians successfully claimed legal jurisdiction over the three million acres of former reservation lands that were either homesteaded by the whites or transferred to the Forest Service in the early years of the century. This was "'Indian Country' as a matter of federal law," wrote Federal District Court Judge Bruce S. Jenkins, whose opinion was upheld when the U.S. Supreme Court refused to hear the case in 1986.

What this judgment possibly meant was that the Utes, if they chose to, could exert civil jurisdiction over most of the Uintah Basin, and by this paper victory partially recoup what they had lost in 1905. Title to the lands did not change. What was now up for grabs was governmental jurisdiction over such important civil matters as oil and gas revenues, sales taxes, law enforcement, hunting and fishing regulation, and land use. But who had gained exactly what was not clear, and time was needed to sort it all out.

The Utes were restrained in their victory statements. They knew there would be more legal actions, and, indeed, initiated one themselves a few months later when they filed a suit that challenged the state's right to tax oil and gas produced on the one million acres held in trust for the Indians by the federal government. Also, white legislators could always take the issue to Congress, as Utah Senator Jake Garn almost did. The whites were strongest in the legislative arenas, while the Indians had the best chance of prevailing in the federal courts. Whites and Indians had to live in close proximity to each other in the basin, so it was best not to antagonize each other unnecessarily. The two cultures were unwillingly locked in a mutual embrace of the land.

To the whites in the Uintah Basin, control by the Indians was anathema. The Utes' attorney, Martin Seneca, referred to the whites' scenario of what might happen as "the parade of terribles." What also rankled the predominantly Mormon population was the fact that the tribe received energy revenues and federal and state tax advantages, yet benefited greatly from welfare and other public services. "This is a very rich tribe, but it is continually receiving huge amounts of money paid by the American Taxpayer," said the Roosevelt city fathers.

Where before there was certainty that favored the whites, now there was uncertainty, and a current of racial fear and hatred ran just underneath the surface of the public statements. There were unsubstantiated stories of whites beating up Indians and Indians patrolling the reservation's roads with automatic weapons. Similar rumors had circulated in the basin when the reservation was about to be opened to homesteading in the early years of the century. At that time the whites wanted into the basin. Emotions were now exacerbated by the hard times. Unemployment was high, and for the whites who wanted to escape the basin it was an almost impossible time to sell a home.

The Indians had united against the whites to do legal battle, but were divided among themselves. There was the nagging question as to who was a real Ute, since the definition, based on the amount of Indian blood (five-eighths or more constituting true Indianness), determined who got what slice of the tribal income. The bulk of the income came from oil and gas revenues. The second-largest source was grants and contracts awarded to the tribe by outsiders, both from the private and public sectors. The remainder was pumped into the reservation by the Bureau of Indian Affairs.

The tribal population had also increased in recent years, but not directly because of any increased prosperity brought on by the energy boom. Less than a dozen Indians were employed by that industry at the height of its activity during the early eighties. Most of the Indians were poorly educated, lived at or near officially declared poverty levels, and were employed by the tribal government. Very few chose to live off the reservation in the strange, hostile world of the white man. In this manner they maintained their traditional separateness.

The growing intensity of the seventies was also given a decided boost by implementation of the Federal Land Policy Management Act of 1976 and the election of Jimmy Carter as President. It was a double whammy for the West. The act greatly increased the powers of the Bureau of Land Management, which had been emasculated over the years to the point where the agency exercised only a custodial role over the bulk of public lands. An outgrowth of the environmental concern of the early seventies, the act empowered the agency to regulate land use on the 473 million acres under its control for the first time and gave it enforcement powers. Particularly nettlesome to western land users were the provisions that tightened grazing regulations, required that mining claims be recorded with the federal government, and called for a study of BLM lands for possible wilderness designation. Turmoil followed the change in rules as it had done before.

Then all hell broke loose in the West when President Carter announced his "hit list" of questionable water projects in early 1977. The President and his environmentally conscious aides then managed to painfully jerk the udders of almost every sacred cow in the West, including the 160-acre water limitation, hard rock and surface mining, grazing fees, wilderness areas, clean-air requirements, and a host of lesser issues. It was all construed as a war on the West, and the western states decided to kick back.

What became known as the Sagebrush Rebellion briefly came into existence. The real goal was to rein in and control the administrators, but the outright state ownership of federal lands became the public rallying cry. By making a lot of noise, and in the process venting some real anger, western resource users hoped to force the bureaucracy to back away from its increasingly meddlesome role. By February of 1981 five western states had passed nonenforceable laws that asserted ownership over BLM lands, and one state also claimed Forest Service lands. While the rurally dominated legislatures were enthusiastic in their support, most of the more realistic governors were only lukewarm or neutral about the paper rebellion.

Spreading out from Nevada, where it was personified by the jut-jawed Dean Rhoads, a rancher and state legislator who was taken aback by the avalanche of attention that he received after dumping his bill in the hopper, the movement attracted the brief attention of the media on both coasts, who believed the rhetoric. Lou Cannon of the Washington *Post* ended his story with the prediction: "If the Sagebrush Rebellion succeeds, this particular trail could lead to the biggest land takeover in the history of the West," a phrase reminiscent of DeVoto.

Closer to the reality of the situation, which was far less dramatic, was the assessment of Maitland S. Sharpe, environmental-affairs director of the Isaak Walton League of America, who said, "The real goal of the Sagebrush Rebellion is to put range management under local political control, and the real danger is that it will succeed." It did, and that was the main result of the movement, which was more indicative of the uneasiness of the times than the outgrowth of any substantive complaints.

All of this activity would not have meant much—just so many westerners letting off steam—had not President Ronald Reagan, Interior Secretary James G. Watt, and a Republican-controlled Senate taken office in early 1981. Reagan sent a message to the "rebels" that he was one of them; and the rules changed again.

Watt, a Wyomingite, became the lightning rod for the Reagan Administration in its early years because he lacked a soothing manner and political sensitivity. At his first meeting with state BLM directors the Interior Secretary said, "I know you state directors understand. I don't know if our Washington crew understands the hostility toward the BLM. And it needn't be that way. For years and years the BLM worked as a good neighbor and was a vital part of every community. We never had friction. But I tell you, there is justification for the Sagebrush Rebellion and the responsibility falls right in this room. You are the [1976] act. And my job is to defuse that rebellion." Those who did not want to adhere to the new policies were urged to find employment elsewhere. "I want to come across today as a hardliner with a delicate touch," said the Interior Secretary.

This time the environmentalists squawked, and rather stridently at times. Such overblown phrases as "environmental Armageddon," the Washington "disaster area," "extreme agenda," "desecration of our wilderness lands," "defunding of our national park system," and "anti-environmental juggernaut" were used to solicit members, contributions, and signatures on petitions to dump Watt. One appeal for funds from the Sierra Club said of the Reagan Administration, "Their goal is all-out development. They want to lease, sell, drill and dig in every possible place." That was a tall order, and not one that even a westerner like Watt either wanted or was able to fulfill.

The clamor increased and Watt eventually left, to be replaced by less-contentious advocates of the same policies. Then the West settled back into more quiet, albeit harder times.

This was the last pause before my descent to Spirit Lake. The sun was warm on the open, bouldered slope, and the sound of the trickle, fed by a snowbank from above, was comforting. It was time to collect myself.

I felt a bit frayed, as were the mountains and the countryside surrounding me. There was no telling when that process began: perhaps with the Indians, certainly with the trappers, and positively by the time the settlers loosed their livestock upon the range, including the headwaters of Sheep Creek below me.

The natural scene has been greatly imposed upon here and

elsewhere in the West. There is a tilt toward impending disaster, a tilt that could become a decided lean considering the increasing tempo of the process. The mountains are refreshing, but at the same time they are also diseased. I have already spoken of *giardia* and Mormon crickets. There are other chemical and biological intrusions.

Radioactive clouds blew northeast on the prevailing winds from the Nevada Test Site and fallout dusted the Uintas in the 1950s and the early years of the next decade. It rains heavier over mountains, and since the Uintas were the first range of consequence in the path of the fallout, the mountains got more than their fair share of the contaminants, which also descended over the entire West and other parts of the country. One of the places where relatively high amounts of radioactive isotopes were measured was in the small community of Altonah on the south slope, where residents subsequently sued the federal government for the cancers that they believed were caused by the fallout.

Robert C. Pendleton, a native Utahan, was familiar with the mountains and fallout, since he had worked for the Atomic Energy Commission and was director of the Department of Radiological Health at the University of Utah. An avid hunter and fisherman, Pendleton in the sixties collected samples of wildlife from the Uintas and tested them for their radioactive content. He said he would not eat the brook trout because they contained such high amounts of cesium-137, and the mountain lions and mule deer that he shot were similarly infected.

Over time the potency of radioactive isotopes lessens; and since the tests went underground more than twenty years ago, the levels of radioactivity must have greatly diminished by the time of my visit. However, a residue of that lethal heritage undoubtedly remains.

Much more tangible than the invisible isotopes is the destruction caused by mountain pine beetles and acid rain. To the east of where I sat large patches of a dried-blood color were mixed in with the dark green of a normal evergreen forest. Those patches were dead or dying lodgepole and ponderosa pine trees. Further on was a huge uneven black hole where a forest fire, spreading quickly through trees weakened or killed by mountain pine beetles, had burned fiercely for days this summer.

The beetles, which decimate trees by girdling their inner bark, have been around ever since there were pine trees. They were first known to have appeared in Utah in the late eighteenth century and were first noticed in a western national forest shortly after 1900. Large-scale devastation by the beetles was not recorded in the Ashley National Forest until after World War II. In 1952 it was estimated that a half million trees had been killed in the previous five years. Periodic epidemics in sections of the forest were noted after that, and in the early seventies the general infestation, much like a cancer, began to spread throughout the forest.

The beetles have been known to kill more than three million trees in a year within a national forest. At the peak of the current infestation at the eastern end of the Uintas, officials of the Ashley National Forest estimated that between three and four million trees were killed in 1981 and 1982. Spraying with the pesticide Sevin and selective logging slowed the beetles, but it certainly did not stop them. The effects of the treatments were haphazard. It worked in some places and had no effect elsewhere.

Earlier in 1985 a Forest Service pest-management expert flew over the area and estimated that 2.8 million trees had been killed. "Tree mortality is occurring in all susceptible lodgepole pine stands on the north and east slopes of the Uinta Mountains," he reported to his supervisor. Whole hillsides turned rust red, as if they were populated by deciduous trees in autumn. The place seemed out of whack with the season. The disease might eventually engulf both national forests. And what would the forests and mountains be without trees?

For the same atmospheric reasons that mountains received radioactive fallout, they were susceptible to acid rain. While I was on my journey, it had been announced that the effects of acid rain in the Uinta Mountains were greater than had been thought. The Forest Service and Environmental Protection Agency decided to follow up that preliminary finding with a sampling of a few lakes.

As in other wilderness areas in the West, trees and lakes were beginning to show damage from sulfur-dioxide and nitrogen-oxide emissions that spewed forth from downwind copper and steel smelters, coal-fired power plants, and natural-gas processing plants. The snow-capped Uintas were ringed by such facilities and were in the path of emissions from more remote sources in Arizona and Mexico.

I subsequently read that the sampling program had been completed at fifteen lakes within the wilderness area. Four were unnamed, and I did not recognize the names of the remaining eleven lakes. Perhaps I should have given as much thought to nuclear fallout and acidity as to *giardia* when I was in the mountains, but actually I found all the possibilities of poisoning rather confusing and chose to concentrate on the pleasures of the immediate journey.

I took a couple of sips of the remaining water in my cup, rose, hoisted my pack onto my back for the last time, and descended to the trail that led to Spirit Lake, just outside the wilderness area.

Dean Chew was no lover of officially declared wilderness areas, although he spent a great deal of time in them. The Chew clan had been part of this landscape for longer than any bureaucrats, legislators, or conservationists. They, too, were endangered.

The Chews came to Utah from Lancashire, England, where they were recruited by the Mormon Church in the early 1860s. Jack Chew grew up in Nephi and, after a short stretch in the state prison for grand theft, moved up to the isolated refuge of Browns Park in 1900. Jack's wife, Mary, who eventually bore him fourteen children, arrived with some members of the large family in tow the next year, and they lived in various parts of the park while eking out a living ranching.

Douglas Chew, the eleventh child, was born in 1902 in Browns Park. His father, who assisted at the birth, dislocated the child's jaw. A fourteen-year-old sister departed on a 120-mile ride to Vernal and back in order to fetch some rubber nipples so that her baby brother could nurse. She rode hard for two full days and returned exhausted with the nipples. It was that kind of life.

Little Douglas learned to ride at the age of four and seldom left the saddle thereafter. As a young man he acquired the money that was needed for a herd of sheep by staking oil-shale claims in the Uintah Basin during one of the periodic booms in that illusive commodity. Douglas married Eleanor Wilkins in 1926. The couple had $2.50 left after paying for the wedding dance in Browns Park. Then began a slow, relentless climb toward middle-class respectability.

Chew took out a loan for one hundred aged ewes, and lost all but fifteen the first winter of their marriage. Their first child, Dean, was born in 1927. They accumulated over one thousand sheep, then lost three hundred in another hard winter. When the monument was enlarged in the thirties Chew felt hemmed in, so he rented and purchased more ranch lands that included grazing rights within the park boundaries. Borrowing more money, Chew bought the Daniels ranch bordering the Green River in 1941 for $12,000.

During his ranching career, he was not out of debt until 1951. Shortly after Douglas handed the ranch over to his oldest son, he wrote an autobiographical note: "I haven't really wanted for much—a good dog, a good horse, a good ranch, a good wife, a good family. I've had them." The couple, friends and neighbors of the Bassett women and Harry Ratliff in their times, lived on into their sixtieth year of married life, teaching grandchildren and great-grandchildren how to ride at the age of four.

When Dean Chew purchased his father's holdings in 1967 he received 244 acres of the home ranch along the bottomlands of the Green River and slightly less than 1,300 acres in scattered homesteads that bordered on or were within the national monument. Dean had gotten his start by working for his father, with whom he gradually became a partner. As Dean's family grew to four sons and three daughters, the Utah land base became too crowded for both families. So Dean bought a ranch in Clark, Colorado, just up the road from Steamboat Springs and the old Ratliff homestead. The livestock were trucked up from the hot Utah desert to the Colorado high country in the early summer. There they grazed on a mix of Chew and Forest Service lands and returned in the fall to roam over a mixture of Chew, Park Service, and Bureau of Land Management lands.

The goal was to keep the four sons in the family ranching business. The girls had to marry into ranching if they wanted to remain with it. Dean and Laura were successful in keeping the family together as a unit, though countless other western ranch families had been dispersed over the years. To stay ahead of the demands of the bank, Dean Chew had to gross $1,000 a day. There were a few years when the family grossed over $400,000.

They were cash poor but land rich. Yet they realized that if they sold the land they would be less than poor. They would be nothing. "Land gets in your blood. Once gone, it is gone forever," said Dean Chew. A mixture of public and private lands, a lot of good luck, and hard work were needed to survive as a family unit in these fractured times. There were no real vacations, just business trips to stockmen's meetings. Chew's suntan ended abruptly at his hat line.

Family interests needed to be protected by active participation on governmental advisory boards and in the hierarchy of trade associations. One of Dean's sons, Scott, had testified against changing the monument's name; and his father saw a threat to the family's ranching operations if certain BLM lands should be designated as wilderness. These were lands that five generations of Chews had ridden horses across almost every day of their lives. They felt a proprietary interest in them.

Dick Carter, who headed the Utah Wilderness Association, was of the opposite persuasion. Carter pointed out that present-day conservationists were not the first to recognize the wilderness values of the Uintas. John Wesley Powell had celebrated the "grand view" of the mountains in 1869 when he set off down the Green River. But it would take more than the words of a one-armed Civil War major to change the designation from primitive to wilderness. A political decision and a court case set the proposal in motion.

In the early eighties Representative John F. Seiberling of Ohio, a champion of wilderness areas and chairman of the Subcommittee on Public Lands and National Parks, decided that the best approach to declaring wilderness areas in the West under the provisions of the 1964 act was not the previous omnibus bills that lumped everything together, but a careful state-by-state approach. Such a tactic, said Seiberling, would be administratively and politically more manageable since the bills would not be submitted until they were shaped for approval. A federal court suit had forced the Forest

Service into the possibility of a third round of wilderness-area reviews, and the various commercial interest groups in Utah did not want to stagnate while yet another study was completed. The alternative was to create their own destiny.

When the next session of Congress began in early 1983, Utah Senator Jake Garn announced his intention to introduce a wilderness bill that the whole congressional delegation and Governor Scott M. Matheson could support. Matheson agreed, stating that there was a need "to designate deserving Forest Service areas and free other areas to traditional multiple use management." When he introduced the bill, Garn spoke for most westerners. He said: "Utahans want limited wilderness designations for those areas which truly deserve protection. They also want to be able to productively and responsibly develop the natural resources which nature has provided for us and which make possible the comforts of life which we enjoy." A similar bill calling for the creation of eleven wilderness areas in the state, including the High Uintas, was introduced in the House by the three Utah representatives.

At about this time Carter wrote a note to himself titled "Wilderness Thoughts." The paeans of Thoreau and Muir came down to these practical considerations:

Utah had no wilderness heritage, nor did Utahans appreciate political activism. The omnibus approach involved bloodletting and outsiders. The Garn bill was hard to fight. It was easier to pass a bill with a united delegation, although it might not be the ideal bill. A little wilderness at a time would not scare anyone and would keep the politicians in front of the television cameras. It would be difficult if not impossible to get a lot of wilderness. We don't publicly endorse; we quietly push. If it becomes a bad bill we back out quietly. If we act openly, we will find ourselves outside the negotiating process. The national conservation groups would object to a state bill shaped by state conservationists and not themselves, Carter noted. The differences between the state group and national preservationists were kept under wraps, but there was bitter infighting.

At the congressional hearings in Washington the talk flowed back and forth along traditional western lines. Dick Carter argued for more wilderness acreage, stating that the Uintas were the largest undesignated roadless area administered by the Forest Service in the contiguous states. Nothing in Utah and only a few areas in the West matched the size, diversity, and wildness of the Uintas, said Carter. Garn noted that in his ten years in the Senate he had had a very difficult time explaining the differences of the West to his eastern colleagues. It was an arid land. Two-thirds of the surface area of Utah was owned by the federal government, the senator pointed out.

Alton N. Moon, a Uintah Basin rancher and county commissioner, was concerned that wilderness status would hinder maintenance work on the small dams in the mountains. Too much land was being given over to wilderness, he said. The mountains were preserved and protected by God, who had created them for the enjoyment and use of man. On the north slope the dominant concerns were expressed by the energy companies, who cited economic arguments; there was a national need for energy.

The oil and gas companies attempted to hold the wilderness line as high on the north slope of the Uintas as possible. A few years earlier their arguments would have been persuasive. Now prices were slipping and an energy glut was developing.

Carter, congressional staffers, Forest Service personnel, and representatives of the energy companies flew over to the north slope in helicopters on April 13. The line descended a bit, at least far enough so that Carter could report to his membership: "There is a strong temptation to say, 'this is a bad bill, and why support it if we can't get what we want?' The answer to that question, as in the Rolling Stones' song, is that we can get what we need. Utah needs a base of wilderness areas we can build on, and this legislation is the only way to get that."

Other whites spoke of sheep and Boy Scouts. The Indians did not speak at the hearings, nor did anyone recall that once the wilderness had briefly belonged to them. The chairman of the subcommittee, Representative Seiberling, read a poem by the nineteenth-century English poet Gerard Manley Hopkins that contained the line: "When we hew or delve: After-comers cannot guess the beauty been."

With the addition of a few last-minute compromises, a final bill was shaped and passed by the House and Senate and signed by President Reagan in late September, 1984. The total acreage of Utah wilderness areas had been increased twenty-five times, and the High Uintas Wilderness Area was now 460,000 acres. The House report on the bill stated: "In summary, from a wildlife, primitive recreation, and watershed standpoint, the High Uintas are Utah's most significant wild area, and indeed, are one of the most diverse and interesting wildland ecosystems in the entire nation." The description was a bit overblown but necessary to justify all the words that had been expended.

Carter was singled out on the floor of the Senate by Garn, who, in a statement that was unusual for a western legislator, cited "the sincere and responsible efforts of conservationists in Utah." The senator continued, "Were it not for the constant efforts of Mr. Dick Carter of the Utah Wilderness Association, there would likely not be such a broad-based system of wilderness in Utah."

Such internal cohesion was a model for the remainder of Sagebrush Country. There was, after all, not that much difference between a Dean Chew and a Dick Carter.

Like the proverbial pot of gold at the end of the rainbow, the recurring western dream appeared at the end of my journey at Spirit Lake Lodge. This dream, too, involved a cosmetic name change. That the dreamer had no knowledge of the mythical tribe that the Spanish envisioned living on the shores of Utah Lake, or of subsequent mirages that were endemic to this land, was symbolic of the shortness of memory hereabouts.

Steve Pedroza, who wore cowboy boots and smoked a pipe, had just bought the ramshackle lodge and cabins at the end of the long dirt road from McKinnon on the north slope. The log structures had been built as a family summer resort in simpler times. He planned to upgrade and rename it The Lodge at Spirit Lake, a name, I suppose, that owed its derivation to similarly designated structures at posh ski resorts.

The plans of the auctioneer–cum–lodge owner were in keeping

with the new nomenclature. There would be a helicopter landing
pad in the meadow for monied passengers from the Salt Lake
airport two hundred miles distant. The guests would then be
obliged to walk a few hundred feet to the newly carpeted lodge,
where they could rest in their suites before being served drinks and
dinner by bartenders and waiters. For relaxation there would be a
deck on which to sun, hot tubs, a gazebo for family picnics, and
horses or skimobiles, depending on the season.

For $2,000 a week guests could rent horses and be furnished a
guide and a cook to hunt in the mountains. Pedroza had purchased
a half-dozen horses earlier that week for a scheduled pack trip that
had failed to materialize. I had seen him playing with the horses. "It
was just like a rodeo all day today," he said. Horses were a necessary
part of any such western dream.

All these amenities and more were part of Pedroza's five-year
plan, as he outlined it to me on the bench outside the lodge that
first evening following my descent from the wilderness. It all seemed
like a futile exercise in unreality; but it was difficult for me to judge
clearly, since I had been away from civilization for some time. I was,
to tell the truth, somewhat overwhelmed by his wordiness, that
being a trait of his occupation. After all, I had lived the silent life
of a monk for nine days. It seemed as if I was disoriented for the
better part of that last day.

As a child and young man Pedroza had hiked, hunted, ridden,
and fished in the Uintas, and a slicked-up lodge was his passport to
a life of profitable play. That the dream depended on the Forest
Service for fulfillment was not mentioned. What the auctioneer of
heavy equipment and onetime bartender had purchased less than
a week before was the improvements, not the land that was leased
from the federal government.

At the present time, however, things were a bit lean for Steve and
his girlfriend, Kathy. They were eating frozen chicken pot pies with
ketchup for dinner and Kathy had broken one of her long purple
fingernails. They had a malamute puppy named Sage that seemed
to go with the scene. Steve, who was sporting the meager start of a
beard, seemed overly dependent for advice on his manager, who had
more ranch savvy and a teenage daughter who was about ready to fly

the coop. They all planned to spend the coming winter at the isolated lodge.

The winters could be cruel in that place. I silently wished them luck, but doubted that they would make it. I thought they might give up or go broke, but I could be wrong.

Others had made it there in smaller ways. The lodge was not far from the Stewart homestead. Success in the West is a matter of perceiving the reality of the place, bringing the right stuff to it, and applying the appropriate scale of development.

On that balmy August evening, Steve surveyed his newly acquired kingdom from the bench outside the lodge. There were the meadow, corral, horses, lake, rental boats, cabins, lodge, dog, and woman.

"It's just like owning land," he said.

I thought that all those people who had settled upon or crossed this landscape were just brief tenants and passersby. That they owned a piece of it was an illusion. A place was just borrowed for a short period of time, and then, inexorably, it must be surrendered. We were, all of us, transients on these lands. It was time for me to move on.

The next day was the start of the bow-hunting season and the nearby Forest Service campground was filling up with hunters in their oversized recreational vehicles. My friend who would drive me back to Salt Lake City, from where I would depart in a few days for California, was due to arrive that day.

I shook hands with Steve, wished him luck, and went back to the stuffy log cabin that I had rented and spent a restless night in the short bed. By the time my ride arrived, I was ready to leave the mountains.

ACKNOWLEDGMENTS

The idea for this book crystallized on a sun-filled day in September, 1981, when I stood on an unnamed peak at the 12,418-foot level of the crest of the Uinta Mountains and gazed, alternately, at the north and south slopes. The next day, at my campsite in the Enchanted Basin, I outlined the two-slope theory in a pocket notebook, and then went fishing.

Indirectly I had been gathering material for this book since 1970, when I began to write in a concentrated manner about land and water in the West. Some of the material and ideas were left over from a book on water and the West, *A River No More: The Colorado River and the West,* that was published in May, 1981. But there was a great deal more information to gather.

Since that first trip into and around the Uintas, I have searched for additional material in archives and libraries in Washington, D.C.; Berkeley, California; and the Sagebrush states of Colorado, Utah, and Wyoming. Those repositories of information were administered by the federal government, state governments, universities, historical societies, city and county libraries, nonprofit organizations, private businesses, and individuals. Invariably, the custodians were helpful and I thank them for their patience and the use of their photocopying machines.

I tended to rely on secondary sources of information up to 1900 and then dug increasingly into primary sources after the turn of the century. Since so much has been written about the frontier, I did not think it necessary to reinvent the wheel—only to shape the material into a meaningful form.

Besides the people named in this book, there were countless others who provided me with information from their stores of personal knowledge. Once again I was taken aback by the generous amounts of time people put aside to talk to a stranger about themselves, their families, their jobs, or the places where they lived or played. There was usually an initial reticence, then a flood of words, and always the ubiquitous cup of weak coffee to lubricate the process.

Virginia Buchanan, Milton Voigt, and Genevieve Atwood of Salt Lake City provided me with hospitality and friendship during my extended stays in the region. Milt drove me into the mountains for my odyssey, and Genevieve brought me back. Ashbel Green, senior editor at Knopf, has guided me through the publishing process—twice successfully. His standards are exacting. The copyeditor, Margaret Cheney, caught some grievous mistakes, and Marty Knapp printed the photographs.

As with the river book, Gary Weatherford, a multifaceted expert on western land and water issues, read the entire manuscript. Dianne Fradkin, my ideal of the intelligent lay reader, did the same. To make sure my suppositions were correct, I asked Wallace Stegner to read the preface, which at that time was more unwieldy but made the same points. He replied with some encouraging words, as is his wont. Kathryn L. MacKay of Salt Lake City helped with some last-minute research on the Ute Indians. While not so long ago it was proper to acknowledge the help of a typist, I can only say that my new word processing program did not fail me too often; and the spelling checker was undoubtedly an aid to those who had to edit the manuscript. Needless to say I, and not the above named or the personal computer, am responsible for the final product.

PHILIP L. FRADKIN
Inverness, California, January, 1988

SELECTED
BIBLIOGRAPHY

This partial listing of sources favors commercially published books and thus slights the many memoranda, reports, letters, interviews, and other informal materials that give a sense of immediacy to history. However, since many of those materials are difficult to locate and this bibliography is designed to lead the average reader in the direction of further information on land and the West, they have generally been omitted. The few exceptions are works that fill a noticeable gap in the published literature and that are of government origin, thus assuring survival in some repository. The list also includes a few novels and nonfiction books that evoke a vivid sense of time, place, and people without sacrificing the gritty reality of the West.

GENERAL

Abbey, Edward. *Desert Solitaire: A Season in the Wilderness.* McGraw-Hill, 1968.

Banham, Reyner. *Scenes in America Deserta.* Peregrine-Smith, 1982.

Bartlett, Richard A. *The New Country: A Social History of the American Frontier, 1776–1890.* Oxford University Press, 1974.

Billington, Ray Allen. *Westward Expansion: A History of the American Frontier.* Macmillan, 1974.

Bowden, Charles. *Blue Desert.* University of Arizona Press, 1986.

Caughley, John W. "The Insignificance of the Frontier in American History or Once Upon a Time There Was an American West." *Western Historical Quarterly,* January, 1974.

Conoway, James. *The Kingdom in the Country.* Houghton Mifflin, 1987.

Cronon, William. *Changes in the Land.* Hill and Wang, 1983.

Crump, Donald J., ed. *A Guide to Our Federal Lands.* National Geographic Society, 1984.

DeVoto, Bernard. *The Course of Empire.* Houghton Mifflin, 1952.

Doctorow, E. L. *Welcome to Hard Times.* Random House, 1960.

Doig, Ivan. *English Creek.* Atheneum, 1984.

——. *This House of Sky: Landscapes of a Western Mind.* Harcourt Brace Jovanovich, 1978.

Ehrlich, Gretel. *The Solace of Open Spaces.* Viking, 1985.

Fisher, Ron. *Our Threatened Inheritance: Natural Treasures of the United States.* National Geographic Society, 1984.

Fradkin, Philip L. *A River No More: The Colorado River and the West.* Alfred A. Knopf, 1981.

Garreau, Joel. *The Nine Nations of North America.* Houghton Mifflin, 1981.

Gates, Paul W. *The History of Public Land Law Development.* Public Land Law Review Commission, 1968.

Gressley, Gene. "Whither Western American History? Some Speculations on a Direction." *Pacific Historical Review,* November, 1984.

High Country News. Lander, Wyoming, and Paonia, Colorado. All issues, 1969 to the present.

Hine, Robert V. *The American West: An Interpretive History.* Little, Brown, 1973.

Lamar, Howard R. "Persistent Frontier: The West in the Twentieth Century." *Western Historical Quarterly.* January, 1973.

——, ed. *The Reader's Encyclopedia of the American West.* Thomas Y. Crowell, 1977.

Lavender, David. *The Great West.* The American Heritage Press, 1985.

Maclean, Norman. *A River Runs Through It.* The University of Chicago Press, 1976.

MacMahon, James A. *Deserts.* Alfred A. Knopf, 1985.

McPhee, John. *Basin and Range.* Farrar, Straus & Giroux, 1980.

Marsh, George Perkins. *Man and Nature.* Harvard University Press, 1965.

Merk, Frederick. *History of the Westward Movement.* Alfred A. Knopf, 1978.

Nash, Gerald D. *The American West in the Twentieth Century: A. Short History of an Urban Crisis.* University of New Mexico Press, 1977.

Nichols, John. *The Milagro Beanfield War.* Holt, Rinehart and Winston, 1974.

Peffer, E. Louise. *The Closing of the Public Domain: Disposal and Reservation Policies, 1900–1950.* Stanford University Press, 1951.

Rabkin, Richard, and Rabkin, Jacob. *Nature in the West.* Holt, Rinehart and Winston, 1981.

Robbins, Roy. *Our Landed Heritage: The Public Domain, 1776–1970.* University of Nebraska Press, 1976.

Shanks, Bernard. *This Land Is Your Land: The Struggle to Save America's Public Lands.* Sierra Club Books, 1984.

Smith, Henry Nash. *Virgin Land.* Harvard University Press, 1950.

Steffen, Jerome, ed. *The American West: New Perspectives, New Dimensions.* University of Oklahoma Press, 1979.

Stegner, Wallace. *Angle of Repose.* Doubleday, 1971.

——. *The American West as Living Space.* University of Michigan Press, 1987.

——. *The Sound of Mountain Water.* Doubleday, 1969.

——. and Stegner, Page. "American Places." *Atlantic Monthly,* April, 1978.

Turner, Frederick Jackson. *The Frontier in American Society.* Henry Holt, 1920.

U.S. Congress. Public Land Law Review Commission. *One Third of the Nation's Land.* Government Printing Office, 1970.

U.S. Department of Interior, Bureau of Land Management, *Public Land Statistics.* Government Printing Office, current year.

Webb, Walter Prescott. *The Great Plains.* University of Nebraska Press, 1981.

Whitney, Stephen. *Western Forests.* Alfred A. Knopf, 1985.

Wyant, William K. *Westward in Eden: The Public Lands and the Conservation Movement.* University of California Press, 1982.

Zaslowsky, Dyan, and the Wilderness Society. *These American Lands: Parks, Wilderness, and the Public Lands.* Henry Holt, 1986.

PREFACE

Bancroft, Hubert Howe. *History of Nevada, Colorado, and Wyoming, 1540–1888.* History Company, 1889.
——. *History of Utah.* History Company, 1889.

A RECENT YEAR

Burnham, William A. "Artificial Increase in Reproduction of Wild Peregrine Falcons." *Journal of Wildlife Management,* March, 1978.
Everhart, William C. *The National Park Service.* Westview Press, 1983.
Runte, Alfred. *National Parks: The American Experience.* University of Nebraska Press, 1979.
Sax, Joseph L. *Mountains Without Handrails: Reflections on the National Parks.* University of Michigan Press, 1980.
U.S. Department of Interior, National Park Service, Dinosaur National Monument. *Natural Resources Management Plan.* 1983.
U.S. Department of Interior, National Park Service, Dinosaur National Monument. *General Management Plan.* Government Printing Office, February, 1986.
Wirth, Conrad L. *Parks, Politics, and the People.* University of Oklahoma Press, 1980.

INDIANS

Bolton, Herbert E. *Pageant in the Wilderness.* Utah State Historical Society, 1950.
Davis, Mel, ed. *High Uinta Trails.* Wasatch Publishers, 1974.
Gunnerson, James H. "The Fremont Culture." *Papers of the Peabody Museum of Archeology and Ethnology.* Harvard University Press, 2 (1969)
Hansen, Wallace R. *The Geologic Story of the Uinta Mountains.* Government Printing Office, 1975.
Hayward, C. Lynn. *The High Uintas.* Monte L. Bean Life Science Museum, 1983.
Jennings, Jesse D., ed. *Prehistory of Utah and the Eastern Great Basin.* University of Utah Press, 1978.
Lindsay, James B., ed. *Geologic Guidebook of the Uinta Mountains.* Intermountain Association of Geologists, 1969.

Shimkin, D. B. "Wind River Shoshone Ethnology." *Anthropological Records*. University of California Press, 3 (1947).

Smith, Anne M. *Ethnography of the Northern Utes*. Museum of New Mexico Press, 1974.

Stewart, Omer C. "Ute Indians: Before and After White Contact." *Utah Historical Quarterly*, Winter, 1966.

Trenholm, Virginia Cole, and Carley, Maurine. *The Shoshonis*. University of Oklahoma Press, 1964.

Tyler, S. Lyman. "The Myth of the Lake of Copala and Land of Teguayo." *Utah Historical Quarterly*, October, 1952.

——. "The Spaniard and the Ute." *Utah Historical Quarterly*, October, 1954.

Warner, Ted J. *The Dominguez Escalante Journal*. Brigham Young University Press, 1976.

Wheat, Carl I. *Mapping of the Transmississippi West*. Institute of Historical Cartography, 1957.

TRAPPERS

Chittenden, Hiram Martin. *History of the American Fur Trade*. Francis P. Harper, 1902.

DeVoto, Bernard. *Across the Wide Missouri*. Houghton Mifflin, 1947.

Evans, Laura, and Belknap, Buzz. *Dinosaur River Guide*. Westwater Books, 1973.

Frémont, Brevet Capt. J. C.. *Narrative of the Exploring Expedition to the Rocky Mountains in the Year 1842: and to Oregon and North California in the years 1843–1844*. L. W. Hall, 1846.

Gilbert, Bil. *Westering Man*. University of Oklahoma Press, 1985.

Goetzmann, William H. *Exploration and Empire*. Alfred A. Knopf, 1966.

Hafen, LeRoy R. "Fort Davy Crockett: Its Fur Men and Visitors." *Colorado Magazine*, January, 1952.

——, ed. *Mountain Men and Fur Traders of the West*. University of Nebraska Press, 1982.

Jackson, Donald, and Spence, Mary Lee, ed. *The Expeditions of John Charles Frémont, Volume I, Travels from 1838 to 1844*. University of Illinois Press, 1970.

Lamar, Howard R. *The Fur Trader on the American Frontier.* Texas A & M University Press, 1977.

Morgan, Dale L. *Jedediah Smith and the Opening of the West.* Bobbs-Merrill, 1953.

Morgan, Dale L., ed. *The West of William H. Ashley.* Old West Publishing Company, 1964.

Snow, William J. "Utah Indians and Spanish Slave Trade." *Utah Historical Quarterly,* July, 1929.

Wishart, David J. *The Fur Trade of the American West.* University of Nebraska Press, 1979.

Zwinger, Ann. *Run, River, Run.* Harper & Row, 1975.

EMIGRANTS

Alter, Cecil J. *Jim Bridger.* University of Oklahoma Press, 1962.

Gowans, Fred R., and Campbell, Eugene E. *Fort Bridger.* Brigham Young University Press, 1975.

——. *Fort Supply.* Brigham Young University Press, 1976.

Holliday, J. S. *The World Rushed In.* Simon and Schuster, 1981.

Stegner, Wallace. *The Gathering of Zion: The Story of the Mormon Trail.* McGraw-Hill, 1964.

Vestel, Stanley. *Jim Bridger.* University of Nebraska Press, 1970.

RAILROADERS

Athearn, Robert G. *Union Pacific Country.* University of Nebraska Press, 1976.

Chisum, Emmett D. "Boom Towns of the Union Pacific." *Annals of Wyoming,* Spring, 1981.

Dodge, Major General Grenville M. *How We Built the Union Pacific Railway.* Sage Books, 1965.

Hebard, Grace Raymond. *Washakie.* Arthur H. Clarke, 1930.

Larson, T. A. *History of Wyoming.* University of Nebraska Press, 1978.

Lent, John A. "The Press on Wheels." *Annals of Wyoming,* Fall, 1971.

Rence, Mary Lou, and Homsher, Lola M. *Ghost Towns of Wyoming.* Hastings House, 1956.

Reps, John W. *Cities of the American West.* Princeton University Press, 1979.

Toponce, Alexander. *The Reminiscences of Alexander Toponce.* University of Oklahoma Press, 1971.

SETTLERS (NORTH SLOPE)

Burroughs, John Rolfe. *Where the Old West Stayed Young.* Bonanza Books, 1962.

Dary, David. *Cowboy Culture.* Avon, 1981.

Davis, Jr., William N. "The Sutler at Fort Bridger." *Western Historical Quarterly,* January, 1971.

——. "Western Justice: The Court at Fort Bridger, Utah Territory." *Utah Historical Quarterly,* April, 1955.

Dunham, Dick, and Dunham, Vivian. *Flaming Gorge Country.* Manila, Utah: Dagget County Lions Club, 1977.

Ellison, R. S. *Fort Bridger.* Wyoming State Archives, 1981.

McClure, Grace. *The Bassett Women.* Swallow Press/University of Ohio Press, 1985.

Stewart, Elinore Pruitt. *Letters of a Woman Homesteader.* Houghton Mifflin, 1982.

——. *Letters on an Elk Hunt.* University of Nebraska Press, 1979.

Tennent, William L. "John Jarvie of Brown's Park." *Cultural Resources Series No. 7.* Bureau of Land Management, Government Printing Office, 1981.

Willis, Ann Bassett. "Queen Ann of Brown's Park." *Colorado Magazine,* April, 1952.

SCIENTISTS

Bartlett, Richard A. *Great Surveys of the American West.* University of Oklahoma Press, 1962.

Colbert, Edwin H. *The Great Dinosaur Hunters and Their Discoveries.* Dover Publications, 1984.

Conrow, Robert. *The Great Diamond Hoax and Other True Tales.* Johnson Books, 1983.

Darrah, William Culp. *Powell of the Colorado.* Princeton University Press, 1951.

Ford, Worthington Chauncey. *Letters of Henry Adams.* Houghton Mifflin, 1930.

Harpending, Asbury. *The Great Diamond Hoax.* University of Oklahoma Press, 1958.

Hayden, F. V. *Fourth Preliminary Report of the United States Geological Survey of Wyoming and Portions of Contiguous Territories.* Government Printing Office, 1872.

King, Clarence. *Systematic Geology.* Government Printing Office, 1878.

McGinnis, Helen J. *Carnegie's Dinosaurs.* Carnegie Museum of Natural History, Carnegie Institute, 1982.

McNierney, Michael. "The Great Bone War." *American West,* May–June, 1982.

Powell, John Wesley. *Report on the Geology of the Eastern Uinta Mountains and a Region of Country Adjacent Thereto.* Government Printing Office, 1876.

——. *Report on the Lands of the Arid Region of the United States: With a More Detailed Account of the Lands of Utah.* The Belknap Press of Harvard University Press, 1962.

——. *The Exploration of the Colorado River and Its Canyons.* Dover Publications, 1961.

Stegner, Wallace. *Beyond the Hundredth Meridian: John Wesley Powell and the Second Opening of the West.* Houghton Mifflin, 1954.

Wilford, John Noble. *The Riddle of the Dinosaur.* Alfred A. Knopf, 1985.

SETTLERS (SOUTH SLOPE)

American Indian Policy Review Commission. *Final Report.* Government Printing Office, 1977.

A Report of the U.S. Commission on Indian Rights. *Indian Rights.* Government Printing Office, 1981.

Arlington, Leonard. *Brigham Young: American Moses.* Alfred A. Knopf, 1985.

——. *The Mormon Experience.* Alfred A. Knopf, 1979.

Conetah, Fred A. *A History of the Northern Ute People*. Duchesne, Utah: Uintah-Ouray Ute Tribe, 1982.

Deloria, Jr., Vine and Clifford M. Lytle. *American Indians, American Justice*. University of Texas Press, 1983.

——. *The Nations Within: The Past and Future of American Indian Sovereignty*. Pantheon Books, 1984.

Dillman, Mildred Miles. *Early History of Duchesne County*. Art City Publishing Company, 1948.

Gottlieb, Robert, and Wiley, Peter. *America's Saints: The Rise of Mormon Power*. G. P. Putnam's Sons, 1984.

MacKay, Kathryn L. "The Strawberry Valley Reclamation Project and the Opening of the Uintah Indian Reservation." *Utah Historical Quarterly*, Winter, 1982.

McLaughlin, James. *My Friend the Indian*. Houghton Mifflin, 1910.

O'Dea, Thomas F. *The Mormons*. University of Chicago Press, 1957.

O'Neil, Floyd A. "A History of the Ute Indians of Utah Until 1890." Ph.D. dissertation, University of Utah.

——. "The Reluctant Suzerainty: The Uintah and Ouray Reservation. *Utah Historical Quarterly*, Spring, 1971.

—— and MacKay, Kathryn L. *A History of the Uintah-Ouray Ute Lands*. University of Utah Press, 1979.

Peterson, Charles S. *Utah: A History*. W. W. Norton, 1977.

Rogers, Kristen Smart. "William Henry Smart, Uinta Basin Pioneer." *Utah Historical Quarterly*, Winter, 1977.

Smart, William B. "William H. Smart, Builder in the Basin." *Utah Historical Quarterly*, Winter, 1982.

Stegner, Wallace. *Mormon Country*. University of Nebraska Press, 1981.

Taylor, Theodore W. *The Bureau of Indian Affairs*. Westview Press, 1984.

U.S. Congress. Senate Committee on Indian Affairs. *Hearings on Leasing of Indian Lands*. Government Printing Office, 1902.

Works Progress Administration. Utah Historical Records Survey. *Inventory of the County Archives of Utah, No. 24 Uintah County (Vernal)*, November, 1940.

REGULATORS

Abbot, Carl, et al. *Colorado: A History of the Centennial State.* Colorado Associated University Press, 1982.

Athearn, Robert G. *The Coloradans.* University of New Mexico Press, 1976.

Fox, Stephen. *John Muir and His Legacy: The American Conservation Movement.* Little, Brown, 1981.

Frome, Michael. *The Forest Service.* Westview Press, 1984.

McCarthy, G. Michael. *Hour of Trial: The Conservation Conflict in Colorado and the West (1891–1907).* University of Oklahoma Press, 1977.

Peterson, Charles S., and Speth, Linda. *A History of the Wasatch-Cache National Forest.* Utah State University Press, 1980.

Pickford, G. D. *History of the Routt National Forest.* Department of Agriculture, Routt National Forest, Steamboat Springs, Colo., 1948.

Ratliff, Harry. *J. H. Ratliff Experiences 1905–1914.* Manuscript furnished by Gifford Pinchot for his Library of Congress record, 1944.

Sprague, Marshall. *Colorado.* W. W. Norton, 1976.

Voigt, Jr., William. *Public Grazing Lands: Use and Misuse by Industry and Government.* Rutgers University Press, 1976.

Young, Robert G., and Young, Joann W. *Colorado West.* Wheelwright Press, 1977.

PRESERVERS

Arnold, Ron. *At the Eye of the Storm: James Watt and the Environmentalists.* Regnery Gateway, 1982.

Bowan, Catherine Drinker, et al. *Four Portraits and One Subject: Bernard DeVoto.* Houghton Mifflin, 1963.

Cole, Walter E., and Amman, Gene D. *Mountain Pine Beetle Dynamics in Lodgepole Pine Forests.* U.S. Department of Agriculture, Forest Service, Intermountain Forest and Range Experiment Station, Ogden, Utah. 1980.

DeVoto, Bernard. *The Easy Chair.* Houghton Mifflin, 1955.

Hugel, Avvon Chew. *The Chew Bunch in Browns Park.* Scrimshaw Press, 1970.

Jenkins, Bruce S. *Memorandum of Opinion: the Ute Indian Tribe v. the State of Utah.* June 19, 1981.

Lamm, Richard, and McCarthy, Michael. *The Angry West: A Vulnerable Land and Its Future.* Houghton Mifflin, 1982.

Lash, Jonathan, et al. *A Season of Spoils: The Story of the Reagan Administration's Attack on the Environment.* Pantheon Books, 1984.

Nash, Roderick. *Wilderness and the American Mind.* Yale University Press, 1982.

Stegner, Wallace. *The Uneasy Chair: A Biography of Bernard DeVoto.* Doubleday, 1974.

——, ed. *The Letters of Bernard DeVoto.* Doubleday, 1975.

——, ed. *This Is Dinosaur.* Roberts Rinehart, 1985.

Stratton, Owen, and Sirotkin, Phillip. *The Echo Park Controversy.* University of Alabama, 1959.

U.S. Commission on Civil Rights. *Indian Tribes: A Continuing Quest for Survival.* Government Printing Office, 1981.

U.S. Congress. House. Report of Interior and Insular Affairs Committee. *Utah Wilderness Act.* Government Printing Office, 1984.

U.S. Congress. House Subcommittee on Public Lands and National Parks. *Hearings on Additions to the National Wilderness Preservation System.* Government Printing Office, 1984.

U.S. Department of Interior, Bureau of Land Management. *Final Environmental Impact Statement, Uintah Basin Synfuels Development.* February, 1983.

Utah State Energy Office. *Final Socioeconomics Technical Report for the Uintah Basin Synfuels Development Environmental Impact Statement.* February, 1983.

Vale, Thomas R., and Vale, Geraldine. *U.S. 40 Today: Thirty Years of Landscape Change in America.* University of Wisconsin Press, 1983.

Weatherford, Gary D., et al. "Legal-Political History of Water Resource Development in the Upper Colorado River Basin." *Lake Powell Research Bulletin.* National Science Foundation, 1974.

Wiley, Peter, and Gottlieb, Robert. *Empires in the Sun: The Rise of the New American West.* G. P. Putnam's Sons, 1982.

INDEX

A Note on the Type

This book was set in a typeface called New Baskerville. The face itself is a facsimile reproduction of types cast from molds made for John Baskerville (1706–1775) from his designs. Baskerville's original face was one of the forerunners of the type style known to printers as "modern face"—a "modern" of the period A.D. 1800.

Printed and bound by Fairfield Graphics,
Fairfield, Pennsylvania.

Composed by Superior Type
Champaign, Illinois

Typography & binding design by
VAL ASTOR

A Note About the Author

Philip L. Fradkin grew up in New Jersey and graduated from Williams College in 1957. He was a reporter for various California newspapers, ending up on the Los Angeles *Times* where he shared a Pulitzer Prize for the paper's coverage of the Watts riot, covered the Vietnam War, and was an environmental writer. He was assistant secretary of the California Resources Agency during the administration of Governor Edmund G. Brown Jr., and later served as western editor of *Audubon* magazine. The author of four books, including *A River No More: The Colorado River and the West* (1981), he has taught writing at Stanford University and the University of California at Berkeley and is the editor and publisher of Redwood Press in Marin County, California.